VOID

Library of
Davidson College

ARTHURIAN STUDIES XVII

REWARDS AND PUNISHMENTS IN THE
ARTHURIAN ROMANCES AND LYRIC POETRY
OF MEDIAEVAL FRANCE

## ARTHURIAN STUDIES

I: ASPECTS OF MALORY
Edited by Toshiyuki Takamiya and Derek Brewer

II: THE ALLITERATIVE *MORTE ARTHURE*:
A Reassessment of the Poem
Edited by Karl Heinz Göller

III: THE ARTHURIAN BIBLIOGRAPHY
I  Author Listing
Edited by C. E. Pickford and R. W. Last

IV: THE CHARACTER OF KING ARTHUR
IN MEDIEVAL LITERATURE
Rosemary Morris

V: PERCEVAL
The Story of the Grail
Chrétien de Troyes
Translated by Nigel Bryant

VI: THE ARTHURIAN BIBLIOGRAPHY
II  Subject Index
Edited by C. E. Pickford and R. W. Last

VII: THE LEGEND OF ARTHUR IN THE MIDDLE AGES
Edited by P. B. Grout, R. A. Lodge,
C. E. Pickford and E. K. C. Varty

VIII: THE ROMANCE OF YDER
Edited and translated by Alison Adams

IX: THE RETURN OF KING ARTHUR
Beverly Taylor and Elisabeth Brewer

X: ARTHUR'S KINGDOM OF ADVENTURE
The World of Malory's *Morte Darthur*
Muriel Whitaker

XI: KNIGHTHOOD IN THE *MORTE DARTHUR*
Beverly Kennedy

XII: LE ROMAN DE TRISTAN EN PROSE
Tome I
Edited by Renée L. Curtis

XIII: LE ROMAN DE TRISTAN EN PROSE
Tome II
Edited by Renée L. Curtis

XIV: LE ROMAN DE TRISTAN EN PROSE
Tome III
Edited by Renée L. Curtis

XV: THE ARTHURIAN BIBLIOGRAPHY
III  Supplement 1979–1983
Author Listing and Subject Index
Edited by Rex Last

XVI: THE CHANGING FACE OF ARTHURIAN ROMANCE
Essays on Arthurian Prose Romances in memory of Cedric E. Pickford
Edited by Alison Adams, Armel H. Diverres, Karen Stern and Kenneth Varty

ISSN 0261–9814

# REWARDS AND PUNISHMENTS IN THE ARTHURIAN ROMANCES AND LYRIC POETRY OF MEDIAEVAL FRANCE

*Essays presented to Kenneth Varty
on the occasion of his sixtieth birthday*

EDITED BY

PETER V. DAVIES AND ANGUS J. KENNEDY

D. S. BREWER

© Contributors 1987

First published 1987 by D. S. Brewer
240 Hills Road, Cambridge
an imprint of Boydell & Brewer Ltd
PO Box 9, Woodbridge, Suffolk IP12 3DF
and Wolfeboro, New Hampshire 03894-2069, USA

ISBN 0 85991 250 7

British Library Cataloguing in Publication Data

Rewards and punishments in the Arthurian
romances and lyric poetry of medieval
France: essays presented to Kenneth Varty
on the occasion of his sixtieth birthday.
——(Arthurian studies, ISSN 0261-9814; 17).
1. French literature——To 1500——History
and criticism
I. Varty, Kenneth    II. Davies, Peter V.
III. Kennedy, Angus J.
840.9′001      PQ151
ISBN 0-85991-250-7

Library of Congress Cataloging in Publication Data applied for

Rewards and punishments in the Arthurian romances
and lyric poetry of mediaeval France.
(Arthurian studies, ISSN 0261-9814; 17)
English and French.
Bibliography: p.
1. French poetry—To 1500—History and criticism.
2. Arthurian romances—History and criticism.
3. Rewards (Prizes, etc.) in literature.  4. Reward
(Psychology) in literature.  5. Punishment in
literature.  6. Varty, Kenneth.  I. Varty, Kenneth.
II. Davies, Peter V.   III. Kennedy, Angus J.
IV. Series.
PQ155.R48R48  1987       840′.9′355       87-707
ISBN 0-85991-250-7

Printed in Great Britain by St Edmundsbury Press, Bury St Edmunds, Suffolk

# Contents

| | |
|---|---|
| List of plates | vii |
| Preface | ix |
| Kenneth Varty | xi |
| Selective Bibliography of Kenneth Varty's Published and Forthcoming Works | xiii |
| Jean Renart's *l'Escoufle* and the Tristan Legend: Moderation Rewarded<br>ALISON ADAMS (*University of Glasgow*) | 1 |
| Récompense et Châtiment dans la structure narrative de la généalogie du *Tristan* en prose<br>JANET H. CAULKINS (*University of Wisconsin-Madison*) | 9 |
| Tristan and Iseut's Condemnation to the Stake in Beroul<br>A. H. DIVERRES (*University College, Swansea*) | 21 |
| L'épreuve du siège vide: esquisse d'une lecture croisée d'un épisode du *Joseph* et du *Merlin* de Robert de Boron<br>LILIANE DULAC (*Université Paul Valéry, Montpellier*) | 31 |
| The Tristan Illustrations in MS London, BL Add. 11619<br>TONY HUNT (*University of St Andrews*) | 45 |
| Punishment in the *Perlesvaus*: the Theme of the Waste Land<br>ANGUS J. KENNEDY (*University of Glasgow*) | 61 |
| The Triumph of Pragmatism: Reward and Punishment in *Le Roman de Silence*<br>HEATHER LLOYD (*University of Glasgow*) | 77 |
| La tête maléfique dans la littérature médiévale, étude d'une croyance magique<br>PHILIPPE MENARD (*Université de Paris-Sorbonne, Paris-IV*) | 89 |
| Punishments and Rewards of the Questing Knights in *La Queste del Saint Graal*<br>EITHNE O'SHARKEY (*University of Dundee*) | 101 |

| | |
|---|---|
| Reward and Punishment in Chrétien's *Erec* and Related Texts<br>D. D. R. OWEN (*University of St Andrews*) | 119 |
| Le châtiment et la mise à l'épreuve du jeune Lancelot<br>MICHEL ROUSSE (*Université de Rennes 2, Haute Bretagne*) | 133 |
| The Troubadour's Vassalage: an Axiology of Courtly Love<br>ARIE SERPER (*University of Jerusalem and Université de Paris-Sorbonne, Paris-IV*) | 143 |
| Sin and Retribution, and the Hope of Salvation, in Rutebeuf's Lyrical Works<br>RICHARD SPENCER (*University College, Cardiff*) | 149 |
| Punishment and Reward in Christine de Pizan's Lyric Poetry<br>CHARITY CANNON WILLARD (*New York*) | 165 |

# List of Plates

*The Tristan Illustrations in MS London, BL Add. 11619*
  1. Mark's court (f.6r)
  2, 3. Tristan at the Irish court; the combat with the dragon (f.6v–f.7r)
  4, 5. Tristan slays duke Morgan; the tryst in the orchard (f.7v–f.8v)
  6, 7. The sea-crossing (f.8v–f.9r)
  8. Mark, Isolde and Tristan (?) f.9v

*La tête maléfique dans la littérature médiévale, étude d'une croyance magique*
Bibliothèque Nationale, Paris, MS fr. 2164, f.34a

## *Preface*

In recent years Kenneth Varty's research has focused on the legal background to twelfth-century French literature, notably the Beast Epic; so it was quite natural that, when the editors invited Kenneth to propose a theme for the present volume, he should suggest 'Rewards and Punishments', adding that both terms of the antithesis could be interpreted in a variety of ways. In view of Kenneth's forthcoming publications, study of the theme here is restricted to two of the fields in which he has been so active, namely, the Arthurian romances and lyric poetry of medieval France.

The editors are extremely grateful to the British Branch of the International Arthurian Society for a most generous loan from the Vinaver Trust Fund to assist with the cost of publication.

P.V.D.

# Kenneth Varty

This volume honours a distinguished scholar who, for over thirty-five years, has worked assiduously and fruitfully in the field of medieval and Renaissance studies. The greater part of Kenneth Varty's career has been spent in four main centres of learning: Nottingham, Keele, Leicester and Glasgow. Born on 18 August 1927 at Calke, near Melbourne in Derbyshire, he attended Bemrose Grammar School, Derby, and entered the University of Nottingham in 1948, having completed three years' service in the Royal Air Force (1945–48). His First Class B.A. Honours Degree in French (1951) was followed up in 1954 by a Ph.D. thesis for Nottingham University, directed by Lewis Thorpe and entitled 'Aspects of the Life and Work of Louise Labé, with special reference to her ideas and imagery'. Appointed Assistant Lecturer in French at Keele in 1953, then Lecturer in 1956, he moved in 1961 to Leicester, where he was Senior Lecturer 1965–68 (and also Visiting Lecturer at Warwick during session 1967–68). He came to the University of Glasgow in 1968, to be the first occupant of the recently established second chair, the Stevenson Chair of French Language and Literature, an appointment that was to mark the beginning of perhaps the most active and most distinguished period of his career both as academic and as administrator.

Although heavily committed as Joint Head of what was, and probably still is, the largest non-collegiate Department of French in the United Kingdom, he served on almost all of the Councils of the University, as a member of Faculty and Senate, as Convenor of the Board of Studies for Modern Languages and, most importantly of all, as Dean of the Faculty of Arts 1979–82, a particularly testing time which saw the beginnings of retrenchment and contraction within Higher Education as a whole. Faculty was fortunate to have as its head during these difficult years someone able to combine sound leadership with a humane concern for individuals. Developments within the Department, undertaken at his initiative, led to the establishment of a Single Honours Degree in French alongside the existing Joint Honours courses, and the setting-up of a highly successful 'lecteur' exchange scheme with the University of Caen. He was solely responsible for organising two Colloquia at the Department, the first on Mallarmé in 1973, in honour of Professor Austin Gill, and the second, on the Beast Epic in 1975;

and along with Dr Alison Rawles, he played an important part in bringing the XIII International Arthurian Congress to Glasgow in 1981. Outwith Glasgow, in addition to his ever-increasing tasks as External Examiner at both undergraduate and post-graduate level, he served as a member, then as Treasurer, of the Executive Committee of the Society for French Studies; along with Lewis Thorpe, he edited the *Bulletin Bibliographique de la Société Internationale Arthurienne* for the period 1967–75; he acted as Secretary of the British Branch of the International Arthurian Society from 1969 to 1976, and as co-compiler of the annual British Bibliography, 1968–74. To these many and varied commitments he gave most generously of himself and of his time.

His interests as a scholar and teacher remained, and remain, admirably wide-ranging in an age of ever-narrowing specialisation. As a dedicated teacher in the fields of Medieval, Middle and Renaissance French literature, the History of the Language, phonetics, stylistics, dialects, and Modern French language, he has been unstinting in the help and encouragement he has given both to undergraduate students and post-graduate researchers. His academic achievements are detailed in the selective bibliography that follows. Suffice it to say here that to Arthurian studies, the medieval lyric, the medieval drama, the iconography and textual criticism of the *Roman de Renart* (a domain he made distinctively his own), he brought a blend of enthusiasm, competence and originality that was to win him national and international status as a scholar of the highest reputation. A series of awards and honours accompanied the steady publication of his academic work: Fellow of the Society of Antiquaries in 1969; Visiting Research Fellow at Merton College, Oxford, in 1973; President of the International Beast Epic, Fable and Fabliau Society since its formation, on his initiative, in 1975; Visiting Professor at the University of Jerusalem in 1977; Vice-President of the British Branch of the International Arthurian Society since 1979; Visiting Research Fellow, Clare Hall, Cambridge, in 1983; Associate Fellow of Clare Hall (Life Membership), Cambridge, since 1985. In June 1987 he was awarded the Degree of D.Litt. by the University of Keele, in recognition of his contribution to scholarship.

Yet, when all these achievements have been noted, the best has not been said. For Kenneth Varty, international scholarship has always been more, much more, than the sum of one's published work. It provided an opportunity for friendship and collaboration, for the forging of new links and the consolidation of the old. This volume is offered not just in appreciation of the scholar, but of the man, whose warmth, generosity, enthusiasm and unfailing courtesy have won him countless friends, many of whom have had the pleasure and privilege of being most hospitably welcomed into his home by himself, Hety, and their two daughters, Anne and Catherine. Kenneth Varty's friends and colleagues offer him this volume of studies as a mark of their deeply felt esteem and affection.

A.J.K.

# Selective Bibliography of Kenneth Varty's Published and Forthcoming Works

## 1956

'Accents and capital letters in French', *Modern Languages*, XXXVII, pp. 113–14.

'The emphatic negative in French', *Modern Languages*, XXXVII, pp. 152–4.

'Louise Labé and Marsilio Ficino', *Modern Language Notes*, LXXI, pp. 508–10.

## 1957

'The future tense in Anouilh's *Antigone*', *Modern Languages*, XXXVIII, pp. 99–101.

'A note on the expression "not to care for" ', *Notes and Queries*, CCII, p. 508.

## 1958

'Louise Labé's theory of transformation', *French Studies*, XII, pp. 5–13.

## 1959

'The Life and Legend of Louise Labé, *Nottingham Mediaeval Studies*, III, pp. 78–108 (an abbreviated translation of this appeared in *Cahiers d'Histoire*, VI (1961), pp. 5–16).

## 1960

*Le Jeu de Robin et de Marion précédé du Jeu du Pèlerin*, London: Harrap, 147 pp.

## 1962

'Reynard in Leicestershire and Rutland', *Transactions of the Leicestershire Archaeological Society*, XXXVIII, pp. 1–8.

## 1963

'Reynard the Fox and the Smithfield Decretals', *Journal of the Warburg and Courtauld Institutes*, XXVI, 347–54.

'Teaching the past historic and the imperfect in French', *Modern Languages*, XLIV, pp. 74–80.

## 1964

'The controversy about the origin of the impersonal pronoun "on" in French', *Archivum Linguisticum* (with D. Cloud), XVI, pp. 125–32.

'The pursuit of Reynard in medieval English literature and art', *Nottingham Mediaeval Studies*, VIII, pp. 62–81.

## 1965

'Deschamps's "Art de Dictier" ', *French Studies*, XIX, pp. 164–8.

*Christine de Pisan: Ballades, Rondeaux and Virelais: an anthology*, Leicester: Leicester University Press, xl + 188 pp.

## 1966

'The death and resurrection of Reynard the Fox in mediaeval literature and art', *Nottingham Mediaeval Studies*, X, pp. 70–93.

'French Literature: the sixteenth century', *Encyclopaedia Britannica*, Vol. IX, pp. 885–8.

'Etienne Pasquier', *Encyclopaedia Britannica*, Vol. XVII, p. 433.

'Maurice Scève', *Encyclopaedia Britannica*, Vol. XIX, p. 1147.

'Jean Vauquelin de la Fresnaye', *Encyclopaedia Britannica*, Vol. XXII, p. 924.

'The Virelai', *Encyclopaedia Britannica*, Vol. XXIII, p. 35.

## 1967

'Index of Authors', pp. 104–8; 'Index of Subject Matter', pp. 109–15; 'List of Members', pp. 152–202, in *Bibliographical Bulletin of the International Arthurian Society*, XIX, Oxford: Alden Press (Assistant Editor).

*Reynard the Fox: a study of the fox in medieval English art*, Leicester: Leicester University Press, 169 pp. and 169 plates.

## 1968

'Index of Authors', pp. 109–14; 'Index of Subject Matter', pp. 115–21; 'List of Members', pp. 160–210, in *Bibliographical Bulletin of the International Arthurian Society*, XX, Hull: Hull Printers Ltd (Assistant Editor).

## 1969

'The British Bibliography, 1968', pp. 71–87; 'Index of Authors', pp. 94–9; 'Index of Subject Matter', pp. 100–5; 'List of Members', pp. 176–230, in *Bibliographical Bulletin of the International Arthurian Society*, XXI, Hull: Hull Printers Ltd (Assistant Editor).

## 1970

'The British Bibliography, 1969', pp. 59–75; 'Index of Authors', pp. 101–6; 'Index of Subject Matter', pp. 107–12; 'List of Members', pp. 144–204, in *Bibliographical Bulletin of the International Arthurian Society*, XXII, Hull: Hull Printers Ltd (Assistant Editor).

## 1971

*Louise Labé: Poems from 'Euvres' 1556*, Menston: The Scolar Press, 32 pp. (a facsimile edition of Louise Labé's elegies and sonnets).

'The British Bibliography, 1970', pp. 79–97; 'Index of Authors', pp. 112–17; 'Index of Subject Matter', pp. 118–27; 'List of Members', pp. 153–215, in *The Bibliographical Bulletin of the International Arthurian Society*, XXIII, Hull: Hull Printers Ltd (Assistant Editor).

## 1972

'The British Bibliography, 1971' (with Ray Barron, David Blamires, Angus J. Kennedy and Gareth Watts), pp. 81–104; Index of Authors', pp. 119–125; 'Index of Subject Matter', pp. 126–33; 'List of Members', pp. 241–308, in *Bibliographical Bulletin of the International Arthurian Society*, XXIV, Hull: Hull Printers Ltd (Assistant Editor).

## 1973

'The British Bibliography, 1972' (with Ray Barron, David Blamires, Angus J. Kennedy and Gareth Watts), pp. 93–119; 'Index of Authors', pp. 130–6; 'Index of Subject Matter', pp. 137–44; 'List of Members', pp. 211–83, in *Bibliographical Bulletin of the International Arthurian Society*, XXV, Hull: Hull Printers Ltd (Assistant Editor).

## 1974

'Christine de Pisan's *Ditié de Jehanne d'Arc*, Part I' (with Angus J. Kennedy), *Nottingham Mediaeval Studies*, XVIII, pp. 29–55.

'Reynard the Fox in Bristol Cathedral', *Reports and Notes of the Friends of Bristol Cathedral* (1973–74), pp. 13–20.

'The British Bibliography, 1973' (with Ray Barron, David Blamires, Angus J. Kennedy and Gareth Watts), pp. 80–112; 'Index of Authors', pp. 155–61; 'Index of Subject Matter', pp. 162–9; 'List of Members', pp. 225–300, in *Bibliographical Bulletin of the International Arthurian Society*, XXVI (Assistant Editor).

## 1975

'Christine de Pisan's *Ditié de Jehanne d'Arc*, Part II' (with Angus J. Kennedy), *Nottingham Mediaeval Studies*, XIX, pp. 53–76.

'*Vernage*: two corrections to Godefroy' (with Angus J. Kennedy), *Medium Aevum*, XLIV, pp. 162–3.

'Further examples of the fox in medieval English art', *Aspects of the Medieval Animal Epic: Proceedings of the International Conference (Louvain, May 15–17, 1972)*, ed. by Prof. Dr E. Rombauts and Prof. Dr A. Welkenhuysen, Leuven: Leuven University Press; The Hague: M. Nijhoff, pp. 251–6.

'The British Bibliography, 1974' (with Ray Barron, David Blamires, Angus J. Kennedy and Gareth Watts), pp. 105–30; 'Index of Authors', pp. 152–8; 'Index of Subject Matter', pp. 159–64; 'List of Members', pp. 247–303, in *Bibliographical Bulletin of the International Arthurian Society*, XXVII (Assistant Editor).

## 1976

*Proceedings of the International Colloquium held at the University of Glasgow (23–25 September, 1975) on the Beast Epic, Fable and Fabliau*, Glasgow: at the French Department of the University of Glasgow, 139 + iv pp. (Editor).

'New light on the story of the fox's execution and funeral (*La Mort et Procession Renart* – Martin, Branch XVII) in medieval England', *ibid.*, pp. 46–8 (+ 2 figures).

'Towards a new edition of the *Roman de Renart*: "Renart and Chantecler", an episode from MS. Varia 151 of the Biblioteca Reale in Turin' (with Anthony Lodge), *Nottingham Mediaeval Studies*, XX, pp. 41–63.

'Paintings of Reynard the Fox in Gloucester Cathedral and some other related examples' (with E. Clive Rouse), *The Archaeological Journal*, CXXXIII, pp. 104–17 (and Plates IX–XIV).

## 1977

*Christine de Pisan: 'Ditié de Jehanne d'Arc'* (with Angus J. Kennedy), Oxford: Society for the Study of Mediaeval Languages and Literature ('*Medium Aevum* Monographs', New Series IX), 103 + iv pp. (+ VIII plates).

## 1978

'An *état présent* of *Roman de Renart* studies', *Mélanges de Philologie et de Littératures romanes offerts à Jeanne Wathelet-Willem*, ed. Jacques De Caluwé, Liège: Marche Romane (*Cahiers de l'A.R.U.Lg.* [Association des Romanistes de l'Université de Liège]), pp. 699–716.

'First list of recent publications and research in progress for 1975–76–77', *Epopée Animale, Fable et Fabliau* (Actes du Colloque de la Société Internationale Renardienne, Amsterdam, 21–24 octobre, 1977) = *Marche Romane*, XXVIII (*Cahiers de l'A.R.U.Lg.*; Mediaevalia 78), nos. 3–4, pp. 225–46.

## 1980

'The earliest illustrated English editions of *Reynard the Fox* and their links with the earliest illustrated continental editions', *Reynaert, Reynard, Reynke: Studien zu einem mittelalterlichen Tierepos*, hgg. von Jan Goosens und Timothy Sodmann, Köln/Wien: Böhlau Verlag ('Niederdeutsche Studien', 27), pp. 160–95, 365–444.

'The Lion, the Unicorn and the Fox', *Proceedings of the Centenary Conference of the London Folklore Society (London, 1978)*, London, pp. 412–18 (and Plates 18–21).

'Le mariage, la courtoisie et l'ironie comique dans le *Jeu de Robin et de Marion*', *Mélanges de Langue et Littérature françaises du Moyen Age et de la Renaissance offerts à Charles Foulon*, vol. II = *Marche Romane*, XXX (*Cahiers de l'A.R.U.Lg.*; Mediaevalia 80), nos. 3–4, pp. 287–92.

## 1981

*An Arthurian Tapestry: Essays in Memory of Lewis Thorpe*, Glasgow: at the French Department of the University of Glasgow, 401 + xi pp. (Editor).

'Pierre de Saint Cloud's *Roman de Renart*: Foulet's thesis re-examined' (with R. Anthony Lodge), *Third International Beast Epic, Fable and Fabliau Colloquium (Münster, 27–29 October, 1979): Proceedings*, ed. by Jan Goosens and Timothy Sodmann, Köln/Wien: Böhlau Verlag ('Niederdeutsche Studien', 30), pp. 189–95.

'Jeanne Wathelet-Willem: une appréciation (Allocution prononcée à Bruges le 11 juin, 1978, à l'occasion de la remise des *Mélanges* à Jeanne Wathelet-Willem)', *Marche Romane*, XXXI, nos. 1–2, pp. 97–101.

## 1982

'The iconography of the medieval beast epic: from manuscript to printed page', *The Medieval Alexander Legend and Romance Epic: Essays in Honour of David J. A. Ross*, ed. by Peter Noble, Lucie Polak and Claire Isoz, Millwood, New York: Kraus, pp. 243–58.

## 1983

'Love, marriage and family relationships in the *Ysengrimus* and the *Roman de Renart*', *Le Roman de Renard: On the Beast Epic* = *Canadian Journal of Netherlandic Studies / Revue Canadienne d'Etudes Néerlandaises* (Windsor, Ontario), vol. IV, no. 1, pp. 39–52.

*The Legend of Arthur in the Middle Ages: Studies presented to A. H. Diverres by Colleagues, Pupils and Friends*, Cambridge: D. S. Brewer ('Arthurian Studies', VII), 253 pp. (Co-editor with P. B. Grout, R. Anthony Lodge and Cedric E. Pickford).

'On birds and beasts, "Death" and "Resurrection", renewal and reunion in Chrétien's Romances', *ibid.*, pp. 194–212, 253.

## 1984

'Le viol dans l'*Ysengrimus*, les branches II-Va, et la branche I du *Roman de Renart*', *Amour, Mariage et Transgressions au Moyen Age (Université de Picardie, Centre d'Etudes Médiévales: Actes du Colloque des 24, 25, 26 et 27 mars, 1983)*, publ. par les soins de Danielle Buschinger et André Crépin, Göppingen: Kümmerle Verlag ('Göppinger Arbeiten zur Germanistik', Nr. 420), pp. 411–24.

## 1985

'Back to the beginning of the *Romans de Renart*', *Nottingham Medieval Studies*, XXIX, pp. 44–72.

## 1986

*The Changing Face of Arthurian Romance: Essays on Arthurian Prose Romances in Memory of Cedric E. Pickford – A Tribute by the Members of the British Branch of the International Arthurian Society*, Woodbridge: Boydell Press ('Arthurian Studies', XVI), 168 + xxiv pp. (Co-editor with Alison Adams, Armel H. Diverres and Karen Stern).

'The giving and withholding of consent in late twelfth-century French literature', *Reading Medieval Studies*, XII, pp. 1–24.

'La mosaïque de Lescar et la datation des contes de Renart le goupil', *Revue des Langues Romanes*, XC, no. 1, pp. 1–12.

*Awaiting publication:*

'Les qualités poétiques de la prose de Louise Labé', *La Renaissance à Lyon: Actes du Colloque de Macerata*, mai 1985.

'Pictorial anthologies of scenes from the medieval Beast Epic featuring the fox', *Actes du sixième Colloque de la Société Internationale Renardienne (Spa, septembre 1985)*.

*Bibliography*

'The role of the anthologist-storyteller in the *Roman de Renart*', *Mélanges . . . Gasca Queirazza.*

*The Earliest Branches of the 'Roman de Renart': A Critical Edition of Branches II–Va* (with Anthony Lodge), Lochee Publications Ltd.

*A la Recherche du 'Roman de Renart': Essais de Critique*, Lochee Publications Ltd.

*Une petite introduction aux contes médiévaux de Renart le goupil et aux Romans de Renart*, Lochee Publications Ltd.

# *Jean Renart's* L'Escoufle *and the Tristan Legend: Moderation Rewarded*

## ALISON ADAMS

Jean Renart's *L'Escoufle* has been criticised recently for its lack of unity, lack of cohesion, in the sense that the characters' aspirations and actions are not ultimately responsible for the outcome of the tale.[1] The lovers are reunited and reconciled not because they have strived towards that end, as the similarity between this poem and the group of romances, the so-called *romans idylliques*, based on the *Floire et Blancheflor* type of story would suggest,[2] but because destiny, borne out by a series of coincidences, arranges it for them. Norris Lacy argues that: 'both the randomness and the apparently coincidental nature of the events create a tension which increases until the work threatens to collapse' (Lacy, p. 155). Though evidently still finding the text somewhat unsatisfactory, Lacy considers that this 'collapse' is avoided by a pattern of repetition and reiteration of scenes and motifs within the poem. Important as such internal patterning may be in providing links between different parts of the work, it seems to me that it is the pattern of allusion to an external source, the Tristan legend, which in fact successfully unifies *L'Escoufle* and indeed furnishes the clue to the poem's meaning.

It has long been recognised that *L'Escoufle* displays a high degree of familiarity with the Tristan legend, making extensive reference to both Béroul and Thomas, as was pointed out by L. Sudre as early as 1886.[3] On account of the purity of the natural love shown to exist between the main characters,

---

[1] Norris J. Lacy, 'The composition of *L'Escoufle*', *Res Publica Litterarum*, 1 (1978), pp. 151–8.
 References are to Jean Renart, *L'Escoufle*, ed. by Franklin Sweetser, T.L.F., Geneva: Droz, 1974.
[2] See my article 'The Shape of Verse Romance' in *The Legacy of Chrétien de Troyes*, ed. by K. Busby, D. Kelly and N. J. Lacy, to appear.
[3] L. Sudre, 'Les allusions à la légende de Tristan dans la littérature du Moyen Age', *Romania*, XV (1886), pp. 540–2. Cf. Sweetser, pp. xxiv–xxv. See also R. Lejeune, 'La coupe de la légende de Tristan dans *L'Escoufle* de Jean Renart' in *The Medieval Alexander Legend and Romance Epic. Essays . . . David J. A. Ross*, ed. by P. Noble, L. Polak and C. Isoz, New York/London: Kraus International Publ., 1982, pp. 119–24.
 References are to Beroul, *The Romance of Tristran*, ed. by A. Ewert, Vol. 1, Oxford: Blackwell, reprint 1963 and Thomas, *Les fragments du roman de Tristan*, ed. by Bartina H. Wind, T.L.F., Geneva/Paris: Droz, 1960.

Guillaume and Aelis, as against the fated and adulterous love of Tristan and Iseut, Sweetser sees it as an anti- or super-Tristan but surprisingly he, like other critics, fails to examine the relationship between the text and the legend in any detail or to consider its implications for our fuller understanding of the poem.

The most extended explicit reference to the legend is the first to occur: it consists of a description of a chalice bearing illustrations of the Tristan story which Rita Lejeune has shown to be comparable at times with Béroul, and at times with Thomas, but on occasion to be independent of either of them (ll. 580–616). She suggests that the explanation for this might lie in Jean Renart referring not to a Tristan poem but to an actual chalice he had seen, but that of course only sets one stage further back the relationship this description may bear with any archetype for the legend. This problem is, however, of limited relevance to an understanding of the poem. The chalice concerned is mentioned at an early stage in the text, when it is offered by Guillaume's father, Richard of Normandy, as a gift at the altar of the Holy Sepulchre in the Holy Land. Although the pattern of preceding the main story with that of the hero's (or in this case the hero and heroine's) parents seems to be derived from the legend and it will later be seen that Jean Renart uses the parents' story, as does Chrétien in *Cligés*, to put the lovers unequivocally in the right from the outset, at this point no thematic parallel with the Tristan story has emerged. Nevertheless such an explicit and detailed reference makes an impact on the reader and must serve to alert us to briefer and less obvious allusions later on, irrespective of what version is concerned.

Were it not for this passage near the beginning of the text, most of the explicit references to the legend, at least taken in isolation, might well appear no more than stereotypes, of little significance for a general interpretation of the poem. The heroes of the Tristan story are drawn on for comparison in the same way as they are in a number of other romances of the period. So, for instance, when Guillaume's father is married Jean Renart comments:

> N'ainc la ou rois Mars prist Yseut
> N'ot tant de joie com la eut
> Ou li quens Richars prist sa feme.     (ll. 1715–17)

Similarly later on, when Guillaume and Aelis are separated, Guillaume recalls Aelis' great beauty, a reality, and compares it with the famed beauty of Iseut:

> Ne puis le tans Yseut la blonde
> Ne fu mais vostre pers veue;
> Ceste chose est par tout seue.
> On dist k'Yseus fu bele et sage:
> Ce ne set nus fors par usage,
> Car cascune dist: Je l'oï dire;
> Mais en vos en cui biautés mire,
> Si com je sai et com je voi . . .     (ll. 3450–7)

These two examples are characteristic of the superlative quality commonly ascribed to the heroes of a particular work.

There are other points where Guillaume compares himself with Tristan, but although he formulates the comparison in a similarly conventional way, it is of greater importance because it underlines certain parallels between the two stories. Separated from his beloved as Tristan was from Iseut, he longs for the guile which allowed Tristan and Iseut to go on seeing each other:

> Diex! fait il, com fu sage Yseus
> Et Tristans; tant sorent de gile
> K'ainc ne fu tant n'en bos n'en vile
> Gardee par si grant destrece
> K'il, par lor sens et par prouece,
> N'assamblaissent malgré lor roi,
> Ml't sorent andui de lor roi,
> K'il ert hardis et ele sage.
> Las! jo n'ai sens ne ele aage
> De faire autel comme Tristrans.      (ll. 3122–31)

And he goes on to recall how Tristan and Kahedin resorted to disguises in pursuit of their love. When the kite has seized Aelis' ring, he adopts a similarly melancholy tone, bewailing the fact that, unlike Tristan, he was unable to keep his lady's ring safe:

> Or me dira je ne fui mie
> De la cortoisie Tristran
> Qui en ot .j. gardé maint an
> Por l'amor la roïne Ysout . . .      (ll. 4616–19)

Such explicit and relatively conventional references to the Tristan legend take their place within a fabric of implicit allusion which might not immediately be apparent to us if the story were not explicitly recalled at regular intervals. This underlying relationship with the Tristan story not only unifies the text and creates a fascinating texture from the blending of familiar and unfamilar elements, but also, and ultimately in the differences rather than the parallels which emerge, provides the key to our understanding of *L'Escoufle*.

The parallelism starts early on in the poem, when Guillaume's father Richard finds himself in a situation reminiscent of Tristan at Mark's court. Richard has come to occupy a special position at the Roman court because of the role he played in bringing freedom and peace to the realm. As among Mark's barons, there are some who grow to resent the favour bestowed on an outsider, although the bad feeling is only voiced openly to the Emperor once Richard has died. The disloyal counsellors are castigated by Renart as traitors and *losengiers* (ll. 2660 and 2920; cf. Béroul l. 464). So it comes about that, although Guillaume and Aelis' love was at first sanctioned by the Emperor, who is Aelis' father, and the young couple are actually formally betrothed, they then find themselves forced to flee together when the Emperor orders them to stop seeing each other.

The series of episodes in which the ring which Aelis receives from her mother, and subsequently gives to Guillaume, is lost, snatched away by a kite, the *escoufle* of the title, is permeated by allusion to the Tristan legend, and more particularly to Béroul rather than the combination of traditions found in the pictures on the chalice depicting the scenes relevant to this episode. Obviously there is no precise source for the story within the Tristan texts, but at different points it bears some relationship both to the scene where the lovers take their leave of each other when Iseut is returned to King Mark, and to the occasion when Mark surprises Tristan and Iseut in the forest. We have already seen that after the ring has been snatched away Guillaume compares himself with Tristan and feels that he has failed. But an indirect allusion can be detected much earlier, when Aelis first receives the ring from her mother, who of course has no idea that Aelis and Guillaume are planning to flee together. Aelis takes the ring and kisses it:

> Ele le baise et si en fait
> Grant joie a cele departie.
> Ensi s'est la bele partie
> De sa mere l'empereris.　　　(ll. 3822–5)

These lines recall passages in Béroul: when Tristan thinks of his forthcoming separation from Iseut, he uses the word 'departie':

> 'Dex!' dist Tristran, 'quel departie!
> Molt est dolenz qui pert s'amie!　　　(ll. 2681–2)

and shortly afterwards, after the exchange of the ring and the dog, Béroul comments:

> Tristran en bese la roïne,
> Et ele lui, par la saisine.　　　(ll. 2731–2)

The two 'departies' are of course very different: Aelis is about to leave triumphantly with her beloved, and her kiss is for the ring, whereas Tristan in his suffering embraces the mistress from whom he is to be parted. Thus over the ring which Aelis receives from a mother who has no idea of what is to ensue hovers the threat of another, tragic 'departie', another separation.

It is the scene which actually brings about this separation, when the kite flies off with the ring and is pursued by Guillaume, that draws on Mark's discovery of the lovers in the forest. Once more there are certain verbal similarities which seem close enough to suggest direct influence. Jean Renart describes the oppressive heat of the day: 'le chaut qui li grieve et nuit . . .' (l. 4414); cf. Béroul: 'Li chauz fu granz, qui molt les grive' (l. 1794). The heat is such that Aelis, like Iseut, removes much of her clothing (though not all as in the description of Tristan and Iseut on the chalice at the beginning of

*L'Escoufle*). Guillaume on this occasion plays the role normally associated with Mark when he wants to shade his beloved from the sun. But most important for the action is the theme of misunderstanding present in both scenes. Tristan and Iseut misinterpret the signs of friendship left by Mark and take to flight, and Aelis, when she finds that Guillaume is nowhere to be seen (in fact he is pursuing the kite which has stolen the purse containing the ring), concludes that he has abandoned her and so goes off on her own in pursuit, as she thinks (ll. 4686–864). So the tragic separation of the couple is brought about.

If narrative elements in this episode seem to be related to Béroul, Aelis' psychological reaction when she finds that Guillaume has disappeared is reminiscent of Thomas: her misplaced anger and pain as she assumes that Guillaume's declarations of love and loyalty were false (ll. 4686–758 and ll. 5352–71) recall Tristan's unfounded doubting of Iseut when he is in Brittany (Sneyd[1] ll. 5–48, 83–158). When it comes to the episode where Guillaume and Aelis find each other again, however, the parallel is not with Béroul or Thomas but the *folie* poems. Aelis' hesitation in recognising Guillaume even when she hears him tell his whole story and sees him standing before her is similar to Iseut's delayed recognition of Tristan in the *folies*, even when she has heard him reveal details of their love which nobody else could know. Neither Iseut nor Aelis can believe the evidence of their ears, or in Aelis' case her eyes either, but in *L'Escoufle* the situation is no game or contrived testing of love; instead Guillaume is as unaware of Aelis' identity as she is of his, so that in a sense he too can be compared with Iseut. We can then even see a point of comparison with Husdent's easy and immediate recognition of Tristan which, in the *folies*, is used to contrast with Iseut's failure to see Tristan beneath his unfamiliar guise. The scene is transposed, however, into a previous episode in which Guillaume immediately notices Aelis' mule when he comes across it by chance, even though later he will have difficulty in recognising its owner.

It is especially the motivation for the recognition scene, bringing Guillaume and Aelis together again after their long period of separation, which has been criticised. Not only are they surprisingly slow in recognising each other, given the grief we have seen them both displaying at their loss, but they have actually stopped looking for each other and settled down with at least relative equanimity to earn a living. It is chance and chance alone which brings about their meeting and reconciliation. How, then, can this work be regarded as any kind of idealised love story, an anti- or super-Tristan? None of the web of allusion to the Tristan legend which we have observed so far, however fascinating, is sufficient of itself to provide an overall reading of the poem which accommodates this apparent anomaly in the pattern familiar from other texts of the *Floire et Blancheflor* type, and indeed virtually demanded at the psychological level. The solution is found in an explicit reference to the Tristan legend in which Tristan's love is compared with Guillaume's, to

Guillaume's advantage. The passage occurs just at the beginning of the string of coincidences which brings Guillaume to Aelis, after he has seen the mule which, he is told, had been bought six years previously from a lady called Aelis:

>Or n'ama mais en tel maniere
>Nus hom ja; si fist viaus Tristrans.
>Ml't ot il ore plus ahans,
>Ains qu'il fust mors, pour la roïne,
>Car ce fu pour la medecine
>Que Brangiens li dona a boire,
>Dont fu ce force: force voire!
>K'il n'i ot onques point de grace ...  (ll. 6352–9)

Guillaume's love, being of natural origin, unlike Tristan's, is less extreme, more rational and controlled, and this Jean Renart judges favourably, as is emphasised in the reference to Piramus immediately following the allusion to Tristan:

>Et Piramus qui la crevace
>Trova, ne fu il mors d'amours?
>Ce ne sai jou que je'en die,
>Se ce fu folie u amors.
>.................
>Le cuidier et la sospechon
>Deust il bien oster ançois
>K'il s'ocesist, qu'en nule[s] lois
>Ne doit hom pas vengement faire
>De cuidier ...  (ll. 6360–76)

Clearly, Jean Renart has no sympathy with the uncompromising *amour passion* of Tristan and Iseut or of Piramus. What he seems to be suggesting is that Guillaume and Aelis' moderation in, eventually at least, accepting their situation and adapting to it is positive. They have their feet firmly on the ground and are able to come to terms not only with the reality of their loss but with the demands of everyday living. Aelis herself emphasises this sense of realism when she decides to settle down and stop hunting for her beloved:

>En plorant dist: 'A moi que monte
>De mon lignage? c'est du mains,
>Quant il m'estuet a mes .ii. mains
>Gaaigner dont je puisse vivre.'  (ll. 5434–7)

In these circumstances, of course, the happy ending which is not only demanded by the expectations of the genre but deserved, because of the young couple's suffering and finally admirable resilience, has to be brought about by some external agency. The very qualities which make them worthy of the reward of being reconciled with each other, mean that they give up striving to attain it. Chance, destiny are the only methods left for the author to bring his tale to a satisfactory conclusion.

But in this poem, the tale does not stop at the point where the couple are reunited. As if to balance the opening section of the poem in which the story of Guillaume and Aelis' parents is related, Jean Renart is not even satisfied with a rapid account of wedding festivities as is so often the case in the closing scenes of other romances. Indeed the wedding is not even celebrated until Guillaume has been welcomed back as his father's heir in Normandy, and Jean Renart goes on to tell us how three years later the couple are recalled to Rome where Guillaume is crowned Emperor after all. Apart from the obvious structural importance of mirroring the beginning of the work, this conclusion, though perhaps unexpectedly protracted,[4] underlines the fact that the young couple's virtue will not allow them to lose out socially. One might even take an interpretation along these lines a little further, by suggesting that in the end Guillaume and Aelis achieve the social position for which they had been destined before Aelis' father's death because of their own merits and not because of lineage or patronage. This fits in not only with Aelis' insistence on earning her own living rather than depending on her noble birth, but with a possible symbolical reading of the story of the ring. Aelis obtains the ring from her mother under false pretences to help Guillaume and herself when they run away from the court. But what is intended to be of advantage to them turns out to be quite the opposite, bringing about the tragic separation which means they have to make their own way, falling back on their own individual resources.

Also in keeping with this overall interpretation of *L'Escoufle* is a facet of Jean Renart's work which has often attracted critics' attention though it has sometimes been viewed as in some way independent of the plot, that is the gift for realistic description which puts Jean Renart at the beginning of the long tradition of the *roman de moeurs*.[5] Once a realistic attitude to life is seen as lying at the heart of *L'Escoufle*, the detailed descriptive passages treating different elements of normal everyday life can and must be seen as integral at least to this poem. Guillaume and Aelis' moderation in love, rather than the extremes of emotional behaviour of Tristan and Iseut, allows the work to be brought to a happy conclusion, at both a social and a personal level:

> Lor regart ont entrelardé
> Parmi les fenestres des eus
> L'un cuer de l'autre: onques Yseus
> Ne Tristrans n'orent mais tel vie.      (ll. 7820–3)

---

[4] Sweetser for instance wonders how best to justify the last 1200 lines of the poem: 'L'histoire proprement dite termine avec la scène de reconnaissance et la réunion des amants' (p. xxxi).

[5] Cf. for instance G. Charlier, '*L'Escoufle* et *Guillaume de Dole*', *Mélanges de philologie romane . . . offerts à Maurice Wilmotte*, Paris: Champion, 1910, Vol. I, pp. 81–98: 'La vie féodale prise sur le vif, décrite non seulement sous ses plus brillants aspects, mais jusque sous les faces les plus modestes, dans sa banalité journalière, tel en est, à notre avis, le véritable sujet' (pp. 93–4).

# *Récompense et Châtiment dans la Structure Narrative de la Généalogie du* Tristan *en Prose*

## JANET H. CAULKINS

> Aucun récit n'est naturel, un choix et une construction présideront toujours à son apparition; c'est un discours et non une série d'événements.[1]

> Technique d'analyse littéraire, la sémiologie du récit tire sa possibilité et sa fécondité de son enracinement dans une anthropologie.[2]

La généalogie du *Tristan* en prose fournit d'excellents exemples du système oppositionnel de récompense/châtiment.[3] C'est un système oppositionnel qui jusqu'ici n'a pas reçu l'attention qu'il mérite, en ce qui concerne les romans en prose. Notre intention dans cet article est d'examiner de près l'idée de rétribution pour montrer non seulement sa centralité, mais aussi la façon dont elle engendre un schéma narratif qui se répète et se modifie tout au long du roman; notre intention est aussi de suivre au cours de notre analyse le plaisir du texte.[4]

Nous analyserons en détail la première partie de la généalogie qui traite des

---

[1] Tzvetan Todorov, *Poétique de la prose*, Paris: Le Seuil, 1971, p. 68.
[2] Claude Bremond, 'La logique des possibles narratifs,' *Communications*, VIII (1966), pp. 60–76, voir p. 76.
[3] Pour une bibliographie sur l'identité de l'auteur ou des auteurs, voir Caulkins, 'La *joie* de Tristan dans le *Tristan* en prose: disjonction, invention et jeux de mots,' à paraître dans *Romania*.
[4] La généalogie du *Tristan* en prose reste la partie du roman la moins appréciée par la critique moderne, voir Caulkins, 'The Genealogy of the *Prose Tristan* and the Theme of a Debased Knighthood,' dans *The Medieval Court in Europe, Houston German Studies*, VI, 1986, pp. 105–22, voir p. 120, n. 8. En 1886 Gaston Paris juge la généalogie du *Tristan* 'aussi ennuyeuse que longue et inutile,' dans 'Note sur les romans relatifs à Tristan,' *Romania*, XV, pp. 597–602, voir p. 601; en 1891 Eilert Löseth parle d'une 'fastidieuse introduction,' dans *Le Roman en prose de Tristan, le roman de Palamède et la compilation de Rusticien de Pise, analyse critique d'après les manuscrits de Paris*, New York: Burt Franklin, 1970: réimp. Paris, 1891, p. XVIII et malgré la grande contribution d'Emmanuèle Baumgartner aux recherches sur le *Tristan* en prose, notamment son livre *Le Tristan en prose: essai d'interprétation d'un roman médiéval*, Genève: Droz, 1975, en 1982 Colette Storms parle du 'malaise qu'on [continue à éprouver] à lire les aventures de Sador et de Chelinde,' dans sa thèse 'Aventures querant et le sens du monde,' Université de Louvain, 1982, p. 37.

aventures de Sador et de Chelinde,[5] comme introductrice au reste du *Tristan en prose*,[6] avant de dégager de façon plus générale les grandes lignes du thème de la rétribution, telles qu'elles ressortent dans la suite de l'oeuvre.

Claude Bremond explique que les lois narratives 'relèvent de deux niveaux d'organisation: (a) elles reflètent les contraintes logiques que toute série d'événements ordonnée en forme de récit doit respecter sous peine d'être inintelligible; (b) elles ajoutent à ces contraintes, valables pour tout récit, les conventions de leurs univers particulier, caractéristique d'une culture, d'une époque, d'un genre littéraire, du style d'un conteur ou, à la limite, de ce seul récit lui-même.'[7]

La fonction narrative qui ouvre la séquence de la généalogie du *Tristan en prose* est le refus de Sador d'être guidé comme ses autres frères par son oncle Joseph d'Arimathie en ce qui concerne le choix d'une épouse. Joseph questionne Sador avec surprise et mécontentement: 'Comment! . . . ne veus tu pas estre desoz mon chastiement ausi cum sunt ti autre frere tuit?' (§3, l. 3–4). Sador lui répond: 'de totes choses veil je bien ovrer a vostre volenté, fors que de feme prendre solement. Mes de cele chose voudrai je ovrer a mon sens' (§3, l. 4–6). Le refus de Sador qui va contre une convention de sa culture et de son époque, indique la déficience de Sador. Ce dernier va à l'encontre de l'autorité d'un représentant de l'Eglise. Bien qu'il s'agisse ici d'une oeuvre laïque, Sador payera très cher cette volonté – tout comme Adam et Eve dans la Bible. La faute de Sador est tolérée par son oncle qui répond à son tour: 'puis que ce veus faire a ta volenté, je m'en soferrai. Mes je dout que tu en la fin ne t'en repentes' (§3, l. 7–8). Cet épisode est fondateur de la fonction narrative qui engendre le récit généalogique en ouvrant tout un réseau de possibilités narratives. Les injonctions relatives à la conduite à tenir ou aux événements à prévoir indiquent les conséquences virtuelles d'un amour-passion. De la même façon, le troisième livre du *De Amore* élabore sur les effets de la passion amoureuse, lorsqu'André le Chapelain conseille à l'amant néophyte, de rejeter complètement l'expérience de l'amour charnel.[8] La fonction narrative initiale

---

[5] Pour toutes références textuelles au *Tristan en prose*, voir Renée L. Curtis, *Le Roman de Tristan en prose*, dans *Arthurian Studies*, XII, XIII, XIV, Woodbridge: Suffolk, 1985: XII: réimp. Munich, 1963; XIII: réimp. Leyde, 1976. A partir du §940, fin du 3 volume de Curtis, voir Löseth.

[6] La question de la date de la composition de la généalogie par comparaison avec le reste du *Tristan en prose* n'a pas été résolue. Il se peut qu'elle ait été composée après le reste du roman. Pour notre présent article nous examinons le texte tel qu'il se présente dans l'édition de Curtis et nous utilisons le mot 'précurseur', étant donné que la généalogie est placée avant le reste du roman.

[7] Bremond, art. cit. p. 60.

[8] 'Amor praeterea inextricabiles consuevit hominibus et mortales guerras parare ac perpetuae pacis foedera removere. Saepe quoque urbes magnas et egregias arcesque munitas et castra tutissima subvertit et multam divitiarum fortunam sine possidentis largitione ad egestatis infortunia ducit multosque cogit commissum luere crimen, quos peccatum nec sui nec parentum potest (ulla) ratione contingere,' Andreae Capellani, *De Amore*, Havniae: Gadiana, 1892, pp. 330–31.

de la généalogie réalise sa virtualité lorsqu'avec le consentement de son frère aîné, Naburzadan, Sador se marie avec Chelinde, la demoiselle de son choix: 'Je la vel prendre a feme par vos otroiz' (§7, l. 2–3), A ce moment de la narration, une certaine amélioration est sensible pour Sador aussi bien que pour Chelinde.

A la suite de leur mariage pourtant, un processus de dégradation atteint le jeune couple. Le point de départ de cette déchéance est le viol de Chelinde par le frère de Sador, Naburzadan. Ce dernier: 'prist Chelynde et la mena en sa chambre, ausi com s'il vosist conseillier a li. Quant il la tint leanz, il jut a li ou elle vosist ou non' (§9, l. 13–14). Le viol se passe au château de Naburzadan où Sador et sa femme demeurent alors que Sador est parti à la chasse. Il s'y fait d'ailleurs blesser par un porc sauvage. Au lieu de récompenser l'affection particulière que Sador lui a toujours témoignée, Naburzadan profite de l'absence de Sador 'pour faire ses volentez' (§7, l. 10). C'est-à-dire que Naburzadan satisfait son *amor concupiscentiae*, par le biais de la tromperie. Il simule des intentions pacifiques envers Chelinde qui: 'ne se prist garde de tot ce, car ele ne poist croire qu'il l'amast si folement' (§7, l. 11–12). Chelinde commet l'erreur imprudente de ne pas faire attention à ce qui se passe, défaut qui se retrouve souvent comme *topos* dans la littérature médiévale.[9]

Sador est mis au courant accidentellement, alors que Chelinde, isolée dans un jardin, se plaint à haute voix: 'cele fu tant dolente de cele aventure que ele eüst autant amé qu'il li eüst la teste copee' (§9, l. 15–16). Elle ne garde plus le silence par lequel elle s'était soumise au *statu quo* et à l'autorité de son agresseur. Se trouvant incitée à déclamer sa douleur par un instinct de révolte contre Naburzadan, Chelinde s'exclame en se lamentant: 'Hé! Naburzadan, chevaliers mauvés et deleax, felons et enuieus, com tu m'as honie et aviliee, tant te devroit haïr Sador tes freres! Tu li as honte porchacié et a moi, si que je n'avrai jamés honor' (§11, l. 5–8). Par hasard – selon les *topoi* des romans médiévaux – son mari, couché dans une chambre qui donne sur la prairie, entend les paroles de sa femme. Sous la menace de la décapiter, il lui fait avouer le crime de son frère: 'Or tost! a dire vos estoit que mes freres vos a mesfait, qui si vos en pleigniez. Se vos nou me dites, morte iestes' (§11, l. 15–17). Laissant de côté une analyse freudienne sans doute déplacée dans ce contexte, nous relevons par contre le motif de l'épée nue avec laquelle Sador menace de décapiter sa femme. Dans la généalogie elle est signe d'une agression qui fait naître un sentiment d'attente angoissée, surtout que la violence est dirigée contre une femme. Apprenant ce qui s'est passé, Sador déclare: 'Honi m'a mes freres, mes je le honirai; aseür en puet estre' (§12, l. 3). A ce moment Naburzadan arrive. Il est surpris de voir l'attitude menaçante de

---

[9] Pour une analyse de la présentation de Chelinde voir Caulkins, 'Chelinde et la naissance du *Tristan* en prose,' à paraître dans *Le Moyen Age*.

Sador contre sa femme. Sans tarder, Sador adresse la parole à son frère: 'Naburzadan ... por quoi m'avez vos honi? Vos me deüssiez avant avoir desfié, enz que vos m'eüssiez si dou tout ma honte porchaciee. Vos m'avez honi sanz desfier, je vos rehonirai après cest desfiement' (§12, l. 6–9). Immédiatement, Sador s'exclame: 'Je vos desfi!' (§12, l. 10), mais Sador ne donne pas le temps à son frère de se défendre, et il l'assassine d'un coup de son épée. L'auteur n'est pas préoccupé par le fratricide, ni par les problèmes religieux. Il s'intéresse uniquement aux principes chevaleresques. Chelinde ne semble être l'objet d'aucune inquiétude. Seul le dommage infligé à Sador par Naburzadan est pris en considération.

Selon la perspective de Sador, le rétributeur du moment, il y a lieu de punir: en omettant de le défier, son frère n'a pas observé les conventions chevaleresques. Mais Sador ne fait que jouer sur les mots. C'est une absurdité, car Sador, tout chevalier qu'il est, ne se comporte pas comme un chevalier exemplaire. Il ne cherche pas de confrontation formelle. Il dit qu'il a été honni et qu'il veut donc payer Naburzadan de retour, mais ce n'est pas le cas: il ne désire que la vengeance et il tue Naburzadan sans le défier en bonne et due forme, selon les conventions chevaleresques. Le méfait que Naburzadan commet envers Sador et la révélation de l'acte par Chelinde ouvrent un processus de rétribution de la part de Sador dont l'acte initial – le meurtre de Naburzadan – entraîne la condamnation. Ce méfait commis par Sador se qualifie dans la perspective du 'rétributeur' comme clôture du processus de malfaisance contre lui par son frère, mais il marque également l'ouverture d'un autre processus. En effet, Sador et Chelinde doivent fuir pour garder la vie sauve, comme Sador l'explique à Chelinde: 'Alons de ci; des ores mes avons nos ci mauvés reperier, car se mi frere puent savoir ce que je ai fait de cesti, toz li mondes ne me garantiroit de la mort, s'il me pooient tenir' (§13, l. 1–4). S'efforçant de se protéger contre la mort et la dégradation qui le menace, l'esquive agressive de ses responsabilités apparaît à Sador non seulement comme un acte de légitime défense, mais comme une opération justicière. Sador et Chelinde se sauvent à bord d'un bâteau où le processus rétributeur continue. Un dommage est infligé à Sador sous la forme d'une tempête qui désigne aux marins la présence d'un pécheur à bord – un *topos* médiéval. Sador est donc jeté à la mer. Cela est le résultat attendu de la fonction de *méfait commis*, et Sador l'avoue lorsqu'il dit aux marins: 'Se je i peris, ce n'est pas merveille, car je l'ai bien deservi' (§16, l. 9–10). Sador fait son devoir lorsqu'il se montre prêt à se sacrifier pour autrui, et en conséquence, selon un thème qui revient dans la littérature médiévale, on lui apporte bientôt de l'aide. En effet, Sador ne se noie pas, mais avec l'aide de Dieu il nage jusqu'à un rocher où il trouve un ermite qui y demeure en toute pauvreté et en toute obéissance à Dieu. Il se contenterait d'y vivre pour le restant de ses jours: 'se Dieu plest' (§29, l. 19). Ainsi Sador expie ses anciens péchés, surtout celui de la luxure. Pour lui, le processus rétributeur continue pendant trois ans. Le rocher est le lieu de la rédemption pour l'ermite et de la punition pour Sador. Jusqu'au moment de sa réhabilitation, c'est-à-dire jusqu'à ce que son méfait soit totalement rétribué, Sador se trouve obligé de rester sur le rocher en l'absence de la femme qu'il aime et privé de nourriture: 'il enpira et enmesgri tant dedenz celi terme que a poines le poïst conistre sa feme, s'ele adonc le veïst' (§32, l. 6–8). Avec la séparation de Sador et de Chelinde l'artère narrative de la généalogie bifurque, et tandis que l'une des routes suit le sort de Sador, l'autre trace les aventures de Chelinde dont les détails suggèrent des analepses qui évoquent des rappels d'événements antérieurs.[10]

C'est alors qu'un second cycle d'aventures de Chelinde rappelle le premier. Celui-ci sert de modèle au second en permettant à l'invention narrative de légers remaniements. Pour la seconde fois, Chelinde regagne la terre dans un état misérable après un accident en mer. Mais cette fois-ci en Cornouaille, alors que l'autre fois c'était en Grande Bretagne. La première fois elle était naufragée, cette fois son mari a été jeté dans la mer. Malgré ses malheurs – elle pense que Sador est noyé – elle est toujours d'une très grande beauté, et pour la troisième fois quelqu'un désire l'épouser. Rappelons que la première fois elle était destinée à être la femme du roi de Perse; la seconde fois c'était Sador qui l'avait convertie à la religion chrétienne avant de l'épouser; maintenant c'est le roi païen Canor, qui l'épouse contre son gré, mais en lui permettant de conserver sa foi chrétienne.

Comme autrefois pour le mariage de Sador et de Chelinde, la virtualité narrative se réalise pour Canor quand il épouse Chelinde. Son but atteint, le sort du couple s'améliore: 'Li rois l'ama tant merveilleusement qu'il la prist a feme a la loi païenne, et la fist coroner del reaume de Cornoaille,/ ou cele vosist ou non' (§19, l. 11–13). Pour Chelinde, bien qu'elle tienne un rang social plus élevé, puisqu'elle est devenue reine de Cornouaille, alors qu'avant elle n'était que la femme de Sador, cette amélioration selon les conventions de l'univers narré recouvre un processus dichotomique de dégradation. En effet, Chelinde aime Sador et elle n'éprouve pas d'affection pour Canor: 'Mes il li desplesoit tant que se ele le poïst destorner en nule maniere del monde, ele destornast celi fait' (§19, l. 15–16). Son ascension sociale se fait au détriment de son bonheur personnel.

Comme antérieurement, le récit qui suit le mariage de Chelinde marque un processus de dégradation. Sador en était victime, et Canor en souffre de manière semblable après son mariage avec Chelinde. C'est par le procédé d'une prolepse, manoeuvre narrative consistant à raconter ou évoquer d'avance un événement ultérieur,[11] que le récit anticipe la mort éventuelle de

---

[10] Pour une discussion de l'emploi de l'analepse, voir Gérard Genette, *Figures III*, Paris: Le Seuil, 1972, p. 82.
[11] Voir ci-dessus, n. 9 pour une discussion de l'emploi de la prolepse.

Canor par le fils de Sador auquel Chelinde va bientôt donner le jour. Apeuré par un rêve et par l'explication qu'un sage lui en donne, Canor expose secrètement le nouveau-né de Chelinde dans une vaine tentative d'éliminer son futur adversaire. Cette tentative échoue, car l'enfant est sauvé par le chevalier Nicoraut et sa femme Madule qui l'adoptent et l'élèvent comme leur propre fils. Mais l'acte d'agression, le méfait commis par Canor en exposant le nouveau-né, entame le processus de dégradation de Canor à cause de sa lâcheté, tout comme l'assassinat de Naburzadan avait été décisive pour Sador – même si dans ce second cas il s'agissait de raisons contraires, de peur plutôt que de vengeance.

Maintenant mariée à Canor, Chelinde est désirée par un autre homme, tout comme elle l'était après son mariage à Sador. Cette fois-ci il s'agit de Pelias roi de Léonois qui dissimule ses volontés. Comme auparavant lorsque Naburzadan la convoitait, Chelinde ne se rend compte de rien. Canor non plus. Il est intéressant de noter que Canor n'a toujours pas été récompensé de ses services par Pelias, et que Pelias est le meilleur ami de Canor comme Naburzadan était le frère favori de Sador. La traîtrise semble donc amplifiée. Pelias, qui s'est perdu dans la forêt, accepte l'hospitalité de son ami Canor. Cette nuit-là en tant qu'invité de Canor, Pelias épie son hôte, puis il le surprend tenant son épée nue sur lui. Il s'agit là du même acte d'agression que celui de Sador contre sa femme. Apeuré, Canor tombe de la fenêtre de son château dans la rivière. Pelias accomplit alors ses désirs avec Chelinde, qui, n'étant toujours pas sur la défensive, dort sans s'apercevoir de rien. Elle imagine dans l'obscurité que c'est son mari Canor qui est couché à côté d'elle. Tôt le lendemain matin, Pelias part en secret de Cornouaille. Dès qu'il est de retour en Léonois, il déclare la guerre contre la Cornouaille à cause de son *amor concupiscentiae* pour Chelinde: 'Si pensoit qu'il conquerroit le reaume de Cornouaille, et prendroit/la roïne Chelinde, la riens ou monde que il plus amoit. Et se il cele pooit avoir en tel maniere com il pansoit, il avroit adonc acompli toz ses voloirs et toz ses desirriers' (§45, l. 6–9). Contrairement à Sador qui prend la honte de sa femme pour la sienne et défend sa position de mari, Canor perd le droit d'être mari et roi lorsqu'il s'enfuit lâchement, au lieu de rester dans la chambre et de se défendre, même sans armes. La chute dans l'eau de Canor est indicative de sa dégradation continue.

Le projet de Pelias échoue pourtant, et Canor est sauvé par deux mariniers, tout comme le projet de Canor échoue lorsque le nouveau né est sauvé par Nicoraut et Madule. Canor est mis en prison en Léonois par deux chevaliers qui le reconnaissent en lui le roi de Cornouaille et qui espèrent tirer profit de lui. Après la déclaration de guerre contre la Cornouaille par Pelias, les deux chevaliers vont parler au roi de Léonois pour lui dire que Canor n'est pas mort, mais prisonnier dans leur château. Pelias, en admettant avoir commis un méfait, se révèle conscient de son acte d'agression et d'avoir bien mal récompensé son généreux ami, Canor. Pourtant Pelias continue à enfreindre le code chevaleresque. Il agit indirectement d'une façon trompeuse envers Canor en ordonnant aux deux chevaliers de ne rien dire à personne au sujet de l'identité de leur prisonnier: 'Ne le faites asavoir a nul autre que je l'aie en ma terre, car aprés ce que il m'a servi et honoré en sa terre, se je aucun gerredon ne l'en rendoie en la moie, a felonie le porroit l'en tenir. Por ce vel je que vos le gardez, que nus n'en saiche plus noveles, ne que s'il estoit morz. Et quant nos avrons sa terre conquise, et je li fais puis honor, adonc m'en savra il gré' (§46, l. 4–9).

Pelias veut satisfaire ses désirs en épousant Chelinde. Pour ce faire, il choisit d'anéantir la Cornouaille. Pelades, le frère de Canor, se rend compte du péril et s'efforce d'amorcer un processus protecteur. Avec l'aide du conseil d'un sage, Pelades fait échapper Sador de son rocher et le ramène en Cornouaille. Ainsi, l'artère narrative de Sador rejoint celle de Cornouaille. Sador devient bénéficiaire d'un heureux concours de circonstances. Les choses ont bien tourné pour lui, et en reconnaissance d'un service passé, c'est-à-dire pour récompenser les Cornouaillais de l'avoir tiré de son rocher, Sador consent à défendre la Cornouaille contre le Léonois. Il devient le champion de Cornouaille contre Pelias.[12]

Les deux champions se rencontrent sur le champ de bataille et leur lutte entraîne une dégradation volontaire de leur part. En effet, Sador et Pelias se sacrifient: 'Tant a duré li premiers assauz des deus chevaliers q'a force les estoit reposer por recovrer vigor et alaine, qu'il avoient auques perdue de lasseté et de travail' (§57, 1–3). Leur lutte est destinée à payer le prix d'une amélioration.

La victoire de Sador contre Pelias qui le consacre comme 'meilleur chevalier,' est soulignée par son acte de générosité. Sador épargne la vie de Pelias. Dans la même veine pacifique, la négociation qui s'ensuit constitue une forme d'élimination non destructrice de l'adversaire. Le pacte spécifique qui en résulte comprend la libération et la restitution du roi Canor aussi bien que la fin de la guerre entre les deux pays. La réparation de Sador est achevée par son succès contre Pelias. La négociation couronnée de succès de Sador est indicative de ses dons de diplomatie et de la fin d'un cycle. Son manque d'obéissance à Joseph est suivi et réparé par une obéissance totale et chevaleresque au royaume de Cornouaille; sa vengeance contre son frère est suivie par son combat formel devant la cour de Marovex de Gaule et le retour de Canor aux Cornouaillais qui restitue l'ordre du pays.

La réhabilitation de Sador paraît être complète lorsqu'il rentre en Cornouaille, mais voilà qu'après un bref *sursis* qui équivaut fonctionnellement à une phase d'amélioration, le récit continue avec un nouveau cycle et un autre processus de dégradation pour Sador. Canor, qui est de retour en

---

[12] Cf Tristan qui lutte contre Morholt en récompense des services reçus en Cornouaille, notamment celui d'avoir été fait chevalier par Marc.

Cornouaille, grâce à Sador, devine son identité de premier mari de Chelinde. Ayant peur de perdre Chelinde, Canor chasse Sador en exil. Sador trouve que le comportement du roi de Cornouaille constitue une récompense négative pour ses services: 'Mauvés guerredon li ont rendu cil de Cornoaille de lor seignor qu'il lor a/rendu, e de lor terre qu'il lor a mis en pes' (§63, l. 4–6). L'idée de récompense pour un service qui a été raconté en détail dans le texte donne une autre dimension à l'emploi d'analepses en encourageant un rappel des événements antérieurs. L'acte d'agression de Canor, le méfait qu'il inflige à Sador, confirme la prophétie de Joseph et signale le point de départ de la nouvelle phase de dégradation de Sador, qui se voit obligé de partir de Cornouaille à pied, aussi pauvre lors de son présent départ qu'au moment de son arrivée. Il souffre de douleur et de colère, car, n'ayant pas encore vu la reine de Cornouaille et ne sachant pas son identité, il ne se rend pas compte qu'une fois de plus Chelinde (sans le savoir elle-même, car elle n'a pas encore revu Sador non plus), est la cause de ce nouveau méfait commis envers lui.

L'itinéraire narratif de Sador bifurque maintenant vers celui de Canor et rejoint celui de Pelias dans le Léonois. Arrivé en Léonois, le processus de dégradation continue et Sador a très peur parce qu'il a vaincu Pelias (tout comme plus tard Tristan aura peur en arrivant en Irlande après avoir vaincu Morholt). Il craint aussi d'être mis en prison quand il est arrêté injustement pour un crime qu'il n'a pas commis. Le juge lui demande: 'Pourquoi nos as tu si honiz, deleal home?' (§69, l. 9–10). Il pense qu'on parle de sa bataille contre Pelias et il répond: 'Einsi me plot/que je le feïsse' (§69, l. 12–13). En réponse, les Léonois lui déclarent: 'Tu en morras. Tu nos as honiz et nos te honirons,' (§69, l. 14–15) et il leur répond: 'Faire . . . le poez, puis qu'il vos plest, car assez vos ai je mal fait, ce sai ge bien' (§69, l. 14–16). Sador accepte volontiers de se sacrifier. Il ne fait nulle objection à son sort et les Léonois se saisissent de lui: 'Et le moinent par la vile batant, et li font laidure tant com il pueent' (§69, l. 16–17).

C'est alors qu'après un sacrifice volontaire il y a une intervention protectrice, qui appelle à son tour une réparation, et un processus rétributeur recommence (semblable au séjour de Sador, resté trois ans sur le rocher). Pelias, dont Sador avait épargné la vie à l'issue du duel, sent qu'il doit s'acquitter d'une dette envers Sador: 'Et quant tant avez fait por moi, ne gerredon ne vos en rendi, a mauvestié le porroit l'en tenir se je nel vos gerredonoie, et quant je le puis faire, et li besoinz en est venuz' (§77, l. 11–13). Jouant de nouveau avec l'emploi d'analepses qui encouragent des rappels d'événements antérieurs, l'auteur réintroduit Pelias, autrefois ennemi de Sador, maintenant son allié. Pelias se comporte en débiteur du bénéficiaire et fournit de l'aide à Sador. C'est par l'intervention de Pelias que Sador est sauvé du perron des condamnés à mort et que le processus d'amélioration de Sador peut s'effectuer. Au cours de ces développements, Sador est devenu l'adversaire de son ancien allié, Canor, qu'il avait établi en Cornouaille pour réaffirmer l'ordre chevaleresque. Par contre, il est obligé de devenir l'allié de son ancien ennemi, Pelias, à cause d'une série d'échanges de services, tantôt sur le mode de la récompense, tantôt sur le mode du châtiment. Sador consent à enlever à Canor la reine de Cornouaille, dont il ne connaît pas encore l'identité, pour la rendre à Pelias: 'Je vos promet que vos l'avrez, puis que vos la desirez tant' (§84, l. 13–14).

Sador est maintenant embarqué dans un processus dichotomique qui représente une phase d'amélioration dans la mesure où il récompense Pelias, mais c'est aussi une phase de dégradation, car c'est spécifiquement un processus à piège. C'est en ayant recours à la tromperie qu'il se saisit de la reine, l'épouse de Canor. Quand Sador la rend à Pelias, le roi de Léonois est si heureux qu'il dit à Sador: 'Vos m'avez fait le greignor servise que chevaliers feïst onques a home, car or m'avez vos acompli quanque je desiroie. Jamés ne me porrez chose faire qui tant me plese' (§91, l. 2–4). L'ironie de la dernière remarque est que Pelias veut tout simplement exprimer le plaisir qu'il éprouve devant le retour de la reine, tandis que la phrase se vérifiera dans un sens tout autre. Sador et Chelinde se reconnaissent bientôt à la cour de Pelias, et poussé par son désir pour Chelinde, Sador, si récemment l'allié de Pelias, devient de nouveau son adversaire en devenant son rival. Sador a de nouveau recours à la ruse, et il demande un don à Pelias en reconnaissance de son service. Il dit ne rien demander qui soit à Pelias, mais à lui-même. Cependant quand Pelias le lui accorde avec confiance, sans savoir de quoi il s'agit, Sador exige des garanties. Le roi lui jure sur ses dieux et devant ses barons de lui rendre son bien. Mais quand Pelias apprend la nature du don, il est furieux contre son ancien allié, trouvant que celui-ci lui offre une récompense négative pour l'amitié qui lui a été témoignée.

En introduisant de nouveau une pluralité de perspectives, aussi bien que des analepses, la narration amorce de nouveaux espaces, bâtis sur des événements antérieurs. Sador essaie d'expliquer à Pelias le bien-fondé de sa requête en lui disant: 'Rois, ne vos soit ceste chose trop greveuse. Vos l'eüstes par moi, et par moi la devez perdre. Bien me devez tant faire d'amor que vos la moie chose me rendoiz' (§94, l. 20–23). Le roi reste furieux contre Sador et lui dit: 'Vassal . . . trahi m'avez, qui ensi m'avez sorpris par paroles' (§95, l. 3–4). Suivant les conventions de cet univers narratif, Pelias se voit obligé de rendre la reine à Sador parce qu'il a donné sa parole, mais il est très en colère et il se considère honni. Il pense en avoir perdu sa joie: 'quant il a perdu par cele decevance la chose par qui tote la joie li venoit' (§95, l. 12–13). Cette déclaration est lourde d'ironie lorsque l'on considère que Pelias lui-même n'hésite pas à avoir recours soit à la récompense négative soit à la tromperie quand il a un but à atteindre.

Pelias vient de subir un empêchement de l'actualisation de son but, alors que Sador et Chelinde réussissent. Ils réalisent leur but, mais par la tromperie. Cette dernière engendre une séquence complexe au cours de laquelle ils doivent rétribuer leur méfait. Un nouveau processus de dégradation s'ensuit, et ils se trouvent de nouveau devant la nécessité de s'enfuir ensemble. Arrêtés en route par un géant, ils endurent une phase de réparation pendant laquelle ils expient le fait d'avoir trompé Pelias (comme auparavant Sador expie le meurtre de son frère sur le rocher). Avec l'arrivée de Pelias chez le géant, Sador a peur de perdre Chelinde à nouveau, car Pelias la veut toujours. Sador négocie donc et de façon ouverte avec le géant. Il lui fait promettre de les libérer, lui et Chelinde, en échange de l'explication de l'énigme posée au géant par Pelias. De cette façon, il transforme le géant d'adversaire en allié. Ainsi, Sador et Chelinde partent de la forêt.

Leur rencontre en route avec le seigneur de Teriaden marque un *sursis* et un processus d'amélioration pour Sador et Chelinde, car le seigneur reconnaît en Sador celui qui a vaincu Pelias (analepse). Le Seigneur de Teriaden n'a pas d'héritiers, et sa mort prompte laisse tout à Sador. Cet héritage joue le rôle de rétribution pour Sador, qui a défendu la Cornouaille contre le Léonois où il a apporté la paix. Pour ces bonnes actions, Sador et Chelinde passent quinze ans de bonheur ensemble.

Plusieurs cycles ou boucles du récit généalogique sont maintenant fermés. Leur fonctionnement repose principalement sur le motif de récompense/châtiment. Le schéma narratif se développe sur le cycle de l'amélioration, de la dégradation et de la réparation. D'autres boucles vont suivre, ouvrant d'autres améliorations, suivies d'autres dégradations, suivies d'autres réparations selon un cycle qui se répète et se modalise plusieurs fois dans la généalogie et ensuite quasi indéfiniment dans le reste du *Tristan* en prose. Les boucles se hiérarchisent, entrent en dichotomie. Elles répètent des phases d'événements passés et anticipent des séquences à venir. Le réseau de leurs articulations et de leurs rapports mutuels devient de plus en plus complexe et différencié selon un jeu de combinaisons inépuisable qui permet le plaisir de l'art subtil de la composition.

Le discours généalogique, en tant que précurseur du reste du roman en prose, pose un paradigme de logique narrative qui comprend un système de signes oppositionnels de récompense et de châtiment coordonnés et enchaînés de façon à refléter les conventions rétributrices de l'univers chevaleresque du *Tristan* en prose. Il s'agirait, avec le motif de récompense/châtiment, d'une véritable économie du récit, d'un jeu d'équilibre toujours en mouvance vers de nouvelles bifurcations généalogiques du récit.

Si le récit repose bien sur un motif génératif de récompense/châtiment, comme cet article essaie de le démontrer, le texte ne peut se ponctuer qu'à la condition d'un échec relatif à l'opposition dont dépend ce motif. C'est-à-dire que le motif oppositionnel perd de sa clarté: il s'use en quelque sorte à force de multiplications complexes et variées, au point où le récit prend fin.

Cette conclusion que nous avançons laisse entrevoir d'autres possibilités. Prenons, par exemple, l'hypothèse que l'opposition récompense/châtiment dépendrait de celle qui existe entre le bien et le mal. Dans ce cas de figure, cette dernière opposition perdrait de son sens. Ainsi se serait éteint peut-être le genre même du récit chevaleresque. La fin du *Tristan* en prose préfigurerait donc à la fois l'apogée et la fin de l'écriture chevaleresque.

# *Tristan and Iseut's Condemnation to the Stake in Beroul*

## A. H. DIVERRES

One of the striking episodes in the surviving portion of Beroul's version of the romance of Tristan and Iseut is the one in which King Mark sentences the lovers to the stake.[1] The relevant events are as follows. The liaison between the hero and the queen has been discovered by three evil barons, who, jealous of Tristan, urge the king to exile his nephew from the court. Unwilling to accept the accusations and conscious of Tristan's great services to him, Mark demands conclusive proof. In consultation with the dwarf Frocin, it is agreed that, on the following evening, the king will instruct his nephew to take a message to Arthur's court on the next day. In the middle of the night, Mark will leave his chamber, in which Tristan also sleeps, so giving him the opportunity to join Iseut. The floor will have been sprinkled with flour, and thus Tristan's tracks will be betrayed. After the king's departure, Tristan, who has seen the dwarf scatter the flour, leaps over to the queen's bed, a lance's length away, but the strain causes a recent wound to open, staining the royal sheets, the flour on the floor as he jumps back, and his own bed. Mark, who considers that on the evidence of the blood-stains the lovers have been caught *in flagrante delicto*, sentences them both without trial to be burnt at the stake on the following morning, in spite of Tristan's appeal for mercy, in particular for the queen, and for the right to defend himself against his accusers in a trial by combat. Though the sympathy of the populace is wholly for the lovers and there is widespread criticism of his decision, the king remains adamant. At dawn he orders the pyre to be prepared, and even participates enthusiastically in its construction. But he is unable to carry out the sentence because Tristan, who is to be burnt first, escapes on his way to execution, and so Mark allows himself to be persuaded to hand Iseut over to a band of lepers, from whom she will be saved by her lover.

Since no evidence exists that the stake was used as a punishment for adultery in twelfth-century France, Mark's sentence has puzzled many critics. The usually accepted theory about the genesis of the Tristan romances in

[1] Beroul, *The Romance of Tristran*, ed. A. Ewert, Oxford: Blackwell, 1939, Vol. I, ll. 741 ff.

French is that there existed an earlier one, usually known as the *estoire*, but now lost, written probably in the late 1150s or early 1160s, which served as a source for the three main surviving versions, those by Beroul and Thomas, both from the later twelfth century, and the thirteenth-century prose version by an unknown author. It would also have been on this French archetype that Eilhart von Oberge based his German version, dating from around 1170 or 1180. If this theory is correct, and at present it appears more satisfactory than any other, would the *estoire* have contained the episode under consideration? In addition to Beroul, the prose *Tristan* includes the episode, but with some minor differences.² On the other hand, it would appear to have been omitted by Thomas, though two separate lines in the first of the surviving fragments of his romance, which describes part of the lovers' meeting in the orchard, relate Mark's threat to have the lovers burnt alive if he catches them *in flagrante delicto*. They provide quite strong circumstantial evidence in support of the existence of the episode in his source.³ Like Beroul, Eilhart includes it in his version immediately after the flour scene, but with one significant difference; while Iseut is condemned to the stake, Tristan is sentenced to the wheel. Which of the two texts reproduces the details in the archetype? The relevant part of Eilhart survives only in a fifteenth-century recension, and so it is on this that we have to base our speculations. Nevertheless, it remains everywhere very close to the extant fragments of the late twelfth-century text. All that one can say, therefore, is that it looks as if either Eilhart or the reviser altered the detail of Tristan's sentence, perhaps for the sake of greater realism, since the combined evidence collected from Beroul, Thomas and the prose *Tristan* would seem to confirm that in their source both lovers were condemned to the stake.

Pierre Jonin has written a very thorough chapter on legal procedure as described by Beroul. He came to the conclusion that everywhere the romance accurately followed practice in northern France as it existed in the thirteenth century, with one exception, the sentence to the stake for adultery, for which

---

² *Le Roman de Tristan en prose*, ed. Renée L. Curtis, Leiden: Brill, Vol. II, 1976, §§544–5.

³
        Li rois les voit, au naim a dit:
        'Atendés moi chi un petit;
        En cel palais la sus irai,
        De mes barons i amerrai:
        Verront com les avon trovez;
        Ardoir les frai, quant ert pruvez.'

(Thomas, *Les Fragments du Roman de Tristan*, ed. B. Wind, Genève: Droz, 1960, ll. 8–13). The second reference to it is by Tristan, speaking to Iseut a few lines further on:

        Fra nos, s'il puet, ensenble prendre,
        Par jugement ardoir en cendre         (ll. 22–3).

he could find no parallel,[4] and so he fell back on a Celtic source for it. The view that the stake as a punishment for adultery was cited in old Irish literature was first put forward in the late nineteenth century and was taken up by Gertrude Schoepperle.[5] But the three examples that she cites are inconclusive, if not worthless. J. R. Reinhard, in an article entitled 'Burning at the stake in medieval law and literature',[6] examines the problem very much more thoroughly. He has studied the early laws of Wales and Ireland, and nowhere has he found burning stipulated as a punishment for adultery. My own reading of these texts confirms his view.[7] Reinhard has also examined literary texts, and only in one, the story of Herc and his sister Ele, the wife of Fergal, to be found in the late twelfth-century Book of Leinster, has he come across a tale in which the accused woman is actually burnt, and in this case, if guilty, she has committed incest as well. In other tales cited by Reinhard, the accused woman may be sentenced to burning, but she always escapes through divine intervention. On this evidence Reinhard rightly casts doubt on the view that burning for adultery was an autochthonous Celtic custom, and he suggests instead that narrative literature was inspired by the Old Testament, in which the sentence for adultery was death, on at least two occasions death by burning, both cases involving prostitution (Gen. xxxviii, 24; Lev. xxi, 9). Though it seems certain that the *estoire* included the lovers' sentence to the stake, no hard evidence has yet been discovered to support its inclusion in any earlier version of the Tristan story that may have existed. It may therefore be worth considering whether it could not be a twelfth-century accretion due to the adaptation of the tale to meet the preoccupations of the time.

A serious shortcoming of Jonin's treatment of the episode is that he studied it entirely against a background of continental French law, though he included Norman treatises such as the thirteenth-century *Tres ancien coutumier de Normandie* and *Ancien coutumier de Normandie*.[8] What he failed to do was to examine English legal treatises and statutes and so pick out any possible differences with Norman practices, an odd omission in view of Beroul's apparent knowledge of the south-west of England and of the possibility that he

---

[4] No legal texts dating from the twelfth century survive. P. Jonin, *Les Personnages féminins dans les romans français de Tristan au XII<sup>e</sup> siècle*, Aix-en-Provence: Annales de la Faculté des Lettres, 1958, pp. 59–108.
[5] Gertrude Schoepperle, *Tristan and Isolt. A Study of the Sources of the Romance*, Frankfurt: Baer & London: D. Nutt, 1913.
[6] *Speculum*, XVI (1941), pp. 186–209.
[7] The earliest manuscript in which burning is mentioned in Welsh law dates from the thirteenth century, in which it is cited as one of the possible alternative penalties for poisoning (see *Ancient Laws and Institutes of Wales*, London, Public Records, 1841, Vol. II, p. 22, §12). Nowhere is it linked with adultery. I am grateful to Professor Dafydd Jenkins for confirming this view.
[8] *Les Coutumiers de Normandie*, ed. E. J. Tardif, 2 vols, Paris: Picard, 1881–1903.

wrote the romance for an Anglo-Norman patron.⁹ Furthermore, relevant legal texts survive in England, in particular Henry de Bracton's monumental *De Legibus et Consuetudinibus Angliae*, written only in the middle of the thirteenth century, it is true. However, in several places it is an expanded version of *De Legibus et Consuetudinibus Regni Angliae*, which usually goes under the name of Glanvill, written before Henry II's death in 1189 and so virtually contemporary with Beroul. Going further back still, we find *Leges Henrici Primi* (c. 1116). They show how conservative the law is, even during such an important period of innovation as Henry II's reign, and basically how little it changed in its main principles during the twelfth and thirteenth centuries.¹⁰ A final text that could have been advantageously consulted by Jonin is John of Salisbury's *Policraticus* (1159). Recent critics have underlined Beroul's interest in the legal problems raised by adultery in the feudal setting, and Alberto Varvaro sums up the romance succinctly by stating: 'Claims of conscience seem to be replaced by those of the law, which are again respected as a whole and meticulously observed in their detail, with a true lawyer's scrupulousness.'¹¹

The first point that should be examined is whether, according to medieval law, the lovers were in fact caught *in flagrante delicto*. Secondly, if they were, was Mark justified in inflicting the penalty of the stake on them both or on either of them; in other words, were the procedure that he followed and the sentence correct in England? Madame Rita Lejeune asserted that Tristan and Iseut were not really caught *in flagrante delicto*. According to her, the evidence provided by the blood-stained beds and floor was no more than circumstantial, and so there could only be a presumption of guilt.¹² The earliest text to give a clear definition of *flagrante delicto* is Philippe de Beaumanoir's *Coutumes de Beauvaisis*, written in 1283. It was not essential for lovers to be caught in the act of copulation for adultery to be established, as Madame Lejeune implies. It was sufficient for them to be surprised alone in a locked room, or for the circumstances in which they were discovered to make their guilt clear.¹³ The dwarf Frocin's plan was to provide proof which could establish beyond doubt that adultery had been committed. Though no footmark was left by Tristan, the presence of blood-stains in the beds occupied by him and Iseut as well as on the floor between, together with his wounded

---

⁹ In her important review of Jonin's book, Dominica Legge was the first to make this criticism. See *Cahiers de Civilisation médiévale*, III (1960), pp. 511–12.
¹⁰ Dominica Legge also drew attention to the late thirteenth-century *Miroir des Justices* in Anglo-Norman. See *The Mirror of Justices*, ed. W. J. Whittaker, London: Selden Society, 1895, pp. 15, 21.
¹¹ A. Varvaro, *Béroul's Romance of Tristan*, trans. J. C. Barnes, Manchester: University Press, 1972, p. 103.
¹² *Le Moyen Age*, LXVI (1960), p. 147.
¹³ Ed. Am. Salmon, 2 vols., Paris: Picard, 1899–1900. §934, I, p. 473. R. Howard Bloch deals with the point in his *Medieval French Literature and Law*, Berkeley: Univ. of California Press, 1977, p. 55.

leg would certainly have been sufficient to convince a medieval judge that the lovers had been caught *in flagrante delicto*.

What rights had a wronged husband if he found his wife and her paramour in this situation? Philippe de Beaumanoir is quite specific. Should a husband, after forbidding a man to visit his house, catch his wife and the man in the act of union and kill them in the heat of the moment, he would go unpunished.[14] On the other hand, should he delay and then kill them without recourse to justice, their deaths at his hand would be deemed to be culpable homicide and he would be brought to trial. If he were found guilty, and his deed had been committed without witnesses, he would be drawn and hanged, the usual penalty for murder, rape and treason.[15] Had Mark killed Iseut and Tristan immediately on finding the blood-stains, he would have been entirely within his rights, but by delaying and then condemning them to death without first granting them a trial or acceding to Tristan's request for a judicial combat with his accusers, he would, according to thirteenth-century custom, have been committing culpable homicide. Though the *Miroir de Justices*, Bracton and Glanvill contain nothing on this point, the likelihood is that custom in the Angevin kingdom in the second half of the twelfth century was very similar, if not identical, for already the *Leges Henrici Primi* affirm a man's right, after due warning, to defend his womenfolk against predatory males:

> Similiter pugnare potest homo contra eum quem cum despensata sibi uxore post secundam et tertiam prohibitionem clausis hostiis vel sub una coopertura inveniet, siue cum filia sua quam de sponsa genuerit, siue cum sorore sua que de sponsa sit, siue cum matre sua que patri suo fuerit desponsata.[16]

The same treatise also decrees a person's right to present a defence when being tried:

> Nec oportet quemquam iudicari uel dampnari priusquam legittimos accusatores habeat presentes locumque defendendi accipiat ad abluenda crimina.[17]

Strict rules for allowing a defendant to choose a judicial combat as an alternative to a trial by jury are still laid down by Bracton, indicating that this practice was still widely used in the middle of the thirteenth century.[18] It is quite clear that, in Beroul's view, Mark had exceeded his powers by denying the lovers the right to a defence, since he describes, through the mouths of the populace and Dinas, the king's summary refusal as the greatest ingratitude towards Tristan for his services to the crown, and towards Iseut as a

---

[14] *Coutumes de Beauvaisis*, §1637, II, p. 337. Cf. §§1188, 1189, II, p. 112.
[15] Ibid, §934, I, p. 473. *Murdrum* was the name given to homicide without witnesses.
[16] *Leges Henrici Primi*, ed. L. J. Downer, Oxford: Clarendon Press, 1972, cap. 82.8, p. 258.
[17] Ibid, cap. 5, 9a, p. 86.
[18] *De Legibus et Consuetudinis Angliae*, Ed. G. E. Woodbine, Harvard Univ. Press, 1968, Vol. II, pp. 385–6.

deliberate humiliation, since her status as a queen gave her the right to more courteous treatment than that she was receiving from her husband.[19]

Is Mark's failure to observe a defendant's right to a trial which would permit him to defend himself the only point at issue, or does Beroul actually criticise the king's choice of punishment, namely burning alive? If the sentence was for adultery alone, Mark was inflicting a more terrible penalty on both parties than was usual in the later twelfth century. Marie de France was closer to established practice when in *Bisclavret* the unfaithful wife was exiled for her actions. Is Mark's condemnation of Iseut and Tristan to the stake the only example of this choice of punishment for adultery in French romance? The answer is no. In the early thirteenth-century *Mort Artu* Guenevere is condemned to be burnt alive for her adultery with Lancelot.[20] The cases are broadly parallel. Does this merely indicate that the episode in the *Mort Artu* is modelled on Beroul, or do they both reflect contemporary legal practice? The answer lies in the fact that both Iseut and Guenevere are queen consorts, and that queen consorts were, according to English law, guilty of treason if they consented to the violation of their chastity by anybody but their husbands. Unfortunately, Bracton avoids the issue, as do Glanvill and the *Leges Henrici Primi* before him, and so one is unable to find a definition in a legal text of English provenance until we come to *Le Miroir des Justices* (c. 1290).[21] In Wace's *Roman de Brut* (1155), however, Arthur's nephew Modred is described as a traitor for committing adultery with the queen in the king's absence.

[Modred]
Kar cuntre crestïene lei
Prist a sun lit femme lu rei,
Femme sun uncle et sun seignur
Prist a guise de traïtur
(ed. I. Arnold, SATF, ll. 13027–30)

The Galfredian text on which this is based is more ambiguous, and it is not clear whether Modred has committed treason because of his usurpation of the throne or of his adultery with the queen, or both.[22] All this would suggest, however, that, on the evidence provided, Mark was justified in considering that both Tristan and Iseut were guilty of treason towards him since he was unaware of the effect of the magic potion that they had accidentally drunk on their way from Ireland and which absolved them of their responsibility.

Treason was not officially defined as a distinct offence before Edward III's

---

[19] *The Romance of Tristran*, ll. 884–7, 1088–1100.
[20] *La Mort le Roi Artu*, ed. J. Frappier, Genève: Droz, 1954, 93, p. 122.
[21] See note 10 above. The definitions of lèse-majesty and treason are to be found on pp. 15 and 21. The description of lèse-majesty contains the following: 'e par ceux avoutres qi purguissent la femme le Roi, ou la fille le Roi einznesce legitimee einz ces qe ele seit marie en la garde le Roi, ou la norice letaunt le heir le Roi (p. 15).
[22] Geoffrey of Monmouth, *Historia Regum Britanniae*, ed. A. Griscom, London: Longmans, 1929, Book X, 13, p. 496.

Statute of Treason of 1352. During the twelfth and thirteenth centuries it was regarded, however, as the most serious of felonies and a capital offence, for it involved a breach between lord and vassal. Under the growing influence of the study of Roman law, royal lawyers from the middle of the twelfth century onwards often referred to the crime of lèse-majesty, or offence against the sovereign authority, in which a distinction was made between the king and the magnates.[23] How far the stake was used as a punishment for lèse-majesty is uncertain, but in the late Roman Empire it had been used as a penalty for counterfeiting, defined as a crime of lèse-majesty.[24] Was its use in fairly limited cases in Rome behind its adoption in western Europe, particularly from the twelfth century onwards, as a penalty for heresy, considered to be lèse-majesty against God?[25] It seems to have been inflicted on women (not only on witches) more than on men for other forms of treason.[26] It became the punishment for adulterous queens sentenced under Edward III's Statute of Treason of 1352,[27] and was not deleted from the Statute Book until 1790, when it was replaced by hanging. It never seems to have been applied, for it could be commuted to beheading at the sovereign's pleasure, as it was in the case of Henry VIII's second and fifth wives, Ann Boleyn and Catherine Howard.[28]

One of the differences of detail between Eilhart and Beroul's versions of the episode is that, while in the former it is Tinas (the Dinas of the French text) who pleads with Mark to show mercy towards the lovers, Beroul allots this role in the first instance to the citizenry. Of course, it is impossible to be sure which of the two authors was responsible for altering the *estoire* at this point, but there is a likelihood that it was Beroul, who was deliberately expanding

---

[23] The term *crimen laesae maiestatis* does not appear in the *Leges Henrici Primi*, in which we find only the Old English *hlaferdspike* and the Latin *infidelitas* and *proditio*. This suggests that no clear distinction was yet made between treachery towards the state as symbolized by the king and towards one's lord, except possibly in cap. 10, 1, p. 108; cap. 13, 1, p. 116; cap. 55, 3a, p. 174.

[24] See *Codex Iustinianus*, Liber IX, 24, 2. See *Corpus Iuris Civilis*, ed. P. Krueger, Berlin, 1900, Vol. II, p. 384.

[25] This is the view of Maurice Bévenot in articles entitled 'The Inquisition and its antecedents', *Heythrop Journal*, VI (1966), VII (1967).

[26] A. L. Poole states that in twelfth-century England, in the rare cases in which the sentence was death, women culprits were generally burnt. His references are *Curia Regis Rolls*, vi, 306; *Select Pleas*, no. 191; *Rot. Chart.* 86b (see *From Domesday Book to Magna Carta*, Oxford: Clarendon Press, p. 405). Bracton is a witness to it having been used in certain cases in the thirteenth century as a punishment for those plotting against the safety of their lords: 'Igni concremantur qui saluti dominorum suorum insidiaverint' (*De Legibus* . . . , II, p. 299).

[27] *The Statutes*, 3rd revised edition, II, London, HMSO, 1950, pp. 141–2.

[28] The most important case in France is that of Philippe le Bel's daughters-in-law, Marguerite and Blanche, accused of adultery with Gautier and Philippe d'Aunai in 1314. The two brothers were convicted of treason, flayed and, after castration, drawn and hanged. The two princesses were imprisoned at Les Andelys, after having their heads cropped. None of the guilty parties was burnt alive. For an interesting contemporary account, see *La Chronique métrique attribuée à Geffroy de Paris*, ed. A. Diverres, Presses Universitaires de Strasbourg, 1956, l. 5867ff.

his source material. It might therefore be worth considering what purpose the citizenry serve in the episode. The usual explanation offered by critics is that their pleas are used by the author to arouse his public's sympathy for the lovers and to reinforce Tristan's demand for a trial.[29] Doubtless this is true, but are they the poet's only, if indeed his main, purposes? Might there not be an intention directly related to twelfth-century England? Could the remarks of the citizenry be explicit social criticism of Mark's conduct when compared to the ideal of kingship prevalent at the time? Was the monarch above the law, unfettered by the legal restraints imposed on his subjects, as Mark's decision to condemn the lovers without trial suggests? Though, in practice, many a medieval king wielded despotic power, in theory he should have reigned within the framework of established constitutional forms. According to the *Policraticus*, if he exceeded these, he was behaving not as a true prince, but as a tyrant. John of Salisbury returns time and again to the supremacy of the law, and Book IV opens with the following sentence:

> Est ergo tiranni et principis haec diffentia sola vel maxima, quod hic legi obtemperat et eius arbitrio populum regit cuius se credit ministrum.[30]

The ruler must possess a clear knowledge of the law and he must adhere to it strictly in all his dealings with his subjects, taking the greatest care not to exceed its dictates. Once he has abandoned these as the foundations of his government, his rule would inevitably sink into tyranny.[31]

There is no doubt that the evidence of the blood-stains was considered sufficient to establish the lovers' adultery, and also that the sentence passed was one that was sometimes imposed for treason, particularly in the case of women. Where Mark exceeded his powers under the law was to pass sentence without first arranging a trial in which the accused had the right to defend themselves, whether it be a trial by law or, in Tristan's case, a trial by combat. A further point is whether Mark had the right to act as a judge in this case, since he had been a victim of the lovers' conduct, and so could not be objective. According to Bracton, he would not have had this right in the thirteenth century, and would have had to delegate his authority to the judges.[32] Mark's conduct assumes the character of private vengeance, which might have been justifiable in earlier centuries, but which, in theory at least,

---

[29] e.g. A. Ewert's commentary in vol. II of his edition (Oxford: Blackwell, 1970, p. 133).
[30] Liber IV, cap. 1, ed. C. C. I. Webb, Oxford: Clarendon Press, 1909, I, p. 235. 'Between a tyrant and a prince there is this single or chief difference, that the latter obeys the law and rules the people by its dictates, accounting himself as but their servant' (*The Statesman's Book of John of Salisbury*, trans. by J. Dickinson, New York, 1963, p. 3).
[31] See further, *Policraticus*, III, 15; VII, 17, 18; VIII, 17, 20.
[32] 'Et sciendum quod non ipse rex, quia sic esset in querela propria actor et iudex in iudicio vitae et membrorum et exheredationis . . .' (It is clear that it cannot be the king himself in his own suit, for he would thus be both *actor* and judge in a case involving life and members and disherison . . .) *De Legibus* . . ., II, p. 337.

was no longer so in the second half of the twelfth century, by which time it had been firmly established that the king should act within the letter of the law. The element of vengeance is underscored by Beroul in his accounts of Mark's part in constructing the pyre and of his persistence in making Iseut pay the penalty after Tristan's escape and eventually in replacing the stake by the even more humiliating penalty of becoming the lepers' whore. Whose treachery is the greatest? That of the lovers, who are really innocent victims of the potion which has destroyed their ability to make a choice, the three barons, who, motivated by jealousy, act as traditional *losengiers*, or the king, who, in pursuing personal vengeance, is exceeding the powers granted to him by the law and is thus behaving like a tyrant? John of Salisbury says:

> Et, cum multa sint crimina maiestatis, nullum gravius est eo, quod adversus ipsum corpus iustitiae exercetur. (Though treason takes many forms there is none more deadly than that which is aimed against the very body of justice.)[33]

---

[33] *Policraticus*, Liber III, cap. 15, I, pp. 232–3. Translation by J. Dickinson, p. 212.

*L'épreuve du siège vide: esquisse d'une lecture croisée d'un épisode du* Joseph *et du* Merlin *de Robert de Boron*[1]

## LILIANE DULAC

Seuls certains manuscrits du *Merlin* comportent l'épisode du puissant baron immédiatement puni pour avoir tenté de s'asseoir parmi les chevaliers de la Table Ronde, à la place que le prophète avait déclarée interdite. On pourrait s'interroger sur les causes possibles de cette lacune surprenante. Le passage a-t-il paru constituer un doublet par rapport à l'épisode correspondant du *Joseph*? ou bien son contenu était-il de nature à déplaire à certains publics? Nous y reviendrons.

---

[1] Nous nous servons principalement des éditions et études suivantes:

EDITIONS

*Merlin*

Robert de Boron, *Merlin*, éd. par A. Micha, Genève: Droz, 1979 (Textes Littéraires Français, 281). L'épisode du baron occupe le chap. 50. Nous avons suivi la division du texte en 'chapitres' établie par Micha.

*The Vulgate Version of the Arthurian Romances*, ed. by H. O. Sommer, Vol. II, *L'Estoire de Merlin*, Washington: Publications of the Carnegie Institution of Washington, 1908. L'épisode du baron, abrégé, est aux pages 56–7.

*Merlin*, éd. par G. Paris et J. Ulrich, Paris: Firmin-Didot, 1886 (Société des Anciens Textes Français), 2 vols. Episode du baron omis.

Robert de Boron, *Le Roman du Graal*, éd. par B. Cerquiglini, Paris: Union Générale d'Editions, 1981 (Collection 10/18. Bibliothèque Médiévale). *Merlin* pp. 73–115, épisode du baron omis.

*Merlin le prophète ou le livre du Graal*, traduit par E. Baumgartner, Paris: Stock-Plus, 1980 (Moyen Age).

*Joseph*

Robert de Boron, *Le Roman du Graal*, éd. cit., par B. Cerquiglini. L'épisode du 'châtiment de Moyse' se trouve aux pages 57–61.

Robert de Boron, *Le Roman de l'Estoire dou Graal*, éd. par W. A. Nitze, Paris: Champion, 1927 (Classiques Français du Moyen Age, 57). 'Le châtiment de Moyse': pp. 93–6, vv. 2687–752. Version en vers, puis lacune comblée à l'aide d'une version en prose.

ETUDES

F. Dubost, 'Merlin et le Texte inaugural', dans 'Le Moyen Age au cinéma', *Cahiers de la cinémathèque* (Perpignan), XLII/XLIII (1985), pp. 85–9.

A. Leupin, *Le Graal et la Littérature*, Lausanne: Lettera, l'âge d'homme, 1982.

C. Méla, *La Reine et le Graal*, Paris: Seuil, 1984.

Toujours est-il qu'on ne peut guère douter que l'épisode ait fait partie intégrante du récit primitif: il s'insère trop bien dans la trilogie attribuée à Robert de Boron, et surtout les manuscrits mêmes où il fait défaut en comportent parfois deux rappels plus ou moins explicites. L'un se situe dans le *Merlin*, au moment où Uterpandragon, follement amoureux d'Egerne, déplore l'absence du prophète qu'il craint d'avoir durablement mécontenté en cette occasion.

> '. . . Mais je sai bien que Merlins set ma destresce, si crien que je l'aie corrocié de ce que li leus de la table fu essaiez, quar il a molt grant pieche que il ne vint en leu ou je fusse et espoir il li poisse de ce que je aim la femme de mon home . . .'[2]

L'autre apparaît dans la troisième partie de la trilogie lorsque le roi Arthur, pour mettre en garde Perceval, lui apprend que '. . . el liu vuit s'assist ja un faus deciples, qui maintenant que il fu assis fu fondus en terre . . .'[3].

Cette seconde référence, il est vrai, comporte une confusion entre l'histoire de Moyse dans le *Joseph* et celle du baron orgueilleux dans le *Merlin*. Enfin il sera encore largement question du siège réservé de la Table Ronde au début du *Perceval*. Ultérieurement cette histoire deviendra un des 'topoi' arthuriens les plus utilisés. L'épisode du *Merlin* apparaît comme une quasi répétition de celui du *Joseph*, dans lequel Moyse, le mauvais disciple, est anéanti pour avoir voulu occuper le siège vide de la Table du Graal. Mais cette reprise est en même temps une variation, dont de très nombreux éléments, hormis le motif central, sont à l'opposé du premier récit. C'est précisément cet écart que nous voudrions explorer, en nous interrogeant sur l'effet propre de la lecture croisée que l'organisation des deux récits impose nécessairement.

LE MOTIF DU SIÈGE VIDE

Le siège vide laissant la Table Ronde inachevée peut être rapproché d'autres objets prédestinés des romans arthuriens, ceux qui dans l'attente du héros qui en sera digne, conduisent à un sort funeste les téméraires qui on osé s'en

---

A. Micha, 'La Table Ronde chez Robert de Boron et dans la *Queste del Saint Graal*', dans *De la chanson de geste au roman*, Genève: Droz, 1976 (Publications Romanes et Françaises, 139), pp. 183–200.

A. Micha, 'Les Manuscrits du *Merlin* en prose de Robert de Boron', *Romania*, LXXVIII (1957), pp. 78–94 et 145–74.

A. Micha, *Etude sur le 'Merlin' de Robert de Boron*, Genève: Droz, 1980 (Publications Romanes et Françaises, 151).

P. Zumthor, *Merlin le prophète*, Genève: Slatkine Reprints, 1973.

[2] *Merlin* éd. A. Micha, chap. 60, ll. 24–8.
[3] *Perceval* éd. B. Cerquiglini, p. 204.

emparer. Il en est ainsi, dans la Queste del Saint Graal,[4] de l'écu blanc barré d'une croix vermeille qui échoirra à Galaad. Le roi Baudemagu veut se soumettre à l'épreuve, malgré les admonestations des moines qui ont la garde de l'écu, malgré le peu de confiance qu'il a lui-même dans le succès de son entreprise; il n'est pas sans pressentir le malheur qui l'attend; il sera peu après blessé presque mortellement par un chevalier inconnu à l'armure blanche.

Si une telle aventure ne présente qu'une analogie superficielle avec l'essai du siège dans le Merlin, la comparaison n'est toutefois pas dépourvue d'intérêt; elle fait clairement apparaître deux caractères originaux de la séquence qui nous occupe.

Contrairement à Baudemagu, le baron orgueilleux n'est pas averti du danger qu'il court, d'autant que l'interdiction dont le siège est l'objet reste vague; elle ne réside que dans une prophétie que Merlin a faite au roi, qui accepte finalement de laisser tenter l'épreuve.

Enfin alors que Baudemagu est présenté comme un bon et loyal chevalier, nullement blamâble de relever le défi qui s'offre à lui et que Galaad en personne encourage à tenter l'aventure, le baron est décrit comme un traître, l'intrigant le plus fourbe de l'entourage du roi, dont la punition à ce titre est méritée.

La séquence – interdiction de l'objet – épreuve – châtiment – peut donc sembler une forme banale qui ne prend de sens que par d'autres éléments du récit. A cet égard tout concourt à montrer l'importance exceptionnelle de l'épisode du siège vide: sa place au centre du Merlin au moment où vient d'être fondée la Table Ronde, sa durée, sa longueur enfin et surtout sa fonction primordiale qui est de manifester la correspondance des trois tables instaurées à l'image de la Trinité. Cette fonction – là est explicitement signalée par Merlin qui est à la fois le premier narrateur et le premier commentateur de l'histoire par les confidences qu'il fait à Blaise.

> '. . . nos establirons la tierce ou non de la Trinité, car la Trinitez senefie touz jorz par trois.'. . .
>
> (Merlin, éd. A. Micha, chap. 48, ll. 75–7)

Le siège interdit marque donc la concordance de la troisième table, qui achèvera la figure trinitaire, avec les deux autres, celle de la Cène et celle du Graal, possédant chacune une place vide; mais l'épreuve dont le baron trompeur sera victime 'notifie'[5] ce que Merlin appelle la haute et grande 'senefiance' du 'lieu'. Le caractère impérieux de cette 'senefiance' devient alors évident, tandis que son contenu reste hermétique; il ne se découvrira

---

[4] La Queste del Saint Graal, éd. par A. Pauphilet, Paris: Champion, 1949 (Classiques Français du Moyen Age, 33), pp. 26–31. La Quête du Saint Graal, traduit par E. Baumgartner, Paris: Champion, 1979, pp. 41–4.
[5] C. Méla, La Reine et le Graal, o.c. p. 148 et plus particulièrement pp. 109–75. Nous devons beaucoup à cet ouvrage de premier ordre.

qu'à mesure que se dessinera vers la fin de la trilogie la figure du chevalier qui accèdera au Graal.

Nous voudrions tenter de montrer combien cette vérité à venir est implicitement préparée par le récit qui dans son agencement même se trouve porteur d'un sens allant bien au delà des explications de Merlin.

### LE COUPLAGE DES RÉCITS

L'épisode du Merlin doit être lu en rapport avec celui du *Joseph*.

Le parallélisme entre ces deux récits ne se limite pas seulement aux deux actions – faute et châtiment – qui en forment le motif commun. Il est très accentué sur bien d'autres points qui tiennent à l'organisation de la séquence ou ne constituent au contraire que des détails, des éléments secondaires dont la reprise n'est que plus significative.

Dans la première catégorie, il faut ranger les acteurs principaux, qui occupent des positions analogues et ont les mêmes fonctions. Ce sont le Christ et Merlin qui ont prévu, voulu l'épreuve et en dégageront le sens; Joseph et le roi Uterpandragon qui la laissent s'accomplir; Moyse et le baron que leur fourberie rend dignes de figurer la trahison de Juda. Les deux épisodes s'ouvrent d'autre part par l'annonce de ce qui va nécessairement suivre. Lorsque Joseph interroge le Christ sur la réponse à apporter à Moyse qui implore le droit de partager la grâce des compagnons du Graal, la voix de l'Esprit Saint déclare:

> 'Joseph, Joseph, or est venus li tans que tu verras ce que je t'ai dit del siege qui est entre toi et Bron.'
>
> (éd. B. Cerquiglini, p. 59)

Il faut donc que la 'senefiance' s'impose et que la démonstration soit faite. Or Merlin ne dit rien d'autre à Blaise, quand il l'informe de l'intrigue ourdie par des gens 'faus' qui exigent la tentative. Il n'entreprendra rien pour les en empêcher,[6] car cette épreuve doit avoir lieu.

Dans le détail du récit bien des traits se font écho d'un texte à l'autre et souvent de manière littérale. Ainsi le châtiment qui frappe Moyse et le baron à l'instant où ils s'asséient sur ce qu'on appellera plus tard le siège périlleux est évoqué dans les deux cas par le verbe '*fondre*',[7] explicité dans certaines

---

[6] *Merlin*, éd. A. Micha, chap. 50, ll. 41–50.

[7] *Merlin*, éd. A. Micha, chap. 50, ll. 79–81.
'. . . si s'asist et si tost com il mist les cuisses sor le siege, si fondi ausis com feist une ploumee de plom qui fust mise seur une grant iaue'.
*Joseph*, éd. B. Cerquiglini, p. 60.
'. . . Et quant il fu assis, si fu fondus tant tost . . .'
– p. 61:
'. . . Et bien saces que il est fondus en abisme'.
– *Le Roman de l'Estoire dou Graal*, éd. Nitze, p. 96.
'. . . si fu fondus maintenant en terre . . .'.

variantes ou certains rappels par des expressions comme '*fondre en terre*' ou '*fondre en abisme*'.

Le siège fonctionne comme un siège de justice, qui par trois fois disqualifie dans la trilogie un prétendant trop audacieux, Moyse, le baron, Perceval,[8] jusqu'au jour où le héros élu et pur de toute souillure y prendra place. Le siège teste et dénonce l'impéritie de Perceval, mais élimine à jamais les pécheurs endurcis, qui, comme Moyse et le baron, disparaissent dans les entrailles de la terre. Ce genre de punition frappe des misérables qui ont encouru la colère divine. Peut-être faut-il voir là un souvenir du châtiment mortel qui s'abat sur Coré, Dathan et Abiran, coupables de s'être dressés contre le prophète Moïse?[9]

'La terre ouvrit sa bouche et les engloutit, eux et leur famille.'
(*Nombres* 16, 32)

Il est certain que les agissements des deux candidats abusifs peuvent être considérés comme une révolte sournoise contre la volonté divine. Cependant ce châtiment est en lui-même mystérieux, puisqu'il ne comporte ni blessure, ni supplice, ni mort évidente, mais seulement une disparition immédiate.

Bien différent en cela, par exemple, du supplice spectaculaire et de la mort, clairement prédite par Merlin, de Brumant l'orgueilleux[10] qui dans le *Lancelot* périt sur le siège en hurlant au milieu des flammes avec une odeur de chair brûlée.

Le caractère énigmatique de la sanction est souligné dans nos deux récits par la question que posent respectivement Joseph au Christ et le roi à Merlin sur le sort tragique des personnages, victimes de l'épreuve.

'... Sire, je vous proi et requier que vos m'ostés de cuidance et me metés en vraie novele ... que Moÿs est devenus, que je le puisse dire a ceste gent cui vous dounés votre grasse en ma compagnie'.
(*Joseph*, éd. B. Cerquiglini, p. 60)

'Et li rois li demande s'il li plait, qu'il li die que cil est devenuz qui en cel leu s'asist, quar molt en a grant merveille' ...
(*Merlin*, éd. A. Micha, chap. 51, ll. 17–19)

Autre reprise évidente dans le *Merlin* d'un détail inclus dans le récit du *Joseph*, le commentaire en forme de proverbe qui justifie le destin cruel de Moyse et du baron.

'et se il nos engigne, il engignera soi meïsme' (*Joseph*, éd. B. Cerquiglini, p. 58)

'Einsis avient de plusors qui cuident engingnier autres: si engingnent els meismes, ...'
(*Merlin*, éd. A. Micha, chap. 51, ll. 7–8)

---

[8] *Perceval*, éd. B. Cerquiglini, pp. 204–5.
[9] A. Micha, *Etude sur le 'Merlin' de Robert de Boron*, o.c., p. 85.
[10] A. Micha, *Lancelot*, Genève: Droz, 1980 (Textes Littéraires Français, 286) Tome VI, 34–42 (et plus spécialement 38–9).

Au-delà des rappels insistants qui opèrent le couplage, l'épisode du baron orgueilleux signifie aussi par les divergences qui l'éloignent de l'aventure similaire de Moyse et revêt alors une complexité et une densité qui se dévoilent à tous les niveaux du récit: l'action de Merlin, plus construite, est étoffée de circonstances adventices; elle s'échelonne sur une durée plus longue et plus précise; des motivations plus nettes, des calculs habiles sont attribués aux personnages; enfin d'autres acteurs apparaissent, si bien que la matière narrative est largement renouvelée. Si d'un récit à l'autre de véritables échos textuels magnifient la concordance quasi consubstantielle des tables, il reste que cet enrichissement a sa propre valeur, qui, elle, n'est pas explicitement commentée par Merlin.

LE JEU DES CONTRASTES

Dans l'ensemble les deux textes laissent entrevoir des contrastes importants. Le récit du *Merlin* est en général fort concret alors que celui du *Joseph* semble n'avoir rien de terrestre. Ni le temps ni l'espace n'ont la moindre épaisseur, faute de repères; les personnages, qui ne manifestent aucun attachement social ou familial, se réduisent à une caractérisation morale et à des actions également simples; la scène où ils se meuvent est nue, sans arrière-plan et hors de toute société. Cette abstraction fait d'autant mieux ressortir les caractères opposés du récit du *Merlin*.

De ces divergences tout aussi constantes que les éléments répétés qui cimentent fortement les deux épisodes on pourrait citer un exemple très ponctuel, mais représentatif, dans la manière dont est évoqué le châtiment de ceux qui tentent indûment l'épreuve. Nous avons vu que le verbe '*fondre*' est employé dans les deux récits, mais il l'est bien différemment, quoique dans le même sens. En effet dans le *Merlin* ce terme s'accompagne d'une image d'autant plus notable qu'elle est la seule de tout le roman, comme Alexandre Micha le montre avec pertinence.[11] Le baron fourbe est englouti dans l'abîme aussi soudainement qu'un morceau de plomb coule à pic dans l'eau qui se referme sur lui. Apparemment seule la densité du métal explique le choix de cette image. Mais il est probable qu'une autre valeur transparaisse en filigrane. Le plomb comme la cire est souvent associé à l'idée de fusion, que pourtant n'exprime pas ici le verbe '*fondre*'. On pourrait s'y tromper, non sans raison, car le terme '*ploumée*', qui peut désigner un projectile, rappelle indirectement le procédé de fabrication sans doute banal des balles de fronde. Du plomb fondu était précipité dans l'eau où il se solidifiait en petites masses

---

[11] A. Micha, *Etude sur le 'Merlin'*, p. 206.

sphériques. Le récit abrégé de la *Vulgate*[12] reprend la même image mais en l'altérant: *'fondre'* évoque plutôt une fusion qu'un mouvement de chute. C'est donc là une comparaison à connotations techniques dont il ne faut sous-estimer ni la précision ni la consistance; par là elle pourrait servir d'*emblème* à ce qui est le plus caractéristique du récit du *Merlin*.

1. *Le traitement de la durée*

Les enrichissements qui distinguent l'épisode du *Merlin* lui apportent un tour plus concret: tous concourent à une sorte d'humanisation du récit. Il en est ainsi du traitement de la *durée* qui devient un de ses éléments importants. Loin de ne former qu'un simple cadre, la temporalité est étroitement liée à l'action qu'elle contribue à éclairer. Dans le *Joseph* des indications plutôt floues jalonnent le déroulement de l'histoire. Robert de Boron dit surtout que Moyse implore 'maintes fois et longement' avant que les compagnons de la seconde table n'intercèdent pour que son admission au service du Graal soit envisagée. S'agit-il d'heures, de jours, de mois, peu importe!

Dans le *Merlin* la chronologie de l'épisode est soulignée avec insistance. Elle suit le rythme de la vie de cour, réglée par les grandes fêtes de la liturgie, notamment la Pentecôte qui dans les romans arthuriens marque d'ordinaire le moment d'événements décisifs. L'ensemble du récit occupe une durée d'un peu plus d'un an, exactement un an et quinze jours. C'est le temps qui sépare deux apparitions de Merlin à la cour d'Uterpandragon. A la Pentecôte, la Table Ronde est fondée, cinquante[13] chevaliers choisis par Merlin s'y installent, mais un siège reste libre. A la Noël des proches du roi l'interrogent sur cet inachèvement de la table et pressent de permettre qu'on la complète; ce que le roi accepte finalement quand ces mauvais conseillers précisent qu'il ne s'agit pas de tenter l'essai sur l'heure, mais à la Pentecôte suivante, si bien que Merlin aura tout le temps d'intervenir. C'est durant ces six mois de délai que se déploient les intrigues des grands seigneurs en vue de l'épreuve qui aura lieu lors de l'assemblée convoquée par le roi. Quinze jours après la Pentecôte, Merlin réapparaît et tire les leçons de l'événement. Cette chronologie joue un rôle déterminant, puisque c'est la longue absence de Merlin qui permet aux courtisans déloyaux de triompher de la résistance du roi, de fomenter des rumeurs mensongères au sujet de la prétendue mort du prophète. Le temps prend donc à la fois une valeur sociale et dramatique, proche en cela d'une durée romanesque totalement absente du *Joseph*.

---

[12] *L'Estoire de Merlin*, ed. H. O. Sommer, o.c., p. 57, ll. 21–2.
'... et lors fondi ausi comme une plombee de plomb, et ensi fu perdus voiant tous que nus ne savoit qu'il estoit devenus.'
[13] *Cinquante*, chiffre sacré qui commémore le nombre de jours séparant la résurrection du Christ de l'apparition de l'Esprit Saint aux disciples.

## 2. Merlin

La relative complexité de l'épisode dans le *Merlin* tient également au personnage du prophète lui-même et au rôle qu'il y joue, effet paradoxal puisque, comme nous l'avons vu, il est absent du lieu où se prépare et se produit l'épreuve du siège inoccupé. Mais son *abstention* même commande le déroulement de l'événement et le comportement des autres personnages.

Dans le *Joseph*, le Christ se contente d'énoncer ce qui va constituer l'avenir immédiat, il confirme la prédiction qu'il a faite au sujet de la place laissée entre Bron et Joseph et confirme clairement les termes du choix que doit faire Moyse. Merlin, lui, calcule sa décision de laisser tenter l'épreuve, et détermine indirectement les conditions dans lesquelles elle va s'effectuer pour des raisons qu'il explique à Blaise en une sorte d'aparté:

> 'Et Merlins, qui toutes ces choses set le redist à Blaises et li dist la mauvaise pensee que cil avoient qui ceste oevre avoient emprise, si dist qu'il n'iroit pas, que il savoit bien que cil leus devoit estre esprouvez, quar il veut miauz que il l'espreuvent par lor mauvés sens et des faus homes que des bons;'
> 
> (*Merlin*, éd. A. Micha, chap. 50, ll. 41–6)

Merlin désigne quasiment la victime de l'épreuve dont le sort est désormais scellé. Le commentaire de Merlin, qui anticipe sur l'événement, en fait bien percevoir le caractère mystérieux. Commandé par une nécessité qui dépasse la personne même de Merlin, le drame va cependant s'accomplir dans les conditions qu'il a choisies en s'abstenant de paraître. Or ces conditions donnent à l'épisode une double signification.

– un mauvais conseiller qui a voulu abuser le roi et discréditer Merlin qu'il accusait de mensonge va disparaître, victime de son propre complot.

– Mais la véritable finalité de l'événement, ce qui le rend inévitable, est d'un autre ordre, sans rapport avec la fausseté des gens de cour: car Merlin admet que d'honnêtes gens pourraient en faire les frais. C'est en un sens ce qui arrivera à Perceval[14] quand il s'assiéra sur le siège vide avant d'en être tout à fait digne.

La signification de ce fait extraordinaire n'est donc pas essentiellement celle du châtiment d'un félon, mais la notification[15] indispensable, quoiqu'encore obscure, du rôle que le siège et donc la table elle-même sont appelés à jouer. C'est pourquoi au cours du *Perceval*, l'essai sera évoqué à certains moments décisifs; pour toujours il témoigne de ce qui doit s'accomplir. Cette manifestation d'une volonté supérieure est favorisée par Merlin puisqu'il

---

[14] *Perceval*, ed. B. Cerquiglini, pp. 204–5.
'. . . Et tant tost com il fu assis li pierre fendi desous lui et braist si angoisseusement que il sambla a tous çaus qui la estoient que li siecles fondist en abisme. Et del brait que li terre jeta si issi une si grans tenebrors que il ne se porent entreveïr en plus d'une liue.'

[15] Nous renvoyons à l'étude très exhaustive de Charles Méla (ouvrage cité).

importe que l'événement ne soit pas méconnu, comme il le serait si l'on croyait que le prophète peut l'empêcher ou le provoquer au gré de sa magie.

> '... et s'il i aloit, donc diroient il que il i seroit alez por destorber l'essai et li autre qui ceste oevre ont a traire ne creroient pas tant com il lor est mestier que il croient: ...'
>
> (*Merlin*, éd. A. Micha, chap. 50, ll. 46–50)

Si l'attitude et les commentaires de Merlin suggèrent cette disjonction entre les deux valeurs du prodige, qui manifeste d'abord la 'senefiance' du siège vide et en second lieu seulement constitue la punition des fourberies d'un grand, on ne peut aller trop loin dans cette opposition. Car le siège promis au parfait chevalier rappelle celui de Judas. Ainsi le caractère de faute et de trahison donné à l'action du baron accentue la concordance avec l'épisode primordial de la Cène et contribue donc à la 'senefiance' annoncée par Merlin.

Dans le *Joseph*, le méfait et la punition de Moyse sont d'une interprétation plus aisée. Clairement averti de ne s'asseoir à la Table que s'il est au fond de lui-même ce qu'il affecte de paraître, Moyse persiste dans sa tromperie si bien que son châtiment et la démonstration de la pureté exigée des compagnons du Graal se confondent parfaitement.

Il ne peut en être de même du baron qui ignore, ainsi que toute la cour, la signification attachée à la Table, et décide de son action en l'absence de toute mise en garde; le fait de tenter l'épreuve n'est donc pas en soi un crime.

On comprend mieux cette situation en tenant compte d'une autre forme de réserve prêtée à Merlin, réserve qui contribue à créer une certaine opacité très éloignée de la transparence qui détermine dans le *Joseph* les relations et les différents niveaux hiérarchiques où se situent les personnages. Prières et demandes montent de Moyse aux compagnons de la Table, de ceux-ci à Joseph et de Joseph au Christ, tandis qu'en retour les réponses divines à propos du siège réservé ne font jamais défaut. Certes l'Esprit Saint laisse entendre que l'épreuve va avoir lieu. Mais le commentaire qu'il fait de la demande de Moyse est énoncé sous la forme d'un avertissement solennel qu'il suffit aux disciples de transmettre. Certaines informations sont tenues secrètes, notamment sur l'identité du futur occupant du siège, mais dans l'ensemble la communication est toujours assurée de bas en haut et de haut en bas, ce qui projette l'action de Moyse en pleine lumière. Les mêmes observations sont partiellement valables à propos de son châtiment. La voix commente brièvement la mort de Moyse, même si en fait les explications restent sommaires.

> 'Et bien saces que il est fondus en abisme ne de lui ne sera mais parole.'
>
> (*Joseph*, éd. B. Cerquiglini, p. 61)

Il en va tout autrement dans le *Merlin*. Le prophète inaccessible ne peut être consulté par le roi en butte aux pressions de son entourage. Avant même ce moment critique, les informations qu'il avait reçues de Merlin étaient plus floues que celles dont disposait Joseph.

Le roi a seulement appris que le vide de la Table Ronde serait comblé sous le règne de son fils Arthur par un chevalier irréprochable, mais il ignore tout du sort réservé au baron, sort dont il s'est enquis en vain.

> '... "Ce ne te tient riens a querre ne riens ne te vauroit, se tu le savoies" répond Merlin.'
> 
> (*Merlin*, éd. A. Micha, chap. 51, ll. 20–21)

Ces réticences sont d'ailleurs plusieurs fois soulignées par le tour restrictif que Merlin donne à ses révélations:

> 'Et je vos dirai ce que je sai que Nostre Sires volt que vos sachiez' ·
> 
> (*Merlin*, éd. A. Micha, chap. 48, ll. 35–6)

Dans l'ensemble, il est vrai, les renseignements transmis au roi sont à peu près ceux qui sont donnés à Joseph. Mais il n'est pas indifférent qu'ils soient tous marqués comme incomplets, rien de comparable donc avec la communication immédiate que le Christ apporte à Joseph et à ses compagnons. Tout le climat de *Merlin* est affecté par cette opposition qui intensifie la coupure entre le monde terrestre représenté par la cour, sur lequel le récit n'est pas avare de détails, et le monde des vérités célestielles à peine entrevues par le truchement réservé de Merlin.

## 3. *Le trompeur*

Le personnage du baron trompeur est dans le *Merlin* l'élément qui par rapport au *Joseph* reçoit les enrichissements les plus notables. Moyse est en effet une figure d'une grande simplicité; il n'est caractérisé que par sa prétention injustifiée à partager la grâce des compagnons du Graal; sa fausseté réside toute entière dans cette demande réitérée malgré la mise en garde de Joseph. Le baron présomptueux est un personnage beaucoup plus complexe. Loin d'être isolé comme Moyse, il se détache d'un groupe dont l'existence est signalée avant même la fondation de la Table Ronde; celui des seigneurs qui jalousent Merlin et cherchent à le rabaisser dans l'esprit du roi. Ces grands sont gens fourbes qui affectent de l'amitié pour Uterpandragon tout en multipliant manoeuvres et discours fallacieux pour l'induire en erreur. C'est un véritable complot collectif qui se développe avant que le plus puissant d'entre eux, qui est aussi un des principaux conseillers du roi, déclare vouloir tenter lui-même l'épreuve. Cette décision est présentée comme l'aboutissement d'un plan très élaboré et énigmatique: au cas où Merlin se présenterait à la cour, le baron a prévu de lui proposer des hommes à lui pour occuper le siège.

'... si trouva assez qui soufri a asseoir *por lui* et *chevaliers* et *prouvoires* et *gaaigneors* de vile, et il les i avoit fait venir por ce que il cuidoit que Merlin i fust et, se il i fust, que il l'aissaiast de quiels que genz que il vousist des *trois manieres* que Diex a establies en terre.'

(*Merlin*, éd. A. Micha, chap. 50, ll. 66–71)

Peut-être veut-il ôter au mage tout prétexte de refus, si lui-même devait être écarté. Ces dispositions s'apparentent très nettement à une intrigue de cour montée pour se saisir directement ou indirectement d'une place convoitée à cause de la puissance ou du prestige qu'elle confère; rien ne peut mieux montrer l'énorme écart qui sépare de telles menées la haute 'senefiance' de la Quête du Graal qu'annonce le siège réservé.

Le baron puissant et de haut lignage, qui semble incarner à lui seul la duplicité et l'ambition sans scrupule de la chevalerie mondaine, se trouve ainsi rabaissé au rang de principal acteur d'une péripétie qui, sans interrompre en rien les débuts d'une glorieuse histoire mythique, livre littéralement au néant cette fausse grandeur.

L'effet critique et dévalorisant du personnage qui s'étend à tout l'épisode serait-il la cause de son omission si fréquente dans les manuscrits? L'hypothèse est hasardeuse, mais ce moment du récit est sans égal.

Il offre en effet des aspects surprenants sur lesquels nous nous interrogeons.

Le baron n'a-t-il pas explicitement prévu de proposer à Merlin des candidats qui appartiennent aux trois classes de la société et qui, de ce fait, ne soient pas forcément chevaliers? De manière insolite cet 'outrecuidant' bouleverse les structures tripartites qui régissent la société médiévale établie à l'image de la Trinité, en concevant le rôle de ces catégories comme interchangeable, en accordant à celui, quel qu'il soit, que désignerait Merlin, la faculté d'incarner les valeurs chevaleresques les plus élevées. Or les prétentions de ce puissant seigneur agressif et perfide vont dans le sens opposé du nouvel ordre instauré par Merlin. Car la Table Ronde, dont la mission est double, mystique, mais aussi politique,[16] symbolise une autorité monarchique forte qui centralise harmonieusement les pouvoirs dévolus aux trois fonctions.[17]

Avant que le désordre et le mal ne s'introduisent dans le cercle encore ouvert de la Table, image incertaine d'une cité idéale qui préfigure la cité céleste, l'abîme engloutit le baron, damné à jamais, dont les intentions semblent défier le monde divin.

---

[16] Je remercie infiniment mes collègues Georges Devallet et Francis Dubost pour les informations très précises qu'ils m'ont données.
F. Dubost, 'Merlin et le Texte Inaugural' (article cité), pp. 88–9.
[17] G. Duby, *Les trois ordres ou l'imaginaire du féodalisme*, Paris: Gallimard, 1978.
J. Grisward, 'Uter Pendragon, Artur et l'idéologie royale des Indo-Européens', *Europe*, N° 654 (octobre 1983), pp. 111–20.
J. Le Goff, 'Les trois fonctions indo-européennes, l'historien et l'Europe féodale', *Annales Economies Sociétés Civilisations*, 34ᵉ année, N° 6 (nov.–déc. 1979), pp. 1187–207.

## 4. *Les acteurs collectifs*

A côté des grands qui complotent contre Merlin, d'autres groupes interviennent dans le récit ou du moins y figurent plus ou moins allusivement, la cour convoquée à Carduel pour la Pentecôte, le peuple qui assistera à l'épreuve, les gens du baron qui l'entourent et soutiennent ses prétentions, les paysans qui sont supposés avoir tué Merlin.

L'événement se situe donc au sein d'une société qui est celle du royaume de Logres et qui n'a pas d'équivalent dans le récit du *Joseph*. Là n'est pas cependant la dissymétrie la plus significative. La première partie de la trilogie comporte elle aussi une sorte d'acteur collectif, et un seul, constitué par les compagnons de Joseph; il parle et agit, il intercède, il interroge ou il commente.

Or dans le *Merlin* le *groupe* correspondant, celui des Chevaliers de la Table Ronde, est montré au contraire totalement passif au cours de l'épisode. Ces 'prodoms' ne sont mentionnés qu'au moment où le baron s'apprête à s'asseoir sur le siège. Ils se contentent de regarder en silence comme s'il ne leur appartenait pas d'intervenir à cet instant qui est le point d'aboutissement des longues et basses manoeuvres de l'homme qui prétend prendre place parmi eux: curieux jeu de scène qui pourrait marquer l'absence de tout lien, de tout intérêt commun entre ce postulant indigne et les chevaliers choisis par Merlin, si fortement unis et solidaires depuis la fondation de la Table. Au contraire les groupes actifs sont ceux qui sont plus ou moins proches du baron, non seulement le parti des ennemis de Merlin, mais aussi la foule de tous ceux qui, tentés par l'épreuve annoncée, accourent à Carduel. Le baron n'est donc que le premier des postulants à l'occupation du siège vide comme le souligne un détail assez surprenant. A la disparition du baron, les spectateurs

'si furent molt espoanté ne ne sot onques nus que dire'.
(*Merlin*, chap. 50, ll. 83–4)

Mais aussitôt tous se précipitent pour s'emparer du siège si manifestement périlleux, comme si l'interdiction et le danger constituaient un défi insupportable.

'... com il l'orent veu einsis perdre, si se volt chascuns en ce leu asseoir ...'
(*Merlin*, chap. 50, ll. 85–6)

Sur la demande du roi, les chevaliers assis à la table se lèvent pour qu'on ne puisse plus distinguer la place réservée. Mais cette étrange péripétie suffit à dépeindre le baron comme représentatif de la cour qui assiste à l'épreuve et partage ses appétits: car le siège vide, qui laisse la table incomplète, exerce sur les êtres une fascination incoercible et fatale.

Les différents éléments du récit que nous avons considérés pour ce qu'ils apportent de complexité à cet épisode du *Merlin* imposent à l'histoire un climat social et politique couvrant tous les aspects de la narration, le traitement de la durée, l'enchaînement des actions, le système des personnages. L'intérêt de cette transformation est que le récit du *Merlin* reste uni à celui du *Joseph* par des indices multiples et non équivoques qui en font une répétition de la première histoire. Mais cette répétition s'accompagne d'une sorte de renversement: un souffle mystique anime l'épisode du Joseph, qui se développe dans la totale transparence, la pureté désincarnée d'un monde d'ailleurs en constante relation avec le divin. Le récit du *Merlin*, englué dans les complications et les embarras d'une vie de cour toute mondaine, n'a rien de mystique, ou du moins la communication avec le divin est coupée dès que Merlin est absent; tout est emporté jusqu'au roi lui-même par le cours ordinaire des calculs et des intrigues sournoises qui menacent le nouvel ordre monarchique établi par le prophète. Certes, la communauté de la Table Ronde, noyau d'une chevalerie vouée à de nobles ambitions, vient d'être fondée, mais, totalement absente de l'action, elle n'est que le témoin immobile de l'épreuve qui signifie l'impuissance radicale de ce monde éloigné de la vraie gloire, dont le baron trompeur est le symbole. L'épreuve du siège vide est à la fois une condamnation et une promesse, car elle signifie avec éclat une rupture; ce qu'elle annonce paraît infiniment lointain, quoique déjà virtuellement présent par l'existence de la table et de son inachèvement. Mais ce germe inerte d'un avenir mystérieux prédit au monde arthurien est désormais installé en pleine lumière aux yeux de tous.

# The Tristan Illustrations in MS London BL Add. 11619

## TONY HUNT

Kenneth Varty's long-standing interest in the relationship of vernacular literature and medieval iconography[1] would itself be sufficient reason for publishing in his honour a set of romance illustrations. The theme of reward and punishment selected for the present volume strengthens this choice, however, in an unexpected way. Of course the notions of reward and punishment represent important thematic strands of the Tristan story, but less obviously they point to a fascinating problem for students of the reception of the romance. Was it seen in the Middle Ages as an exaltation of human love in which the final reward is an apotheosis represented by the *Liebestod*? Or was it, rather, understood as a monitory tale in which the vanity and instability of human emotions lead to annihilation? The questions are raised in an acute form by the *Tristan* of Thomas. Some years ago I argued,[2] against the critical consensus, that Thomas treats the legend of Tristan and Isolde as a negative *exemplum* in the *contemptus mundi* tradition and that he is 'a pessimistic commentator on the vicissitudes of earthly love'. I further suggested that a dating of his work in the early 1170s, when Henry II publicly acknowledged his adultery with 'Fair Rosamund', would fittingly explain Thomas's choice and treatment of his material. The location of the Tristan illustrations to be discussed below seems to me to strengthen rather than to subvert this view, suggesting that in Thomas's version of the legend the theme of punishment is stronger than that of reward.

The illustrations, which have never been discussed or reproduced, are found in MS London, BL Add. 11619 ff. 6r–9v. In the Catalogue of Additional Manuscripts they are described as 'Picturae quaedam, fortassis ad Romancium de Tristano spectantes',[3] in Ward's Catalogue of Romances as 'Drawings from

---

[1] See most recently 'The Iconography of the Medieval Beast Epic: From Manuscript to Printed Page', in *The Medieval Alexander and Romance Epic. Essays in Honour of David J. A. Ross*, ed. by P. Noble, L. Polak, C. Isoz, London: Kraus International Publications, 1982, pp. 243–58.
[2] 'The Significance of Thomas's *Tristan*', *Reading Medieval Studies*, VII (1981), pp. 41–61.
[3] *List of Additions to the Manuscripts in the British Museum in the Years MDCCCXXXVI–MDCCCXL*, London: British Museum, 1843.

subjects in the Romance of Tristram, washed with purple [sic] green and red'.[4] These are the only references to them which I have been able to discover. Since, in the present context, the location of the illustrations is as important as their artistic value, it is necessary to establish a detailed description of the contents of the MS.[5]

I. THE MANUSCRIPT

The MS comprises 277 folios (f. 275 is mutilated and the blank folio following f. 4 is unnumbered) written mostly at the beginning of the fourteenth century and contains texts written exclusively in Latin and almost entirely of a religious or didactic nature. The folios, which have been cut down, now measure approximately 110 × 80 mm. with the prickings clearly visible in the outer margins. The volume retains its original (fourteenth-century) binding, but it is clear that some folios have been lost near the beginning (see below). The MS was acquired by the British Museum as lot *316 at Sotheby's sale of 18 June 1839. The only mark of previous ownership is the note on f. 4r (repeated verbatim on f. 5r) 'Thomas Addenbrooke bought at Shrewsbury 1772' after which is appended the description 'A collection of essays on various subjects with the Fables of Esop etc'. The MS along with its binding must have been constituted at the beginning of the fourteenth century and displays fore-edge painting with stiff leaf design. The main hands are as follows:

1. small hand of *c.* 1300: ff. 1r–3r, 272r–275r
2. another hand of *c.* 1300: ff. 10r–210r, 234r/v
3. a slightly larger hand, s. xiv in.: ff. 211r–234r
4. a larger hand of s. xiii$^2$: ff. 235r–265v
5. another hand of s. xiii$^2$: ff. 266r–268r
6. another hand of s. xiii$^2$: f. 268r/v
7. small hand of *c.* 1300: ff. 269r–271v
8. hand of s. xiii ex.: f. 277v

The contents of the MS may be described as follows:

1. ff. 1r–3r: miscellaneous sententiae and religious items[6]
   [f. 1r] WI 20639 (7 v.); WI 1068 (6 v.); WP 4287 (2 v.); 'Si Constantino

---

[4] H. L. D. Ward, *Catalogue of Romances in the Department of Manuscripts in the British Museum* vol. 2, London: British Museum, 1893, p. 342.
[5] A brief conspectus is given by Ward, *supra*, pp. 342–3.
[6] WI = H. Walther, *Initia carminum ac versuum medii aevi posterioris latinorum*, Göttingen: Vandenhoeck & Ruprecht, 1959; WP = *id.*, *Proverbia sententiaeque latinitatis medii aevi*, 5 vols., Göttingen: Vandenhoeck & Ruprecht, 1963–67.

pede concultatur equino / istud tantillum quia zelotipaverat illum'; WI 16778 (5 v.)

[f. 1v] 'Concipiens morte parit equa vipera sorte / per que quis peccat merito torquetur eisdem' (WP 3033, cf. WP 21238); 'Serpentis cibus est fenum pulvisque favilla / et caro mactata semen cum gramine terra'; WI 20331 (4 v.); WI 11868 (4 v.); 'Ubi movebatur sepulcrum cum sepulto quando Jonas s. in n. c. . . .' (2 v.); 'In regnum notetur .i. in prelacionem, qui dissipaverit ursum .i. turpitudinem luxurie, qui fregerit ora leonum .i. iracundiam interit, qui cum gladio suo jugulaverit goliam .i. diabolum vel ipocrishim vana gloria occiderit'; 'Non scandalizat iudex doctor bene vivens'.

[f. 2r] prose passage beginning 'Quatuor modis pervertitur iudicium humanum: timore, cupiditate, odio et amore . . .'; WI 17792 (6 v.); short prose passages beginning 'Colerici dicuntur habere quasdam proprietates . . .', 'Melanc(l)olici autem contrariis hiis videntur habere proprietates . . .', 'Sanguinei vero temperati et bene morigerati et affabiles'.

[f. 2v] didactic tale beginning 'In civitate Merrari fuerunt mulieres quedam iuvencule que fecerunt sibi templum ubi sero et mane adorare [MS ad arare] solebant sed adorandi devotionem verterunt in reprobum sensum . . .'; WP 25040.

[f. 3r] short didactic prose tale concerning St Gregory, headed 'De iudicibus', beginning 'Dum quendam regem ad bella properantem vidua interpellaret ut filium suum vindicaret, ille peracto bello se facturum respondit . . .'

[ff. 3v–5v] blank save for marks of ownership indicated above

2. ff. 6r–9v Tristan illustrations
3. ff. 10r–73v: [Alan of Lille's *Summa predicatoria*] [red rubric] *Summa bona et optima de bono et optimo modo predicandi* inc. 'Vidit Jacob scalam a terra usque ad celos attingentem . . .',[7] incomplete (ending at PL 210, 164C 'in multiloquio non deest peccatum') owing to loss of four (?) quires (the surviving ones bear the signatures V–X).[8] There are alternating red and blue initials, red rubrics and paragraph marks.
4. ff. 74r–106v: A set of 21 sermons. The initial red rubric has been carefully erased, the text beginning 'Dominus noster Jhesu Christus in die palmarum Jherusalem iturus congruam elegit viam docens suos eadem via debere proficisci . . .' The quires are marked with signatures I–III, a number of folios being lost after f. 106.

---

[7] See M. W. Bloomfield *et al.*, *Incipits of Latin Works on the Virtues and Vices 1100–1500 AD*, Cambridge, Mass.: Mediaeval Academy of America, 1979, no. 6457.
[8] Capital letters in drypoint appear at the beginning and/or end of quires as follows: A (f. 41v), B (f. 42r), C (f. 49v), D (f. 50r), E (f. 58r).

5. ff. 107r–134v: [A digest of Isidore's *Sententiarum liber* or *De summo bono*] [red rubric] *Isidorus de summo bono* inc. 'Summum bonum est Deus quia incommutabilis est ...'[9] ending at PL 83, 736A ('expletur diebus singulis'). There are alternating red and blue initials, red rubrics and paragraph marks. Folio 120 is damaged. At the bottom of f. 129v has been added in red WI 5627 (4 v.) and on f. 134v, after 'Explicit. Finitur liber, scriptor sit a crimine liber', WP 6059 (2 v.).
6. f. 135r/v: A poem of forty leonine hexameters, [red rubric] *De virtutibus et conflictu viciorum* inc. 'Per me transite qui queritis atria vite ...'[10] Each line begins with a red initial and ends with the name of the relevant virtue or vice in red.
7. ff. 135v–137r: [red rubric] *Incipit tractatus de pueris in claustro nutriendis* inc. 'Quodam tempore cum quidam abbas qui admodum religiosus habebatur, ad Anselmum de hiis que monastice religionis erant loqueretur ...', expl. 'Crescit cenobium illud et intus et extra, intus in sancta religione, extra in multimoda possessione'.
8. ff. 137r–142r: A version of Adso's treatise on the life of Antichrist,[11] here without the dedication and with much extra prefatory matter, [red rubric] *Incipit de Antichristo et eius signis et eius vitae ad Karoldum magnum ab Alchino edita* inc. 'Antichristus in Corothaym [sic] civitate de tribu Dan ex inmundissimo nebulone et scorto procreatus et natus ...', *Explicit vita Antichristi ad Karolandum ab Alchino edita.*
9. ff. 142r–145v: [The Latin Life of Secundus by Willelmus of St Denis] [red rubric] *Vita Secundi philosophi de greco in latinum translatum* inc. 'Secundus fuit philosophus, hic philosophatus, omni tempore silencium conservans et picchagoricam ducens vitam ...'[12] At the top of f. 142v has been added WI 573 (2 v.) and at the bottom of the same folio WP 13518 (4 v.), [red explicit] *Explicit vita Secundi philosophi.*
10. ff. 145v–153r: The *Apocalypsis* of Golias (108 stanzas, without rubric), inc. 'A tauro torida lampade cinchii ...'[13] The verses are set out in quatrains with alternating blue and red initials (red only on ff. 149r–150v and 152r). The guide letters for the rubricator are clearly visible.

---

[9] Bloomfield *et al.*, op. cit., no. 5854.
[10] WI 13948 (wrongly gives ref. as f. 135v, but corrects this in WP 21213).
[11] See D. Verhelst (ed.), *Adso Dervensis, De Ortu et tempore Antichristi*, Corpus Christianorum, continuatio mediaevalis XLV (Turnholti, 1976), pp. 105ff. (our MS described on p. 113).
[12] See B. E. Perry, *Secundus the Silent Philosopher*, American Philol. Assoc., Philological Monographs XXII, Ithaca: The Amer. Philol. Assoc., 1964, pp. 92–100 (Suchier's Latin text) and pp. 23–52 (historical introduction). Suchier's text is found in L. W. Daly & W. Suchier, *Altercatio Hadriani Augusti et Epicteti philosophi*, Illinois Studies in Language and Literature XXIV/1–2, Urbana: University of Illinois, 1939, pp. 152–9 (introd. pp. 147–52). Our MS is recorded (p. 164) in the list of MSS on pp. 162–6.
[13] WI 91.

11. ff. 153r–158v: An incomplete consolatory treatise on the occasion of a death, inc. 'Subtra[c]to illo siquidem per quem mea in domino studia ut cumque libera esse solebant . . .'. After f. 158 a folio has been cut away.
12. f. 159r/v: An acephalous treatise in prose, the first rubric (in red) of which is *De adulacione*.
13. ff. 159v–162r: A set of verses on the seven deadly sins, ending (ff. 161v/162r) with verses on *humilitas* and *caritas*. [red rubric] *Contra superbiam* inc. 'Deicit infatuat condempnat deprimit inflat'.[14] On f. 160r there are red rubrics as follows: *Contra iram et eius effectus*; *Contra invidiam et eius effectus*; *Contra malam tristiciam seculi*; *Contra accidiam sive tedium boni*; *Contra avariciam et cupiditatem et eorum effectus sive quod prosperitas mundane vite sive amor mundi vel apetitus*. In the left-hand margins there are headwords in the ink of the text and the verses following each rubric are largely composed of verbs. At the bottom of f. 160r is written in red 'Temporalium facit hec mala sequentia homini'. The concluding sections (f. 162r) comprise the rubrics *Sunt servanda in edendo* (WI 18347 = 2 v.), *Ista sunt vitanda in dapibus* (WP 164 = 2 v.), *De largisicione elemosine et qualiter danda sit* ('Spontaneum mundum plenumque ferens moderatum / quid cui vel quantum quando cur quomodo dandum').
14. f. 162r/v: [red rubric] *Decimi abusionis gradus* inc. 'Rex ratione carens in iniquis gestibus arcens'.[15] Eleven verses, accompanied to the left by the subject (in red) – *Rex, Episcopus, Senex* etc. – and on the right, also in red, by an epithet or descriptive phrase – *iniqus, negligens, in operibus bonis* etc. On f. 162v follows, without a rubric, the *Abusiones claustri* inc. 'Forma gregis prelis qui despicit actus' (12 v.),[16] with no marginal words.
15. ff. 162v–186v: [A treatise on the seven deadly sins sometimes ascribed to Grosseteste] [red rubric] *De vii criminalibus peccatis et eorum effectibus et de eorum incomodis* inc. 'Superbia est elatio viciosa que inferiorem despiciens . . .'[17] There are many red rubrics and marginal references to Biblical quotations. On f. 186v is written in red WI 19747 (4 v.) followed by 'Explicit tractatus de septem criminalibus peccatis, amen'.
16. ff. 186v–187r: Miscellaneous leonine verses as follows: WI 15948 (7 v.); [f. 187r] WI 13982 (4 v.); WI 5691 (4 v.); WI 10474 (4 v.); 'Triplex stulticie genus est quo proba parantur . . .' (4 v.); WP 33767 (2 v.); 'Sub foliis fructum decet expectare serenum'.
17. ff. 187v–188r: Sermon on Ruth inc. 'Messis quidam multa in Booz, Booz Christus . . .' followed (f. 188v) by miscellaneous notes including an allegory on three harvests and a set of five verses beginning 'Pontificem parium manus excuset duodena'.

---

[14] WI 4225, Bloomfield *et al.*, op. cit., no. 1507.
[15] WI 16762 ('De 12 abusionibus seculi et claustri').
[16] Cf. MS Cambridge, Corpus Christi College 481 (s. xiii), p. 420.
[17] Bloomfield *et al.*, op. cit., no. 5905.

18. ff. 189r–210r: [52 Aesopic fables in monorhyme quatrains based on the 'Romulus Nilanti'] [red rubric] *Incipiunt fabule Esopi* inc. 'Accendentes insule de longo venite'.[18] There are alternating red and blue initials, red rubrics and the explanation of each fable is marked *moralitas* in red. At the bottom of f. 205v is written in red 'Est res enormis cum fuerit hyrcus endormys' and at the bottom of f. 206r, also in red, 'Cum sit deformis bene debuit esse dehor mys'. The coloured initials have not been entered on f. 210r.

19. f. 210r/v: A short prose passage on conjugal duties inc. 'Sex faciunt quod non tenetur homo reddere debitum uxori: suscitatio, corruptio, indignitas, necessitas, defectus, exceptio . . .'. At the bottom of f. 210v are the lines 'Nos morimur strati, victi, cesi, spoliati,/ mentula legati facit ista pati'.

20. ff. 211r–234r: A prose narrative of the Passion of Christ inc. 'Factum est in anno quinto decimo imperii Tiberii Cesaris imperatoris romanorum et Herodis filii Herodis regis Galilee . . .'

21. f. 234r/v: The *Exemplum de dimidio amico* or 'The calf in the sack' from the *Disciplina clericalis* of Petrus Alfonsi inc. '[Q]uidam philosophus dixit filio suo "Fili, quot amicos tibi acquisisti?" . . .', expl. 'Hic est vere amicus qui te adiuvat cum tibi seculum deficit'.[19] The text is followed on f. 234v by WI 2852 (2 v.), WP 19716 (2 v.), WI 4924 (2 v.).

22. ff. 235r–265v: [The *Moralium dogma philosophorum* sometimes attributed to William of Conches] [red rubric] *Incipit liber moralitatis* inc. 'Moralium dogma philosophorum per multa dispersum volumina . . .'[20] There are alternating red and blue initials, but few rubrics.

23. f. 266r: Notes on the Cross inc. 'Bene veneris veteris crux purgatrix celeris lingnum federis in partes anglorum . . .' followed by miscellaneous verses: [f. 266r] 'Ama quod odisti, penas paveas, / si granum novisti, noles paleas'; [f. 266v] WI 5894 (4 v.); WI 03 (parodic poem by Golias); [ff. 267r–68v] WI 2646 (2 v.); 36 hexameters in praise of Alan of Galloway inc. 'Certa dei ratio totum cum ponderat orbem' (WI 2646) and coda of 4 verses (WI 18866); WI 2527 (2 v.); a phlebotomy (WI 17053) including dietary instructions on fowl involving much etymological play.

24. ff. 269r–271v: red rubric *Incipit quoddam stupendum et inauditum miraculum beati Augustini anglorum apostoli* inc. 'Est vicus in pago oxenfordensi sex miliariis distans a loco hac tempestate celebri qui dicitur wdeflix [?] cumetona nomine . . .'

25. f. 272r: Acephalous text consisting of notes on numbers

---

[18] WI 1667; see Ward, *Catalogue* . . ., 2, pp. 343–7.
[19] See *Petri Alfonsi Disciplina Clericalis* I ed. by A. Hilka & W. Söderhjelm, Acta Societatis Scientiarum Fennicae 37/4, Helsingfors, 1911, pp. 3–4.
[20] MS not known to J. Holmberg (ed.), *Das Moralium dogma philosophorum des Guillaume de Conches*, Uppsala etc., 1929 and R. A. Gauthier in *Revue du moyen âge latin* IX (1953), pp. 171–260.

26. ff. 272r–275r: Tract against marriage from Walter Map's *De nugis curialium* inc. 'Loqui prohibeor et tacere non possum. Grues odi et vocem ulule, bubonem et aves ceteras que luctuose hyemis gravitatem luctuose perululant . . .'[20a] The text is incomplete owing to the mutilation of f. 275. On f. 276r is a list of virtues and vices in a post-medieval hand and there are some Latin verses on f. 276v. Folios 275v and 277r are blank.

27. f. 277v: The first fourteen verses of a jest poem on the simple-mindedness of Norfolk people which is usually ascribed to a monk of Peterborough, inc. 'Exiit edictum Augusto Cesare'.[21]

This description of contents is sufficient to demonstrate clearly that MS Add. 11619 is a monastic book designed for edification, combining religious and theological texts with didactic *exempla* such as the Fables of Aesop or the *Disciplina clericalis* of Petrus Alfonsi. We now come to the Tristan illustrations.

## II. THE ILLUSTRATIONS

Surprisingly little work has been done on medieval illustrations of secular romance since the pioneering study of R. S. Loomis.[22] So far as the Tristan is concerned, the most useful recent surveys are those of Doris Fouquet and Hella Frühmorgen-Voss.[23] Hartmann von Aue's *Iwein* has in fact been the subject of the most searching enquiries into the significance of pictures for the

---

[20a] See *Walter Map, De nugis curialium, Courtiers' Trifles*, rev. by C. N. L. Brooke and R. A. B. Mynors (Oxford, 1983), Dist. IV, c. 3, pp. 288–98 (line 11).

[21] See Th. Wright, *Early Mysteries and other Latin Poems of the Twelfth and Thirteenth Centuries*, London, 1838, pp. 91–8 (poem of 256 lines, 'Anonymi Petroburgensis Descriptio Norfolciensium'; introd. pp. xxi–xxiii). Wright knows 3 MSS: Cambridge, Trinity College 0.2.45 (s. xiii), pp. 340f and 0.9.38 (s. xv), f. 59f, and the imperfect copy in MS London, BL, Cotton Titus A XX (s. xiv), ff. 167va–168rb which is followed by the unique text of John of St Omer's answer to the jest, ff. 168va–170vb (Wright, pp. 99–106).

[22] R. S. Loomis, *Arthurian Legends in Medieval Art*, London: Oxford University Press, 1938.

[23] Doris Fouquet, *Wort und Bild in der mittelalterlichen Tristantradition: Der älteste Tristanteppich von Kloster Wienhausen und die textile Tristanüberlieferung des Mittelalters*, Philologische Studien und Quellen 62, Berlin: Erich Schmidt Verlag, 1971, with a summary of Tristan MS illustrations on pp. 16–21; Hella Frühmorgen-Voss, *Text und Illustration im Mittelalter. Aufsätze zu den Wechselbeziehungen zwischen Literatur und bildender Kunst*, München: C. H. Beck'sche Verlagsbuchhandlung, 1975, esp. pp. 119–39 ('Tristan und Isolde in mittelalterlichen Bildzeugnissen') and pp. 140–71 ('Katalog der Tristan-Bildzeugnisse. Zusammengestellt von Norbert H. Ott). See also N. H. Ott, 'Tristan auf Runkelstein und die übrigen zyklischen Darstellungen des Tristanstoffes: Textrezeption oder medieninterne Eigengesetzlichkeit der Bildprogramme?', in W. Haug *et al.*, *Runkelstein. Die Wandmalereien des Sommerhauses*, Wiesbaden: Dr Ludwig Reichert Verlag, 1982, pp. 194–238.

understanding and the reception of the text.[24] Outside Germany there is nothing to compare with the celebrated Munich Tristan[25] and little that is close in date (variously put between 1240 and 1300). The Tristan story remains, however, the most popular secular subject after Charlemagne and Roland,[26] being particularly promoted in France in the fourteenth century.[27] In England, in the period that concerns us, there are only two sets of secular romance illustrations. In MS Cambridge, Trinity College 0.9.34 (s. xiii¹) we have 152 framed tinted drawings illlustrating Thomas of Kent's *Roman de Toute Chevalerie* incorporated in the columns of text.[28] They are of excellent quality and are dated *c*. 1240–50. From the same period, but of much inferior quality, are the 45 framed tinted drawings in MS London, BL Lansdowne 782 (s. xiii¹), where they are set into the text of the *Chanson d'Aspremont*.[29] Tinted drawings were commonly produced in England from the tenth century and though the effective use of colour for the purpose of modelling is somewhat sporadic, the quality of the line drawing is often of the highest. Something of the unevenness of the Lansdowne pictures is found in the illustrations which

---

[24] The literature is assembled and discussed in N. H. Ott & W. Walliczek, 'Bildprogramm und Textstruktur. Anmerkungen zu den 'Iwein'-Zyklen auf Rodeneck und in Schmalkalden', in *Deutsche Literatur im Mittelalter. Kontakte und Perspektiven. Hugo Kuhn zum Gedenken*, ed. by Christoph Cormeau, Stuttgart: J. B. Metzlersche Verlagsbuchhandlung, 1979, pp. 473–500. For the French *Yvain* see R. L. McGrath, 'A Newly Discovered Illustrated Manuscript of Chrétien de Troyes' *Yvain* and *Lancelot* in the Princeton University Library', *Speculum*, XXXVIII (1963), pp. 583–94.

[25] See P. Gichtel, 'Die Bilder der Münchner Tristan-Handschrift (cod. germ. 51). Eine Bestandaufnahme', in *Buch und Welt. Festschrift für Gustav Hofmann zum 65. Geburtstag dargebracht*, Wiesbaden: Otto Harrassowitz, 1965, pp. 391–457. In 1979 Gichtel and U. Montag published a facsimile of the Munich MS. See also J. Hucklenbroich, 'Einige Bemerkungen zum *Münchener Tristan*', in *Diversarum artium studia. Beiträge zu Kunstwissenschaft, Kunsttechnologie und ihren Randgebieten. Festschrift für Heinz Roosen-Runge zum 70. Geburtstag am 5. Oktober 1982*, ed. by H. Engelhart & G. Kempter, Wiesbaden: Dr Ludwig Reichert Verlag, 1982, pp. 55–73; Bettina Falkenberg, *Die Bilder des Münchner Tristan*, diss. Köln, 1986; Julia Walworth, The Illustrations of the Munich Tristan and Willehalm von Orlens (work in progress). I am grateful to Julia Walworth for these and other references.

[26] R. Lejeune & J. Stiennon, *La Légende de Roland dans l'art du moyen âge*, Bruxelles: Arcade, 1966, 2 vols. See also D. J. A. Ross, 'The Iconography of Roland', *Medium Aevum*, XXXVII (1968), pp. 46–65.

[27] See M. A. Stones, 'Secular Manuscript Illumination in France', in C. Kleinhenz (ed.), *Medieval Manuscripts and Textual Criticism*, North Carolina Studies in the Romance Languages and Literatures, Symposia no. 4, Chapel Hill: University of North Carolina Department of Romance Languages, 1976, pp. 83–102.

[28] See B. Foster (with the assistance of I. Short), *The Anglo-Norman 'Alexander' (Le Roman de Toute Chevalerie) by Thomas of Kent*, ANTS XXXII–XXXIII (for 1974–75), London: Anglo-Norman Text Society, 1977, pp. 10–12. The illustrations are described in James's catalogue, vol. 3, pp. 4ff.

[29] See D. J. A. Ross, 'A Thirteenth-Century Anglo-Norman Workshop illustrating secular literary Manuscripts', in *Mélanges offerts à Rita Lejeune* t. 1, Gembloux: Editions J. Duclot, SA, 1969, pp. 689–94. Ross compares the Cambridge and Lansdowne pictures.

*The Tristan Illustrations in MS London BL Add. 11619*

occupy ff. 6r–9v of MS Add. 11619.[30] Whilst nos. 1–4 are assured and refined, no. 5 is poor, nos. 6–7 no more than crude sketches, and no. 8 unfinished and rough in its execution of heads and faces. Whether nos. 5–8 are by the same artist as the first four illustrations it is, of course, difficult to say. No. 8 is obviously comparable to no. 1 in design, but very inferior in execution.

Although the illustrations have been cut down, it is clear that they are not part of a text and were either designed to be interleaved in a text, as in the case of the Munich Tristan, or did not accompany a text at all. After the opening quire of the MS, which consists of six folios (one unnumbered), it is evident that something has fallen out. Since ff. 3v–5v were left blank it is improbable that it is text which is missing and more likely that some Tristan illustrations have been lost. I think it is just possible to discern on ff. 6–9 traces of the fore-edge painting which characterises the rest of the MS, thus suggesting that they were part of the original MS or inserted at a very early stage i.e. in the early fourteenth century. The colours used in the illustrations are yellow,

---

[30] For permission to reproduce these illustrations I am indebted to the Trustees of the British Library.

brown, green, blue and red, as is normal in thirteenth-century tinted drawings. When they do not appear as part of an overall wash they are usually employed to give added relief to folds, but a modest attempt at modelling can be seen in no. 1 in the king's mantle. Whilst the identification of nos. 2, 3 and 5 leaves no room for doubt, that of the others must be regarded as tentative, as is so often the situation in unrubricated secular iconography. References below are to Bédier's edition of Thomas (SATF, 1905) and Hatto's translation of Gottfried (Penguin, 1960).

1. (f. 6r)  A full illustration (frame = 97 × 80 mm) of Mark's court. Tristan is dressed in a distinctive *aumuce* (see also nos. 4 and 5), here coloured green, and a long surcoat the folds of which are accentuated in blue, the same colour as his sleeves. He is accompanied by two bare-headed followers dressed in brown and in green (some attempt at modelling here). On the left, seated, is Mark, bearded and crowned, and with him his counsellors, one in stalked round cap with rolled brim (common throughout the thirteenth century) and the other in a round hat without stalk. Tristan's raised open hand is, to follow Karl von Amira's terminology, simply a 'Redegestus',[31] but the outstretched finger of both Mark and his counsellor hints at something more than merely a sign for attention, being equally typical of a 'Befehlgestus' and 'Gelöbnisgestus'.[32] A likely identification for this picture seems to be the scene at Mark's court, following Tristan's safe return from Ireland, where the king, under pressure from his barons, vows to take a wife and agrees to Tristan's expedition to Ireland to bring back Isolde. The absence of rigidity in the poses is striking, the swirling motion of the king's mantle (yellow with brown lining) is well judged,[33] and the refined execution of the faces is noteworthy. The bold, forward movement of the Tristan figure fittingly conveys his initiative and determination in this scene (it is he who persuades Mark to agree to the barons' proposals). The king's surcoat (with Magyar sleeves) and that of the second counsellor are washed in green, the crown is yellow and the round caps brown. See Béd. XII, pp. 109–10; Hatto 11, pp. 152–4.

2. (f. 6v)  The celebrated scene at the Irish court in which Tristan in the bath anxiously watches as Isolde observes the notch in the blade of his sword and realises that the 'merchant' (in Gottfried the minstrel Tantris) is really the slayer of her uncle, the Morolt. The scene is a popular one in Tristan illustrations and the suppliant gesture of Tristan, hands together,

---

[31] K. von Amira, 'Die Handgebärden in den Bilderhandschriften des Sachsenspiegels', in *Abhandlungen der königlich bayerischen Akademie der Wissenschaften*, Philosophisch-Philologische Klasse 33, abt. 2 (1905), München, 1909 [pp. 161–263] pp. 170ff.

[32] Ibid., pp. 212ff. and 216ff.

[33] For the king's position with legs crossed see the Munich Tristan f. 30r and Fouquet, op. cit., p. 51. The hand on the knee is also illustrated in the Munich Tristan f. 37v and in Nigel Morgan, *Early Gothic Manuscripts [I] 1190–1250*, Oxford: Oxford University Press, 1982, illustr. 272, 274 & 303.

## The Tristan Illustrations in MS London BL Add. 11619

characteristic.³⁴ There is some divergence among illustrators about the identity of the women present, who may be the queen and her daughter Isolde, or Isolde and her handmaiden Brengain.³⁵ The woman in barbette and fillet on the left is surely Isolde (cf. no. 8) who is about to wield the sword against Tristan, whilst the girl with long hair parted in the middle, with circlet and loose flowing locks, certainly the younger and socially less elevated of the two,³⁶ is Brengain. The planks of the bath tub are coloured brown, the cross

---

³⁴ See Loomis, op. cit., fig. 68, 70, 78, 80 & 82.
³⁵ See Loomis, op. cit., p. 50 and fig. 68, 70 and Fouquet, op. cit., pp. 118f and abb. 2. In the Munich Tristan f. 67v the illustrator conflates the two scenes from Gottfried, in which first the queen seeks to prevent Isolde from assaulting Tristan and then 'Brangane' enters and remonstrates with Isolde (depicted twice).
³⁶ See Fouquet, op. cit., p. 70.

bars green, the folds of Isolde's garment are accentuated in red and Brengain's in green (though her arms are coloured red). The faces of both women are touched with red. No attempt is made to depict Isolde's recognition of the truth through her fitting of the missing piece to the notch of the swordblade.[37] See Béd. XIV, pp. 132ff.; Hatto 13, pp. 173ff.

3. (f. 7r)   There now follows the celebrated combat with the dragon by which Tristan obtains Isolde as his prize which he will present to Mark. In Gottfried the hero is described thus: 'Tristan lowered his spear, set spur to his horse and, charging along at speed, thrust the spear through its [= the dragon's] gullet . . .' (Hatto, p. 160). Later Tristan has to finish the beast off with his sword. In the illustration Tristan does not appear to be wearing any leg armour (unless the hatching was forgotten, cf. no. 4) and there is the interesting detail of his rowel spurs, also seen in nos. 4 and 8. Rowel spurs appear to be rare in England before 1300, though they are depicted on Henry III's First Seal (1220).[38] They also appear in MS Dublin, Trinity College 177 (*c.* 1240–50),[39] but in MS Lansdowne 782 f. 6r the radii of the rowel clearly depicted in the tinted drawing are in fact a later addition to the prick spur which is standard in all the illustrations in this MS. By contrast, the rowel is clearly depicted in three of the present Tristan illustrations and this may suggest a date late in the thirteenth century when the rowel was more firmly established. Unlike the rowel, the lion (coloured green) on the hero's shield is a detail shared with the celebrated Chertsey tiles.[40] Loomis comments 'The logical inference . . . is that Thomas . . . attributed to his hero, as his armorial charge, gules a lion rampant or'.[41] Tristan's helm, flat-topped and with crossbar, also closely resembles that depicted in the tiles. The dragon, with its massive claws (given prominence by Gottfried), is coloured green and red and

---

[37] See Loomis, op. cit., pl. 78.
[38] See Hunt in *Zeitschrift für celtische Philologie*, XXXIII (1974), pp. 109ff.
[39] See Morgan, op. cit., ill. 282.
[40] There are 34 positively identified Tristan scenes in this famous set of inlaid tile mosaics which are outstanding for their technical skill and which are generally held to show a debt to Thomas and which have often been dated to *c.* 1260 (Morgan, op. cit., p. 37, n. 59 considers that the figure style suggests a date around the middle of the century).
E. S. Eames, *Medieval Tiles*, London: British Museum, 1968, repr. 1976, p. 9 comments 'Until more is known, any date between 1250 and 1290 would seem acceptable and it is possible that the development of the series lasted throughout that time, the mosaic element becoming progressively simpler until by the 1290s it was abandoned altogether'. On the scenes from Tristan Dr Eames observes (p. 7) 'It is possible that the pictorial roundels were designed for the tiles, but it is more probable that the tile dies were copied from existing decorative roundels illustrating a manuscript of the romance of Tristram and Isolde, although no manuscript with comparable pictures is known to survive'. Pictorial roundels of the Tristan scenes almost identical to those at Chertsey were also used at Hailes Abbey and Halesowen Abbey. See also J. A. Wight, *Mediaeval Floor Tiles: their design and distribution in Britain*, London: John Baker, 1975, pp. 103ff. and, for a detailed technical account, E. S. Eames, *Catalogue of Mediaeval lead-glazed earthenware Tiles in the Department of Medieval and Later Antiquities, British Museum*, vol. 1, London: British Museum, 1980, pp. 141–71 and pl. IVb (colour).
[41] Loomis, op. cit., p. 47 and fig. 43–4 (fight with the Morolt)

## The Tristan Illustrations in MS London BL Add. 11619

stands on a rock (coloured green) inhabited by a rabbit-like creature and a small serpent such as appear in the marginalia of Gothic MSS. To the right of the dragon is a black and white bird, perhaps an omen of death. The fire issuing from the dragon's mouth is, surprisingly, uncoloured. See Béd. XIII, pp. 114ff.; Hatto 12, pp. 159ff.

4. (f. 7v)   The assailant is unmistakably Tristan, with characteristic *aumuce*, rowel spurs, and a sword (but no baldric). His victim is unarmed and is being decapitated. The scene must be that of Tristan's slaying of Duke Morgan who had killed Tristan's father Rivalen. In Bedier's reconstruction Tristan kills Morgan in the main hall after the Duke has struck him in the face. He smites him on the head in the presence of the court and of his own companions. In Gottfried he attacks Morgan whilst the latter is out hunting in the forest, a

falcon on his arm.[42] In the illustration the only colour is red which is used for the blood spurting from the Duke's head and for the faces of Tristan and the companion on his right. The treatment of the folds of Morgan's mantle recalls that of Mark's in no. 1. See Béd. IX, pp. 62ff.; Hatto 8, pp. 111ff.

5. (f. 8r) This is the most popular of all the illustrated Tristan scenes, the assignation in the orchard,[43] with the lovers spied on by Mark concealed in a tree. Tristan and Isolde are depicted making gestures of greeting (Tristan's left hand does not seem to have been executed), whilst the dwarf (Frocin/Melot) spies on them from nearby, apparently with hands clasped. In some

---

[42] See the Munich Tristan f. 37r and Loomis, op. cit., fig. 73 & 83.
[43] See D. Fouquet, 'Die Baumgartenszene des Tristan in der mittelalterlichen Kunst und Literatur', *Zeitschrift für deutsche Philologie*, XCII (1973), pp. 360–70 and Loomis, op. cit., pp. 65f. (pl. 120–34)

illustrations the dwarf joins Mark in the tree (following Gottfried).[44] Whereas in Beroul we have a pine tree and in Gottfried an olive tree, the English illustrator seems to have chosen a pear tree, perhaps for its erotic connotations.[45] The tree is coloured green, Isolde's mantle is red, her gown grey-blue. The pears are an ochre colour. As with the scene depicting the damaged sword, no attempt is made to provide interpretative detail, here the lovers' realisation that they are being spied on as a result of seeing Mark's shadow in the moonlight. See Béd. XXIII, pp. 198ff.; Hatto 22, pp. 234ff.

6/7. (ff. 8v–9r) In two markedly inferior, crude sketches a sea voyage is depicted. The illustrations may present the landing in Wexford, but even the

---

[44] See the Munich Tristan f. 76r.
[45] See Hunt in *Mediaeval Studies*, XL (1978), p. 153 and L. Polak in *Romania*, XCIII (1972), pp. 310–11.

figures cannot really be identified. In no. 6 the figure in the prow wears a knee-length tunic coloured in red. There is no other colour. In no. 7 the figure in the prow is casting the anchor. The only colouring is the green wash applied to the sea. These two scenes seem to have lost more through being cut down than the others.

8. (f. 9v)   A sketch, uncoloured and incomplete, but displaying some reflection of the quality of no. 1. The lady in barbette and fillet, her hair coiled over each ear and held by a crespine, must be Isolde. The king is presumably Mark, depicted in a similar pose to that of no. 1, but here beardless. The central figure is probably Tristan who presents Isolde, brought from Ireland, to her future husband. This scene would then be a pendant to no. 1 in which, as suggested above, Mark agrees to Tristan's wooing expedition to Ireland. The two scenes seem to be designed to complement each other. There has been some retouching of the arm and facial features of the middle character. There is no colour. See Béd. XVIII, p. 156; Hatto 17, p. 206.

I conclude that the Tristan illustrations were admitted into MS Add. 11619 for their didactic value as a reminder of the negative element of the legend received as an exemplum along the lines suggested by my reading of Thomas.

# *Punishment in the* Perlesvaus: *The Theme of the Waste Land*

## ANGUS J. KENNEDY

The physical blighting of Arthur's Kingdom as a form of collective punishment imposed for a variety of reasons (an individual's misdeeds, vengeance, or the miraculous act of devastation wrought by the so-called Dolorous Stroke) constitutes one of the most characteristic and memorable ingredients of the Grail Legend as it developed in France between *c.* 1180 and *c.* 1240. Occurring as it does in nearly all of the Grail texts composed over this period (notably, Chrétien's *Conte du Graal*, the *Elucidation* prologue, the *First* and *Fourth Continuations*, the *Estoire* and *Queste* sections of the *Vulgate Cycle*, the *Perlesvaus*, the Balaain section of the *Suite du Merlin*, and also in the much later Grail-related *Sone de Nansai*[1]), the Waste Land theme has naturally attracted fairly frequent critical attention and discussion over the years.[2] Much of this discussion has tended to concentrate on the question of origins rather than on the literary handling of the theme in individual texts. Jessie L. Weston, for example, taking as her starting-point the sympathetic relationship that

---

[1] Chrétien de Troyes, *Le Roman de Perceval ou le Conte du Graal*, éd. par W. Roach, Genève: Droz, 1956 (Textes Littéraires Français, 71), ll. 3583–90, 4469–83; *The Elucidation, A Prologue to the Conte del Graal*, ed. by A. W. Thompson, Genève: Slatkine, 1982 (Reprint of New York ed., 1931), ll. 26–33, 89–98, 383–400; *The Continuations of the Old French Perceval of Chrétien de Troyes*, ed. by W. Roach, Philadelphia: University of Pennsylvania Press, 1949, Vol. I, ll. 13560–88; Gerbert de Montreuil, *La Continuation de Perceval*, ed. by M. Williams, Paris: Champion, 1922 (Classiques Français du Moyen Age, 28), Vol. I, ll. 312–24, 363–9, 492–501; *Vulgate Version of the Arthurian Romances*, ed. by H. O. Sommer, Washington: Publications of the Carnegie Institution of Washington, 1908–16, Vol. I, p. 290, Vol. VI, p. 147; *La Queste del Saint Graal*, éd. par A. Pauphilet, Paris: Champion, 1949 (Classiques Français du Moyen Age, 33), p. 204; *Le Haut Livre du Graal, Perlesvaus*, ed. by W. A. Nitze and T. A. Jenkins, New York: Phaeton, 1972, 2 Vols. (Reprint of Chicago University Press ed., 1932–37); all subsequent references will be to lines of this edition; *Merlin*, éd. par G. Paris et J. Ulrich, Paris: Firmin-Didot, 1886 (Société des Anciens Textes Fr.), Vol. I, p. 212– Vol. II, p. 60, cp. also *Le Roman de Balain*, ed. by M. D. Legge, Manchester: University Press, 1942 (French Classics); *Sone von Nausay*, hgg. von M. Goldschmidt, Tübingen, 1899 (Bibliothek des Litterarischen Vereins in Stuttgart, 216), ll. 4841–56.

[2] For bibliographical details, see C. E. Pickford and R. Last, *The Arthurian Bibliography*, Woodbridge: Brewer, 1981, 2 Vols.; E. Reiss, L. H. Reiss, B. Taylor, *Arthurian Legend and Literature. An Annotated Bibliography*, Vol. I, *The Middle Ages*, New York and London: Garland, 1984 (Garland Reference Library of the Humanities, 415), *sub.* Waste Land.

seemed to exist in Grail romance between the vitality of the king and the life-forces of his kingdom, and conversely the maiming of the king and the wasting of the land, devoted all her energies to relating her findings in Arthurian romance to oriental nature-rituals, while Loomis, Nitze, Newstead and others, working on more concrete evidence and with more positive results, pointed to fairly clear parallels to and echoes of the Waste Land in the literature and lore of Ireland and Wales, and used these as part of their general argument for the ultimate Celtic provenance of the Arthurian cycle.[3] This kind of approach to the Waste Land theme is best summed-up in the title of Jessie Weston's now famous book, *From Ritual to Romance*, of Nitze's article 'The Waste Land: a Celtic Arthurian Theme', or of the chapter 'Irish *echtrai*: the Waste Land and the Bleeding Lance' in Loomis's *The Grail. From Celtic Myth to Christian Symbol*.[4] Not all studies of the Waste Land, however, have been presented within the framework of theories about ultimate origins – though these still attract, and are likely to continue to attract, scholarly attention (see, for example, the interesting articles on the Maimed King by O'Sharkey and Riemschneider[5]). Invaluable studies by Nitze, Vinaver, Bogdanow, Kelly and Cor, among others, have concentrated less on origins and more on the creative adaptation of material in each successive text, attempting to journey along what Vinaver referred to as 'the steep and adventurous path of creation';[6] and more recently, in an article entitled 'Waste Land and Round Table: the Historical Significance of Myths of Dearth and Plenty in Old French Romance', Bloch has perceptively explored how the Waste Land theme may reflect or project issues of contemporary reality.[7] These studies still leave scope, however, in my view, for a more detailed examination of the Waste Land as it is presented in the *Perlesvaus*.[8] It is the purpose of this article to approach the Waste Land in the *Perlesvaus* from both a literary and historical point of view (though no reference will be made

---

[3] Jessie L. Weston, *From Ritual to Romance*, New York: Doubleday, 1957 (Reprint of Cambridge University Press, 1920); R. S. Loomis, *The Grail. From Celtic Myth to Christian Symbol*, New York: Columbia University Press, 1963; *Perlesvaus*, ed. cit., Vol. II; H. Newstead, *Bran the Blessed in Arthurian Literature*, New York: Columbia University Press, 1939 (Columbia University Studies in English and Comparative Literature, 141).

[4] For Weston and Loomis, see Note 3 above; Nitze, *Modern Philology*, XLIII (1945–46), pp. 58–62.

[5] E. O'Sharkey, 'The Maimed Kings in the Arthurian Romances', *Etudes Celtiques*, VIII (1958–59), pp. 420–8; M. Riemschneider, 'Li rois mahaignies', *Romanistisches Jahrbuch*, IX (1958), pp. 126–38.

[6] E. Vinaver, *The Rise of Romance*, Oxford: Clarendon, 1971, p. 67; *Perlesvaus*, ed. cit., Vol. II; F. Bogdanow, *The Romance of the Grail*, Manchester: University Press, 1966; T. E. Kelly, *Le Haut Livre du Graal: Perlesvaus. A Structural Study*, Genève: Droz, 1974 (Histoire des Idées et Critique Littéraire, 145); M. A. Cor, 'Structure and Theme in the *Perlesvaus*', Ph.D., University of North Carolina at Chapel Hill, 1979 (available through University Microfilms International).

[7] *New Literary History*, XI (1980), pp. 255–76.

[8] For bibliography of *Perlesvaus*, see works by Kelly (pp. 194–8) and Cor (pp. 139–49) cited in Note 6 above.

to questions of origins), in order to bring out more clearly than has been attempted to date something of the author's originality with regard both to the way in which he handles the theme and the 'senefiance' he attaches to it. Given the overtly propagandist nature of the *Perlesvaus*, it is impossible to separate literary and didactic intentions. A useful, overall perspective for this discussion is provided by Vinaver's analysis of the basic ingredients that can occur in various combinations in the presentation of the Waste Land: a miraculous weapon, a wound inflicted upon a knight or king (the Dolorous Stroke), the wasting of the land, the healing of the wound.[9] As will be shown, not all of these motifs are applicable to the *Perlesvaus*, but they do provide a general focus within which the author's priorities can be judged. This survey will examine, firstly, the development of the Waste Land at the level of plot or narrative; secondly, the textual indications that guide us towards interpreting the Waste Land in a certain way; thirdly, the Waste Land as part of a complex pattern of related, criss-crossing themes that all point towards a similar if not identical 'senefiance'.

*1. The Waste Land at the level of plot*

When the story opens, Perlesvaus' first visit to the Grail Castle has already taken place. We learn through a number of retrospective allusions woven into the opening sections of the romance that Perlesvaus has been to the Castle of the Fisher King, that he has seen the Grail and the Bleeding Lance, but has failed to ask what purpose the Grail served and whom it served, and that, as a result of this, the Fisher King has fallen ill, disaster has overtaken the whole of Arthur's Kingdom and all the adjacent islands. Now what the author is at pains to do throughout the rest of Part I of the romance (i.e. up to l. 6271) is to bring these consequences constantly before the reader's attention, and it is in executing this design that he develops his own conception of the Waste Land theme. What strikes the reader as perhaps the most immediately obvious consequence of Perlesvaus' disastrous silence is the physical blighting that overtakes not the Grail Country but Arthur's Kingdom itself. Brief but telling descriptions of the landscape, emphasising above all its bleakness and sterility, are carefully introduced, at all times confronting us and the knights of Logres with the fact of the Grail hero's failure. For example, Gauvain enters into 'la plus orrible forest e la plus hideuse que nus veïst onques; e sanbloit qu'onques verdeur n'i eüst eüe, ainz erent totes les branches nues de fueille e seches, e tuit li arbre noir ausi comme brullé de feu, e la terre par desoz arsice e noire e sanz verdeur e plainne de granz crevaces' (ll. 737–42). At another point Gauvain comes to 'une terre seche et povre et sofraiteuse de toz biens. Et trove un povre chastel et entre dedenz, et le trove molt agasti . . .' (ll. 2529–

[9] Vinaver, op. cit., pp. 56–7.

31). In the course of one of his adventures, Lancelot finds himself in 'une terre gaste et un païs grant et large, ou il n'abitoit ne beste ne oisiax, car la terre estoit si seche et si povre q'il n'i trovoient point de pouture. Lanceloz esgarde devant lui en loig, et voit une cité aparoir, si chevauche cele part grant aleüre, et voit que la cité est si grant q'il senble q'ele porpraige un païs. Il voit les murs qui dechïent environ, et les portes enclinent de vellece. Il entra la dedenz et trove la cité tote voide de gent, et voit les granz palés deschaüz et gastes, et trove les marchiez et les changes toz voiz, et voit les granz cemetires toz plains de sarqex et les iglises totes gastes' (ll. 2857–65). Perlesvaus, passing through 'un païs qui li senbloit estre gastez, car il estoit tot voit de gent' (ll. 4906–07), is told by a hermit that this desolate terrain marks the beginning of the Kingdom of Logres: 'Ceste terre gastee en son ceste forest par ont vos venistes est li conmencemenz dou roiaume de Logres' (ll. 4920–21). Equally indicative of this widespread desolation is the proliferation of the word 'gaste' in the titles assumed by the knights and ladies of the Kingdom: the Chevalier de la Gaste Meson, the Povre Chevalier dou Gaste Chastel, the Seigneur dou Gaste Chastel, or the Dame dou Gaste Manoir.

This concrete picture of the blighting of the land is itself only part of the author's development of the Waste Land theme: the depiction of the blighted land proceeds apace with a description of the moral and spiritual decline of Arthur and his court after Perlesvaus' failure, in such a way that the one is made to reflect and constantly reinforce the other. The theme of Arthur's decline is developed throughout Part I (e.g. in Gauvain's and Lancelot's visits to the Grail Castle or in Perlesvaus' numerous encounters with his sister), but it is presented most clearly of all in the prologue, then in a hermit's severe censure of Arthur during his pilgrimage to a chapel in Wales, and in Arthur's first encounter with the Damoisele du Char. In the prologue the author states: 'par molt poi de parole qu'il (i.e. Perlesvaus) delaia a dire, avindrent si granz meschaances a la Grant Breteingne que totes les illes e totes les terres en chaïrent en grant doleur . . .' (ll. 18–21) . . . 'une volentez delaianz li (i.e. to Arthur) vint, e commença a perdre le talent des largesces que il soloit fere. Ne voloit cort tenir a Noël, ne a Pasques, ne a Pentecoste. Li chevalier de la Table Reonde, qant il virent son bienfet alentir, il s'en partirent e commencierent sa cort a lessier. De trois .c. e .lxx. chevaliers q'il soloit avoir de sa mesniee, n'avoit il ore mie plus de .xxv. au plus. Nule aventure n'avenoit mes a sa cort. Tuit li autre prince avoient leur biensfez delaiez por ce q'il veoient le roi maintenir si foiblement' (ll. 69–76). Then, in the course of his pilgrimage to Saint Austin's Chapel in Wales, Arthur is vigorously upbraided by a hermit for this transformation that has taken place in himself and at his court: 'Car vos estes li plus riches rois du mont e li plus poissanz e li plus aventurex, si devroit a vos toz li mondes prendre essanple de bien fere e de largesse e d'oneur: e vos estes li essanples de vilenie fere a toz les riches homes qui ore sont. Si vos en mescharra molt durement, se vos ne remetez vostre afere o point o vos l'aviez commencié; car vostre corz estoit la sovrainne de totes les corz, e la plus aventureuse; or est la pis vaillanz' (ll. 333–9). Arthur himself is then given, for the first time, an explanation for this decline in terms that clearly recall those of the prologue: 'Mes une granz doleurs est avenue novelement par un chevalier qui fu herbergiez en l'ostel au riche roi Pescheeur, si s'aparut a lui li sainz Graauz e la lance de coi la pointe de fer saine, ne ne demanda de coi ce servoit, ne cui on en servoit; por ce qu'il ne le demanda, sont totes les terres de guerre escommeües, ne chevaliers n'e[n]contre autre en forest q'il ne qeure sus e ocie s'il puet, e vos meïsmes vos en perceveroiz bien ainz que vos partez de ceste lande' (ll. 349–56). And finally, in his encounter with the Damoisele du Char, Arthur (and the reader) is reminded yet again: 'por ce que cil ne volst demander cui on en servoit, totes les terres en furent commeües de guerre; chevaliers n'encontra onques puis autre en forest ne en lande, o il n'eüst contenz d'armes sanz resnable achoison; vos meïsmes vos en poez bien estre perceüz, car vos en avez delaié vostre bienfet grant piece, de coi vos avez esté molt blasmez e tuit li autre baron qui pris ont garde a vos, car vos estes li mireoirs au siecle de bien fere o de mal' (ll. 640–46). It is worth pointing out too that the Damoisele du Char, who speaks these words, seems to embody the decline that each of these passages underlines: once the Grail bearer at the Court of the Fisher King, she is now forced to wander over the face of the earth, her right hand (which she once used to carry the Grail) slung in a gold stole about her neck, her head once adorned with luxuriant tresses now 'tote chauve e sans chevex' (ll. 648–9) as a result of Perlesvaus' failure. For the Damoisele du Char, as for Arthur and his court, Perlesvaus' silence has wrought a dramatic reversal in their fortunes.

Arthur and his court, however, as the Damoisele du Char reminds us in one of the passages just quoted, represent 'li mireoirs au siecle de bien fere o de mal' (ll. 645–6). As part therefore of his development of the Waste Land theme, the author goes on to show us in detail how the woes and calamities that beset Arthur's court are reflected on a much larger scale throughout the whole kingdom. Now the way in which the author chooses to do this is to show us Arthur's kingdom exposed to the ravages of war, both from without and within. This involves him and his readers in a very long and at times highly complicated series of adventures to do with warfare and copious blood-letting, ranging from the Sire des Mares' repeated attacks on the estates of Perlesvaus' mother (e.g. ll. 461, 513, 1076–7), the King of Chastel Mortel's attacks on the Grail Castle (e.g. ll. 1081–5, 2486, 3929–31, 4986), through Perlesvaus' feud with the family of the Red Knight (e.g. ll. 512, 1077, 3046–7) to the conquest of the Chevalier au Dragon Ardant (l. 5913) and the Tor de Cuivre (l. 5960), and the story of Keu's treacherous murder of Loholt, Arthur's son (ll. 4010–12). The inherent complexity of these adventures at times puts additional demands on the reader in that the adventures are not developed in a straight, narrative sequence, but are interlaced with one another in such a way that we are left waiting for the reappearance of some theme held temporarily in suspense whilst already following a second or a third. Yet, however intricate the complexities of the plot or narrative technique, however easy it is for us to lose sight of the central threads amidst all the detail with which the author presents us, it is clear that there is one overall consideration running right through this section, giving shape and coherence to what on the surface may appear to be a meaningless patchwork of bigger and better battles: namely, the cause-effect relationship between Perlesvaus' silence at the Grail Castle and *all* the disasters that overtake the land. Indeed, it is notable that on a few occasions, even when immersed in the detail of some particular feud or battle, the author has taken the trouble to help the reader keep this central consideration in mind. For example, when describing the Sire des Mares' assaults on the estates belonging to Perlesvaus' mother, the author reminds us that it is precisely because of Perlesvaus' failure in the Grail adventure that his mother has no-one available to defend her land (ll. 1076–85): Perlesvaus has withdrawn to a hermitage to recover from the humiliation of his first visit to the Grail Castle, while the Fisher King, who is related to Perlesvaus and his mother and who therefore could be expected to come to her aid, cannot help because he has fallen into languishment, again as a direct result of Perlesvaus' silence. It is evident, therefore, that the account of how Arthur's Kingdom is exposed to the ravages of war is part and parcel of the wasting of the land that results from Perlesvaus' failure at the Castle of the Fisher King.

Considered solely from the point of view of narrative or plot, then, the Waste Land theme is composed of a number of interwoven, criss-crossing strands: the physical blighting of the land, the decline of Arthur's chivalry, the proliferation of war and dissension throughout his Kingdom. The already considerable impact which the reappearance of these various strands must have on the reader, at the level of plot, is deepened by an additional element introduced and highlighted by the author, namely, the striking antithesis which he develops between Arthur's Waste Kingdom and the fertile country of the Fisher King. As was touched upon earlier, although the Fisher King falls into languishment as a result of Perlesvaus' failure, his land escapes the punishment inflicted upon Arthur's territories, and his country is as fertile and plenteous as Arthur's is poor and sterile. When Gauvain arrives at the Fisher King's country, he finds it to comprise 'une terre molt bele e molt ri[ch]e e molt plenteïve' (ll. 1689–90) . . . 'la plus bele terre du mont et les plus beles praeries et les plus beles rivieres que nus veïst onques, et forez garnies de bestes sauvaches' (ll. 2255–7) . . . '[li chastiax] est avironé de granz eues et plenteüreuses de toz biens' (ll. 2267–8). A similar description is given on Lancelot's arrival at the Grail Castle: '. . . et trouva .i. molt bele praerie qui tote estoit chargie de flors, et coroit une molt grant riviere qui molt estoit clere et large, et avoit forest d'une part et d'autre, mes que les praeries estoi[en]t granz et larges entre la riviere et la forest' (ll. 3627–30). Additional details, pointing to the same abundance and fruitfulness, are provided when Arthur arrives at the castle after it has been reconquered by Perlesvaus: 'Li rois . . . esgarda la richoise e la grant habundance qui eu chastel venoit, car il n'estoit riens ou monde qui i faillist, qui covenist a cors de bone gent . . . Il avoit derier le chastel .i. flun, ce tesmoigne l'estoire, par coi toz li biens venoit ou chastel. Icil flun estoit mout beaus e mout plentious. Josephez nos tesmoigne que il venoit de Paradis Terrestre, e avironnoit tot le chastel, e coroit dusqu'en la forest chiés .i. prodom hermite. Iluec perdoit son cors e entroit en terre, mais tot la o il s'espandoit estoit grant la plenté de toz les biens' (ll. 7193–5, 7198–203). The contrast thus established between drought and fertility, dearth and plenty, poverty and wealth, sterility and fruitfulness serves to highlight the seriousness of Perlesvaus' failure and the punishment it has imposed on the whole Arthurian world.

It remains now to look briefly at the Waste Land theme at plot-level in Part 2 of the text (l. 6272–end). After the languishment and death of the Fisher King (l. 5145) and Perlesvaus' reconquest of the Grail Castle (l. 6252), one would have expected the author to orchestrate fully the transformation of the Waste Land to a land of fruitfulness and plenty: the articulation of this theme would have neatly counterbalanced the depiction of the blighting of the kingdom in Part 1 and would have served to underscore the redemptive nature of Perlesvaus' mission and his atonement for his original transgression. Rather surprisingly, however, the theme of the restoration of the land is somewhat muted: it occurs, as will be seen, in Lancelot's regeneration of the Waste City, but there is no general depiction of the land suddenly regaining its fruitfulness. In addition, even after the Grail conquest and Arthur's pilgrimage to the castle, one still finds echoes of the Waste Land theme reverberating throughout the text. Lancelot, for example, approaching Carduel, finds 'la terre gaste e essilliee' (l. 7635). Similarly, Arthur 'trove sa terre gastee en plusors lex, de quoi il est molt dolenz' (7811). The risk of war bringing dissension and ruin is still ever-present: 'Sa[g]ramors, fait Briens, meuz vendroit le roi que il congeast Lancelot un an que il fust por lui gerroiez dis, ne que sa terre fust gastee ne maumise' (ll. 8093–5). Perlesvaus, whose life as a knight is never 'sanz travaill e sanz paine en tant com il vesqui chevaliers' (ll. 8983–4), at one point on his various journeys 'passe .iii. roiaumes e plus, e trove isles gastes e desertes, [d'une part]e d'autre part la mer, quar la nef coroit assez pres de terre' (ll. 9825–7), and later comes across the forest of Noir Hermite once visited by Gauvain: '[La forest] tant est lede e hideuse qu'il n'i a fueille ne verdeur en iver ne en esté, ne chanz d'oisel n'i fu onques oïz, ainz est la terre lede e arsice e les crevaces granz' (ll. 9942–5). Even the Grail Castle itself eventually crumbles away, with only the Grail Chapel being left intact: '. . . commença li manoirs a deschaoir e les sales a agastir, mes onques la chapele n'enpira, ainz fu adés en son buen point, e est encore' (ll. 10167–9).

All of these examples are clearly not directly related to the Waste Land theme as developed in Part 1: there, as has been shown, there was a cause-effect relationship between Perlesvaus' silence and all the calamities that befall the Kingdom. That said and allowed for, these allusions nonetheless constitute an important continuation and echo of the Waste Land throughout Part 2, confronting the reader with the spectacle of a land that (despite Perlesvaus' redemptive mission and Lancelot's restoration of the Waste City) never quite manages to free itself from dissension and the threat of further devastation.

At the level of plot or narrative, then, it can be seen that the author of the *Perlesvaus* has made a highly original use of the material familiar to him, exploiting it as he does to depict the Arthurian world in its collective death-throes, no more than a 'heap of broken images' (to borrow Eliot's phrase from *The Waste Land*), morally and spiritually wasting away as the result of Perlesvaus' failure at the castle of the Fisher King. His handling of the Waste Land reflects too an attempt to simplify and rationalise inherited motifs. For example, he has rejected the Dolorous Stroke as the cause of the Waste Land (as we find it in the *First Continuation*, the *Suite du Merlin* and the later *Sone de Nansai*);[10] he has rejected too as unnecessary a distinction that some texts make (e.g. Chrétien's *Conte du Graal*) between the cause of the Fisher King's malady and the cause of the wasting of the land. In Chrétien's romance, as in the *Perlesvaus*, the calamities that befall the land are explained by the hero's failure: but in Chrétien the illness of the Fisher King is antecedent to and not explained by the hero's first visit to the Grail Castle – we learn in ll. 3509–15 of the *Conte du Graal* how Chrétien's Fisher King came to be wounded in battle. In the *Perlesvaus*, by contrast, the author seems to have regarded this distinction as an unnecessary extra, and in his text it is the hero's failure to ask the appropriate Grail questions that explains both the illness of the King and the wasting of the land. These modifications, together with the fact that there is no healing of the 'Maimed King' (in *Perlesvaus* the Fisher King languishes and eventually dies), reflect a consistent design to highlight the seriousness of Perlesvaus' failure and the punishment that this imposes on the whole Arthurian world. This overall design explains not only the rejection of the Dolorous Stroke and the attribution of the wasting of the land and the illness of the Fisher King to a single cause but also the reason why the author excludes altogether an account of Perlesvaus' first visit to the Grail Castle – he began instead, as was shown earlier, by concentrating on the consequences, i.e. the wasting of the land. All of this confers on the Waste Land in the *Perlesvaus* the status of a major and coherent theme, designed to reflect the moral and spiritual wilderness into which Perlesvaus has brought himself and the rest of the Arthurian world, and worked out with a consistency and seriousness of purpose found rarely in the other texts. That said, there still

---

[10] For editions, see Note 1 above.

remains a number of unanswered questions at the level of plot or narrative: the exact nature of Perlesvaus' sin that causes the wasting of the land is left unspecified; Perlesvaus' failure brings disaster not so much on the Grail Country as on Arthur's Kingdom; the author refrains from giving a full articulation to the theme of the restoration of the land, and instead confronts the reader with the contrast, not between the Waste Land and its regeneration, but between the Waste Land and the rich country of the Fisher King – a contrast echoed in the concluding section of the text in the opposition between the Isle Souffroitose and the Isle Plenteureuse (ll. 9631, 9633); after Perlesvaus' conquest of the Grail Castle, the inhabitants of Arthur's country are not granted the 'reward' of a definitive regeneration of the land: there is evidence to suggest that Arthur's Kingdom is still exposed to the twin evils of physical blighting and devastation caused by warfare. Answers to these problems will emerge when we turn to examine the 'senefiance' that the author has conferred on his theme.

## 2. *The 'senefiance' of the Waste Land*

When one turns now to the task of interpreting the Waste Land theme, it is important to stress at the outset that the *Perlesvaus* belongs to a type of romance that is self-avowedly symbolic, the author's design being to recall or bring to mind the spiritual truths of the New Law of Christianity: '. . . ce nos trete en senefiance li bons hermites por la Novele Loi, en la quele li plusor ne sont pas bien connoissant, si en volt fere remembrance par essanples' (ll. 2184–6). What is particularly important about this statement is not just its suggestion that more is meant in *Perlesvaus* than meets the eye, or even the clear pointer it provides as to the general lines of interpretation we should follow, but rather the warning it contains against making excessive claims for symbolical analysis. All that the author claims he is doing is using the Arthurian material to recall or bring to mind certain truths of the Christian faith: he makes no claim that certain parallels he proposes are precisely worked out in every detail, or that certain identifications made at one point in the narrative need be applied throughout the text.[11] This technique confers on the romance what Tuve calls 'a flickering intermittent clarity of the double senses'[12] or, as Kelly puts it, 'an intermittent allegorical significance'.[13] With this general point in mind, let us look now at the 'senefiance' which the author suggests for the Waste Land theme: through it he tries first of all to direct the reader's mind to the Christian doctrine of the Fall and the consequent legacy of suffering and death it bequeathed to mankind. Through Perlesvaus' failure

---

[11] For a good discussion of technique, see Kelly, op. cit., pp. 91–102.
[12] R. Tuve, *Allegorical Imagery*, Princeton: University Press, 1966, p. 401.
[13] Kelly, op. cit., p. 92.

at the Grail Castle the author brings to mind Adam's first disobedience, while the wasting of the land becomes representative of the punishment and misery which the human race brought upon itself as a result of Original Sin. It must be emphasised that not all of this is explicitly stated by the author, nor at any point does he suspend narration to insert an explanation of the Waste Land; but if the Waste Land is not directly interpreted for us, there are other episodes which are, and it is in the light of these that its significance begins to emerge. Two such episodes will be looked at: Gauvain's adventure at the Castle of Noir Hermite (l. 736 seq.), and Perlesvaus' reconquest of the Grail Castle (l. 6095 seq.), the adventure whereby he redeems himself and makes up for his initial failure. In what follows, no claim is made for any originality in the understanding of the 'senefiance' of the *Perlesvaus* as a whole, or of individual episodes – this has been admirably established by the works on *Perlesvaus* already referred to, particularly Kelly's monograph. What the analysis is designed to bring out is the obliqueness of the author's approach in his handling of the Waste Land, and the quite subtle way in which he works into it a number of overlapping meanings.

During his quest for the Grail Castle and the Fisher King, Gauvain encounters the Damoisele du Char who asks him to conduct her safely past the Castle of Noir Hermite (ll. 716–17). By this point in the narrative the Damoisele du Char has already become a familiar figure to the reader: she first appeared at Arthur's court (l. 596 seq.), robed in silk and gold, attended by two damsels and followed by a richly ornamented cart drawn by three white deer. In her hand she carries the head of a king, sealed in silver and crowned in gold, while one of her attendants carries the head of a queen who, it appears, betrayed not only the king but also 150 knights whose heads, sealed in gold, silver or lead, are in the cart which accompanies her everywhere. When Gauvain begins his task of escorting this strange company past the Castle of Noir Hermite, they are attacked by 152 knights clad in black, exactly the right number, since the assailants can then carry off one head each and bring it back with them into the castle. At a later stage in the narrative, the author gives a detailed interpretation of this adventure (ll. 2173–86): the heads of the king and queen are those of Adam and Eve, while the other 150 represent the souls of the rest of mankind, the Castle of Noir Hermite represents Hell, Noir Hermite is Lucifer, the account of the heads being carried off by the black knights represents the peopling of Hell with the souls of mankind after the Fall. Now this deliberate inclusion on the part of the author of an adventure designed to remind the reader of Adam's first disobedience and its legacy of suffering and death, carefully introduced in the midst of an account of Perlesvaus' sin at the Grail Castle and the consequent misfortunes that overtake the land, positively invites us to see a parallel in the two events, to see in Perlesvaus' sin a representation of the Fall and therefore to see in the wasting of the land a reminder of the consequent punishment inflicted on the whole of mankind. It is this design that best explains why the author does not specify the exact nature of Perlesvaus' sin or point out precisely where his guilt lies. We are left to deduce that his original transgression is representative of Original Sin. This parallelism would perhaps be all the more apparent to an audience versed in the detail of scripture: God's cursing of Cain in Genesis 4:12 ('when thou tillest the ground, it shall not henceforth yield unto thee her strength') would make a link between the Waste Land theme and the Fall all the more readily discernible.

Perlesvaus' reconquest of the Grail Castle from the hands of the King of Chastel Mortel points in exactly the same direction (l. 6095 seq.). The meaning that the author wishes to attach to this, the central event of the whole romance, is quite unmistakable, and there is no need to extract it, as Carman does,[14] by over-rigid attention to detail. There is enough evidence supplied by the author himself that points to a broad parallel between Perlesvaus' victory over the King of Chastel Mortel and Christ's victory over death and sin at the crucifixion: throughout the adventure Perlesvaus wears on his head a Cercle d'or, in his hand he carries a shield with a red cross whose boss contains 'del sanc Nostre Saignor et de son vestement' (l. 5851); in addition to being known as le Bon Chevalier or le Chevalier au Cercle d'or, Perlesvaus also enjoys the name of Par-lui-fez (l. 1647), which seems to be a clear enough reference to the Self-Begotten Son and the Incarnation; and finally, just as Perlesvaus wins his victory over Chastel Mortel and re-establishes the New Law of Christianity, so Christ won his victory over death, thus releasing humanity from the bondage of mortality. Now if Perlesvaus is represented as a figure of Christ at the moment when he redeems himself at the Grail Castle, it is not difficult for any reader familiar with Saint Paul to see him as a figure of Adam at the moment of his failure, and therefore to see the Waste Land as a symbol of humanity punished as a result of man's first disobedience. Further to help the reader establish this link, the author has provided one other important signpost: the contrast already referred to between the Waste Land of Arthur's Kingdom and the rich country of the Fisher King. Given that the river surrounding the Grail Castle comes from the Earthly Paradise (ll. 7200-1), that the names of the castle are Eden, Joy, Souls (ll. 7205-6), one is led to see the Fisher King's rich and plenteous country as a projection of Eden/Paradise, and to see in the contrasting Waste Kingdom a symbol of fallen humanity, as yet unredeemed. The fact that after Perlesvaus' reconquest of the Grail Castle there is no definitive or generalised restoration of the land presents one final problem, best solved by a suggestion put forward by Kelly: the work of redemption and the extension of the New Law are to be seen as representing a slow, gradual process. As he points out, the unspelling

---

[14] J. N. Carman, 'The Symbolism of the *Perlesvaus*', *PMLA*, LXI (1946), pp. 42-83.

of the Waste Land is 'presented as a slow process which, although well under way as the story closes, remains to be completed. By depicting the regeneration of the Waste Land as an unfinished process, our author reveals a keen sense of the reality of Salvation history which is the progressive transmission and extension of the effect of Christ's victory over Sin, His setting aright the disorder caused by the Original Fault.'[15] The Waste Land theme, therefore, is developed in a quite original way as part of a parable illustrating the Fall and progressive redemption of man.

## 3. *The Waste Land and related themes*

This central 'senefiance' conferred on the Waste Land is further reinforced and enriched by the fact that the Waste Land itself is only part of a very intricate pattern of closely interrelated themes, each one echoing and intensifying the other. Two examples will suffice: Lancelot's participation in the Beheading Game at the Waste City, and the author's treatment of the Coward Knight story. Like the Waste Land, these are themes which the author of the *Perlesvaus* inherited from his predecessors, and then adapted and remodelled to suit his own didactic purposes.[16] Given that the Beheading Game is played out within the setting of the Waste City, it enriches the general theme of the Waste Land, inevitably echoing the parable of the Fall and Redemption. The Coward Knight story points to an overlapping but somewhat different 'senefiance': when we view it in conjunction with the Waste Land we are led to see in the latter a representation not just of the punishment mankind had to endure after the Fall, but of what is in the author's eyes the sterility and inferiority of the Jewish faith; and we are led to see in the contrast between the Waste Kingdom and the rich country of the Fisher King a contrast between two faiths, the Jewish and the Christian, between the Synagogue and Holy Church. In addition to bringing to mind the parable of the Fall, the Waste Land becomes indeed the projection of a collective punishment that awaits all those who remain blind to the true rewards of Christ's redemptive death. As it is handled in the *Perlesvaus*, the Waste Land theme is made to form part of a militant, not to say aggressive and intolerant, statement of the overall supremacy of the Christian faith.

The adventure involving Lancelot, the Beheading Game at the Waste City (ll. 2860–923, 6657–733), is one version of a story made familiar to English readers in *Sir Gawain and the Green Knight*. When Lancelot arrives at the Waste City (l. 2860), he is received by a young knight carrying a large axe and is invited to take part in a 'geu-parti': Lancelot will cut off the knight's head with the axe, on condition that one year later, on the same day, at the same place,

---

[15] Kelly, op. cit., p. 178.
[16] *Perlesvaus*, ed. cit., Vol. II, pp. 129 *seq.*

and at the same hour, Lancelot will submit himself to the same test. Lancelot strikes off the knight's head, departs from the Waste City, keeps his covenant by returning in order to receive the blow, but fortunately emerges unscathed (l. 6705), is spared, and the adventure is brought to an end. Although in itself this episode has no inherent connection with the Grail theme, what makes it relevant is, firstly, the author's description of the transformation which the Waste City undergoes as a result of Lancelot's exploits, and secondly, the key position or positions which this episode is given within the narrative as a whole. When the adventure is completed, the Waste City's empty streets are filled with thronging people, rejoicing at this long-awaited deliverance from grief and sorrow: 'Sire, font les damoi[seles], or poez oïr la joie de vostre venue . . . Lanceloz . . . voit popler la cité de la plus bele gent dou mont, e emplir les granz sales, e venir clers e provoires a grans processions, qui loent Deu e aorent de ce qu'il ont pooir de revenir a lor iglises, e donent beneïchon au chevalier par qui il ont pooir de repairier' (ll. 6726–32). When one adds to this the fact that the author has deliberately chosen to divide the Beheading Game into two parts, the first occurring before Perlesvaus' conquest of the Grail, and the second, after, it becomes apparent that the author's account of the desolation and misery prevailing at the Waste City, its deliverance by Lancelot and its return to happiness and prosperity, not only highlights Perlesvaus' achievements but also echoes the central theme: the wretchedness of man after the Fall, Christ's deliverance of mankind, the consequent reconquest of its lost prosperity.

Like the Waste Land and the Beheading Game, the Coward Knight story is brought to bear on the theme of regeneration and deliverance. It is used, however, not so much to contrast the Fall and Redemption (though it does that as well) as to oppose two conflicting sets of belief, the Old Law and the New, the Jewish and the Christian. Apart from his cowardice, the most striking thing about the Coward Knight is his strange appearance: the armour which he wears is in complete disorder, his shield upside down, his spear the wrong way round, his hauberk and greaves strung round his neck, and he rides backwards on his horse (ll. 1354–7). By forcing him to defend two damsels against the attack of a robber-knight (l. 5581), Perlesvaus gives the Coward Knight a taste for action that he had never experienced before, the latter acquitting himself so well that at the end of the exploit he is dubbed the Hardi Chevalier (l. 5616). This transformation had been hinted at, and its significance already glossed, in an earlier episode in which a hermit had explained to Gauvain that the Coward Knight represents the inferiority, confusion and blindness of the Old Law which was 'bestornee devant le crucefiement Nostre Saignor, et tantost comme il fu crucefiez si fu remi[s]e a droit' (ll. 2217–18). It is worthy of note too that the Coward Knight story is itself reinforced by a number of parallel episodes all proclaiming the superiority of Holy Church over the Synagogue, for example, the Damoisele du Char's recovery of her tresses once the New Law is established (ll. 9946–8), or the conversion of the heathen queen Jandree, an immediately recognisable representative of the Old Law in that she is blind, but recovers her sight as soon as she is prepared to be baptised (l. 9216). Given that each of these episodes is, like the Waste Land, a *type* of the theme of regeneration, and perhaps more importantly, given that at plot level all of these themes are closely interlaced with one another, the Waste Land comes to represent in our eyes not just the Fall but all the imperfections that the author associates with the Jewish faith. It is clear, then, that, in the light of what has been said, an appreciation of all the overtones of meaning which the author has obliquely worked into his material requires us to see the Waste Land not in isolation but as part of a rich and intricate pattern of related themes, all pointing in similar but not necessarily identical directions.

The author of the *Perlesvaus*, then, has elaborated a quite distinctive, subtle and original approach to the Waste Land, adapting basically secular material to suit his Christian priorities and preoccupations. The foundations of the 'senefiance' are firmly laid at plot level: what may appear initially to constitute rather puzzling modifications to his basic theme (e.g. the rejection of the Dolorous Stroke, the fact that the Fisher King is never healed but is allowed to languish and die, the contrast developed between the Grail Country and the Waste Land, the latter's partial restoration and the continuing, ever-present threat of further devastation) is seen on reflection to be part of a deftly articulated, interlaced structure designed to prove the wretchedness and misery of man when he turns his back on God. In the execution of this design, the author's talent, like the country of the Fisher King, could be said to be 'rich and plenteous' and 'garnished with all things good'. With regard to the 'senefiance', perhaps the author's most original contribution is his perception that the Waste Land is not so much a geographical location as a dark country of the soul into which, through sin or blindness, man is ever-likely to stray. Through the Waste Land, projected as it is as a form of collective, self-imposed punishment, the author tries to inspire in his readers the conviction that the central event of human history is represented by the crucifixion and resurrection of Christ. This conviction of course forms part of his wider, militant affirmation of the overall supremacy of the Christian faith, whose enduring quality is underscored in the concluding pages of the text when we are told that, amidst the decay that ultimately overtakes even the Grail Castle, the chapel of the New Law alone survives (ll. 10168–9). As I have pointed out elsewhere,[17] whether one prefers, with Nitze, to relate this militancy to Cluny, with Helen Adolf to the Albigensian

---

[17]*Romania*, XCV (1974) p. 69; *Perlesvaus*, ed. cit., Vol. II, pp. 86–8; H. Adolf, 'Studies in the *Perlesvaus*, the historical background', *Studies in Philology*, XLII (1945), pp. 723–40; M. Schlauch, 'The Allegory of Church and Synagogue', *Speculum*, XIV (1939), pp. 448–64.

Crusade, or with Margaret Schlauch to the disputes between Church and Synagogue, there is little doubt that *Perlesvaus* reflects the aggressive, intolerant Christianity of the crusading era. The author's handling of the Waste Land thus reveals considerable literary talent put at the service of the militant advancement of the New Law.

# *The Triumph of Pragmatism – Reward and Punishment in* Le roman de Silence

## HEATHER LLOYD

Edited in 1972 by Kenneth Varty's mentor and friend from the University of Nottingham, the late Lewis Thorpe, *Le roman de Silence* has very recently begun to attract some of the critical attention which it has hitherto lacked and which it undoubtedly deserves. Kathleen J. Brahney has analysed the portrayal of female characters in this romance which, relating as it does the tale of a girl who is brought up believed by everyone to be of the male sex, was destined sooner or later to invite a feminist (albeit it in this case a mildly feminist) reading;[1] and R. Howard Bloch, interpreting the romance against the background of Alain de Lille's ideas in *De Planctu Naturae*, discerns in it an elaborate metaphor of poetic theory.[2] In studying the role of reward and punishment in *Le roman de Silence*, my aim is to distil something of the moral tone of the romance, where a workaday spirit of pragmatism and a strong sense of moral relativity arise from a plot strongly marked by folk-lore themes, which, paradoxically, one might associate with a more rigid type of narrative development and a more black-and-white system of values.[3]

The theme of reward occurs early in *Le roman de Silence* when Ebain, king of England, offers a reward to any knight who can kill a dragon terrorising the region round Winchester. The dragon's vanquisher will receive land and the

---

[1] Kathleen J. Brahney, 'When *Silence* was Golden: Female Personae in the *Roman de Silence*', in *The Spirit of the Court. Selected Proceedings of the Fourth Congress of the International Courtly Literature Society (Toronto 1983)*, ed. by Glyn S. Burgess and Robert A. Taylor, Cambridge: D. S. Brewer, 1985, pp. 52–61.
[2] R. Howard Bloch, 'Silence and Holes: The *Roman de Silence* and the Art of the Trouvère', *Yale French Studies*, LXX (1986), pp. 81–99.
[3] In a footnote to his discussion of the sources of *Le roman de Silence*, Thorpe comments 'So much of mediaeval literature is in absolute essence a repeated statement and re-statement of certain folk-lore themes, which can be traced, usually fruitlessly, across the map of Europe and Asia – the Amazon knight, Potiphar's wife, the substituted letter, birth-marks, the man disguised as a woman, la princesse lointaine, the incubus, the incuba, the incubum. Needless to say, they are nearly all in *Le roman de Silence*.' (*Le roman de Silence. A thirteenth-century Arthurian verse-romance by Heldris de Cornuälle*, ed. by Lewis Thorpe, Cambridge: W. Heffer & Sons Ltd, 1972, p. 35, footnote 92.
All references are to this edition.

free choice of any lady in the kingdom, subject only to her availability (ll. 375–86). The dragon is killed by Ebain's nephew Cador, who burns with undeclared love for Eufemie, daughter of the Count of Cornwall. He hesitates to claim his reward, since he first wants to assure himself that Eufemie will return his love. But on the night following his victory he falls ill from the poison he has absorbed from his fight with the dragon. The king, knowing nothing of Cador's love for Eufemie, sends for her and promises her that if she nurses and cures Cador she may have as a reward the free choice of any baron in the land, as long as he is available for marriage (ll. 599–610).

In such circumstances, a young man and a young woman scarcely need the influence of the Tristan story, which hovers over the narrative at this point, nor the incitement of Ovidian conceits of love-sickness, for the inevitable to happen. Cador is cured of his illness but becomes lovesick for his nurse, while Eufemie is overcome by desire for her patient. Initially, the fact that each has been granted a free choice of partner as a reward for services to Ebain militates against the fulfilment of their mutual love. Eufemie reasons that Cador must already be bespoke to the lady of his choice and that the king may rightfully refuse to grant him to her as the reward (ll. 798–803). But love compels her almost in spite of herself to reveal her feelings to Cador, and after a long dialogue, full of reticences and misunderstandings, their mutual love becomes clear (ll. 879–1154). Now all that is required, it would seem, is for the pair to claim each other as reward from the king, and for the story of Silence (in which, after all, they are to figure only as her parents) to proceed. Indeed, as far as the development of the plot is concerned, Cador and Eufemie could have been granted to one another in marriage on the basis of the reward motif alone, without the elaborate portrayal of the way in which they achieve mutual understanding – though it is a delightful portrayal, and the poet is clearly eager to show his skill in handling one of the great set pieces of courtly romance. Yet once this excursion into courtliness has been allowed for, the audience might be justified in expecting the reward motif to be rounded off by the granting of the lovers to each other without further ado. Far from it. When Cador and Eufemie present themselves to the king, each with a formal, separate claim for the promised reward, Ebain's replies have a suspiciously smooth and urbane ring to them (witness his words to Eufemie, below) and before the two young claimants may reveal their mutual choice, he goes into conclave with his barons, leaving them at a loss to know what will happen next:

> Li rois li dist: 'Ma bele amie,
> Por vos ne mentirai jo mie.
> Mentir a roi n'est mie gius.
> Baron avrés a v(ost)re kius.
> Uns sans calenge m'en trovés:
> Quels que il soit, sil me rovés.

> Amie, ne vus esmaiés:
> Ja n'iert si haus que nel aiés,
> Soit cuens, u dus, u castelains. –
> Ne vos ruis, sire, plus ne mains,'
> Cho li respondi la puchiele.
> Li rois ses barons en apiele
> A un consel moult bielement,
> E cil i vont isnielement.
> Cador remaint et la mescine,
> Sor cui li consals pent et cline.
> Remés sunt andoi en la place.
> Nus d'als ne set preu que il face:
> Criement cil consals ne lor nuise. (ll. 1237–55)

It now becomes clear that Ebain is beginning to regret the terms of the rewards that he has offered Cador and Eufemie in response to the crises occasioned by the dragon and by Cador's sickness. A more prudent calculation of his own best interests is replacing the earlier grand gestures, for he sees in Cador and Eufemie the solution to a current problem of state. This problem in itself has been occasioned by his dramatic response to an even earlier crisis, recounted near the beginning of the narrative. Two knights married to twin sisters had fought each other and died in a bloody and wasteful contest over the question of which of their wives was the true heiress to land. In his grief at this waste of life, and even before the two knights had been buried, the king had promulgated a law cancelling inheritance through the female line (ll. 308–18). But this hastily conceived law has become an inconvenience to Ebain himself, and the purpose of the council meeting is for him to outline to his barons a way of getting round it. Eufemie is the only child of Renalt, count of Cornwall. If Cador could be rewarded with the promise of the countship of Cornwall after Renalt's death, and if it could be arranged for him to marry Eufemie, then the law cancelling female inheritance would not have to be put to the test and the delicate question of succession in the county of Cornwall would be quite neatly solved (ll. 1275–1300).

A new character, the Count of Chester, now briefly comes to the fore. He offers to undertake the mission of persuading Cador and Eufemie to choose each other. Coming upon the young people quietly and being no stranger to love himself (ll. 1409–10, 1445) he realises at once that they are in love. He is presented as being an extremely shrewd operator, out to exploit the situation in a way that will enhance his own good standing. Thus he gives the lovers to believe that he himself has persuaded the king that they should marry each other and inherit Cornwall (ll. 1433–77); and he tries to stop them from going back to Ebain too quickly, so that he is able to take credit in the eyes of the king for having 'persuaded' them, supposedly with difficulty, to accept the idea (ll. 1479–98). The Count of Cornwall is presented humorously (for example, he is depicted sneezing discreetly to make the lovers aware of his presence – ll. 1399–411) and there is clearly no trace of authorial disapproval in the comment that he is 'moult voiseus' (l. 1399). His opportunist approach, sympathetically portrayed, duplicates that of Ebain.

The pragmatic attitude which leads Ebain to modify the terms of his promise of reward to Cador and Eufemie finds distinct echoes in the central part of the narrative in which the story of Silence is presented, even though these echoes occur in episodes concerned with punishment rather than reward. Silence, the daughter of Cador and Eufemie, is being brought up in the guise of a boy (precisely so that she may not fall victim to the law that Ebain has managed to circumvent in the case of her mother). The question of punishment first arises in the romance when the adolescent Silence runs away to Brittany with a pair of minstrels because she wants to learn their arts. When the distraught Cador hears of the circumstances of her disappearance, he issues a decree banishing all minstrels from his territory. By the terms of this stern decree, any minstrel found in Cornwall will be punished by burning or hanging, and anyone who lets a minstrel escape will suffer the same punishment (ll. 3115–26).

In the fullness of time, and unaware of the threat of punishment, Silence returns incognito as an accomplished minstrel. The man who gives her shelter, and the townspeople, starved of entertainment since Cador's decree, are greatly distressed at the thought that they will have to hand her over to their count. Like Ebain's law cancelling inheritance through the female line, Cador's sweeping and dogmatic decision to punish all minstrels by death was clearly rash and ill-conceived. Even he must be aware of this, for when Silence is brought before him, her own straightforward appeal for her life and the grief of the townspeople on her behalf are enough to make him set aside the threat of death in an entirely pragmatic way (ll. 3539–58) even before the revelation that she is his child.[4]

The theme of punishment surfaces again in the next important phase of the story. Cador sends Silence to join the household of King Ebain and there she falls victim to the lustful wiles of the Queen, Eufeme (whose name is so confusingly akin to that of our heroine's mother).[5] Eufeme is furious when the handsome youth, as she believes Silence to be, rejects her amorous advances,

---

[4] Thorpe's summary of the episode – 'She arrives, reveals herself as a jongleur, and is in danger of being executed when Cador recognises her by a birth-mark on her right shoulder' (op. cit. p. 20) – is inaccurate. Cador is alerted to the identity of the minstrel by an observant old man (ll. 3559–610) and recognises the birth-mark (ll. 3647–50) only after he has publicly reprieved Silence:

> Li cuens lor fait une promesse
> Que il nen iert huimais pendus,
> Et il l'en ont grans grés rendus.     (ll. 3554–6)

[5] Bloch, who states that 'The *Roman de Silence* is . . all about misreading', refers to the pair Eufeme/Eufemie as being one in 'a series of graphemic displacements' in the romance (art. cit. p. 98, p. 96).

and she plans to take revenge. She tells Ebain that Silence has tried violently to seduce her and demands that Silence be punished. The king is faced with a dilemma: on the one hand to ignore the queen's accusations would seem to stand in the way of justice; on the other hand, to pursue justice would involve making the matter public and bringing the taint of scandal upon himself. In the face of the queen's rigid demand for punishment, Ebain's approach is pragmatic rather than idealistic, as the narrator notes with clear approval:

>     La roïne fort se demente.
>     Sachiés que moult li est a ente
>     Qu'ele ne voit ardoir en cendre
>     Le vallet, u a forces pendre.
>     *Mais el roi a bon home et sage*
>     *Et atenpret de son corage;*
>     Et set bien de .ii. mals eslire
>     Quels est li mioldres et quel pire.
>     Voit se venjance nen est prise,
>     Foible est, malvaise sa justice.
>     Pis est de honir cel enfant,
>     Car il seroit honis partant,
>     Se honte esparse et esmeüe
>     Ki pas nen est encor seüe.
>     Por cho se violt il miols retraire
>     De la justice que trop faire.         (ll. 4183–98)

In the narrator's own decidedly unidealistic view, the human situation is such that it is often necessary, for one's own welfare, to choose between the lesser of two evils:

>     Et cascuns hom se doit pener
>     Por cho qu'il i puist assener
>     De s'onor salver, se il puet:
>     Et se il voit que lui estuet
>     De .ii. mals tols jors l'un passer,
>     Son sens doit en soi amasser
>     Veïr liquels li puist mains nuire.     (ll. 4199–205)

The account of the king's plan to sidestep the question of punishment simply by sending Silence out of the way to France is prefaced with the comment that he is not the kind of irascible man whose actions will merely make a bad situation worse:[6]

>     N'est pas ireuls a fuer d'Irois
>     Por faire d'un damage .ii.            (ll. 4222–3)

---

[6] Ebain's barons voiced their approval in similar terms when he explained to them his plan to manipulate Cador and Eufemie in their choice of reward:

>     Cho dient tuit: Bien dist li rois.
>     N'est pas irouis, a fuer d'Irois.      (ll. 1301–2)

The opposition between the queen's rigid demand that Silence be punished, and his own more flexible approach, is brought out well in the piece of dialogue that follows:

> 'Biele, se vos me volés croire,
> Bon consel porons de cho prendre. –
> Comment? fait ele. El que del pendre? –
> Oïl! n'avra pas tel martyre. –
> Que li volés donc faire, sire?
> Ardoir, u a chevals detraire? –
> Ne mie, bele; on doit moult faire
> Solvent contre sa volenté.
> Cis est moult de halt parenté,
> Et si est fils a moult prodome.
> Or en gardons tolte la some.
> Cho qu'il a fait est par enfance (ll. 4226–37)

Brahney, commenting on this episode, is much harsher on Ebain than the narrator appears to be:

> Ebain .. is self-seeking and unwilling to avenge his wife's honor if it involves risking his own. Worse yet, from a twentieth-century feminist point of view, he subscribes to a boys-will-be-boys attitude that participates in and perpetuates the abuse of women.[7]

Ebain now makes plans to send Silence to the King of France with a letter of commendation, but the queen is still intent on vengeance and substitutes for Ebain's letter a counterfeit one which asks the King of France to have Silence beheaded for treachery, with the explanation that Ebain, the supposed writer of the letter, thought it impolitic to have him beheaded in England (ll. 4299–364). The King of France's chancellor, called upon to read the letter, is immediately impressed by the bearing and charm of Silence. Just as Ebain had, he sees himself caught between two evils, that of lying to his king about the contents of the letter and saving Silence (in which case he will risk his own skin) and that of reading the letter as it is and bringing punishment upon the young visitor:

> Je ne volroie por Monmartre
> Qu'il m'esteüst lire la cartre:
> Ja se jel di cho iert pechiés,
> Qu'il iert deffais et depechiés.
> Pitiés me rueve a roi mentir;
> Paörs nel violt pas consentir.
> Pitié ai grant se il i muert;
> Paör s'il par moi en estuert.
> De .ii. mals estuet ore eslire
> Le mains malvais, cho est le dire. (ll. 4403–12)

---

[7] Brahney, art. cit., p. 59.

Fortunately the chancellor is able to accommodate his own self-interest with a defence of Silence, by conveying the contents of the letter in such a way as to evoke sympathy for its bearer:

> Sire, encontre vostre plaisir,
> Vos hom, vos parens, vos amis,
> Rois Ebayns le* vos a transmis    *the letter
> Por le vallet faire afoler,
> Que je vos vi ore acoler.
> Por lui honir et damagier
> En a fait, sire, messagier.
> Dex, com mar fu tels creäture!    (ll. 4434–41)

The chancellor's softened way of intimating to the king the harsh contents of the letter leads him to take advice of a council of barons. There, at great length (ll. 4459–878) the claims of friendship that Ebain has over the King of France are weighed against the damage that would be done to the latter's honour if he were to execute Silence after his warm welcoming embrace, and without knowing what the justification for punishment was. Scenes of discussion among barons as to the rights and wrongs of a given case are among the great commonplaces of medieval French narrative;[8] the poet of *Silence*, ever sensitive to life's moral dilemmas, revels in the tradition. The account of the discussion between the king's three barons, the counts of Clermont, Blois and Nevers, is highly authentic in its reproduction of dialogue, in which the various points of view are made to ebb and flow. Authorial comments on the Count of Clermont's measured and astute response to the count of Blois' advice about the paramount claims of friendship confirm in passing the impression that, in the general ethos of the poem, it is the less extreme, more flexible approach to life's problems that is being promoted:

> Li cuens de Clermont s'en aïre.
> En sa main tint un baston brief:
> Si vait runiant de cief en cief.
> A paines qu'il puet dire mot
> De maltalent de cho qu'il ot;
> Mais qu'il refrainst son maltalent
> Com sages hom, si parla gent.
> Ne le violt mie desmentir
> Al premier mot, ne consentir:
> Car cil met le fu en l'estoppe
> Ki al premier le bouce estoppe
> De celui que voel contredire.
> Hom qui cho fait, son plait empire,
> Ainz doit premiers tolt otroier,
> Por miols son per amoloier.
> Si fist li cuens de Clermont donques.    (ll. 4582–97)

---

[8] Famous early examples are in the *Chanson de Roland*, laisses XIII–XVI (Charlemagne consults his barons over Marsile's message) and in the *Roman de Thèbes*, ll. 7797–978 (the trial of Daire).

In the central matter of whether the King of France should mete out punishment to Silence on Ebain's behalf, the less absolute approach again wins the day: the letter is sent back to Ebain with the medieval equivalent of a covering note – 'Some mistake here surely?' (ll. 4841–78). And indeed, when Ebain receives the communication and questions his own chancellor, the truth of the matter eventually becomes clear. But will he punish the queen for her treacherous act? As we have come to expect of Ebain, his prime concern is damage-limitation, even at the expense of truth and justice; and as we have come to expect of the narrator, he pronounces approval of this approach:

> *Li rois n'est pas ne fols ne lors.*
> Il nen a soig de faire rien
> C'on li atort a el qu'a bien,
> Ne de faire tel commençalle
> Ki ait malvaise definalle.
> Ne proise gaires sa venjance
> Qui li acroisce sa viltance. (ll. 5086–92)

The plot receives new impetus when Silence, having won knightly renown in France, is recalled by Ebain to help quell a barons' revolt (ll. 5252–656). There follows yet another attempt at seduction by Queen Eufeme, another rebuffal and another denunciation of Silence to Ebain (ll. 5657–766). This time Ebain bursts out in rage against Silence (ll. 5767–78). He falls in with a scheme conceived by Eufeme for punishing Silence (whom all still believe to be a man) by sending her on an impossible mission. Merlin the magician has taken leave of civilised society and has become a Wild Man who can only be brought back to civilisation 'par engien de feme' (l. 5803). Let Silence be sent to look for Merlin, and not dare to return until Merlin has been apprehended (ll. 5807–15) – which will be, according to Ebain and Eufeme's lights, never.

This new turn of events lies somewhat uneasily with what has gone before. The introduction of a figure such as Merlin, and the idea that Merlin may only be captured by a woman, clash with the tone of most of the rest of the poem which, apart from the early episode of the dragon, has been thoroughly realistic. More importantly, Ebain's angry decision to rid himself of Silence (albeit as discreetly as possible – ll. 5776–8) seems unlikely. True, even the mildest of husbands has a sticking-point. But Ebain has had evidence of Eufeme's dishonesty in the matter of the counterfeit letter. Moreover, for a man who has previously shown himself to be unashamedly open to the dictates of self-interest, it seems inconsistent that Ebain should decide to get rid of a knight who has just proved his great worth in a battle against Ebain's enemies. The explanation of these inconsistencies is not far to seek. As Thorpe suggests in the introduction to his edition:

> The search for Merlin, which forms the final adventure undertaken by Silence, is in essence a re-writing of the story of Grisandoles the Seneschal of Rome, herself

a German princess Avenable in disguise, as we find it narrated in that section of the Arthurian prose-Vulgate which is called *L'Estoire Merlin*.⁹

Thorpe's view is that the poet, Heldris de Cornuälle, wrote the bulk of the poem as the *Enfances Grisandoles-Silence*, 'to lead up to and to explain this final episode'.¹⁰ Expressed thus in terms of its sources, Thorpe's evaluation of the poem does seem to cast a spotlight on the final episode of the poem to the disadvantage of the major part. But it accounts for the rather awkward hiatus at the point where Ebain decides to punish Silence. It also accounts for the fact that, in a work where extremes in the area of reward and punishment are generally avoided or modified, the plot is brought to a conclusion with reward and punishment being meted out in a most resounding way, since this is what happens in the source. Silence, being a woman, succeeds in capturing Merlin. Merlin, with his superior powers of insight, reveals the true nature of Silence and denounces Eufeme. Eufeme is then torn apart by horses (this at the instigation of a king who likes to avoid trouble!) and Silence is married to Ebain and becomes queen in her stead. However, the ending is in some respects in keeping with the spirit of the poem as a whole: Ebain cancels the law whereby women may not inherit (l. 6643) – the very extreme measure which he had introduced at the beginning of the poem and which accounts for the story of Silence and her disguise in the first place; and the narrator, who has permitted himself a number of quite vicious anti-feminist sallies, either directly or on the lips of his characters (ll. 667–73; 4266–70; 6398–406) ends on a conciliatory, albeit condescending, note intended for the ladies:

> Maistre Heldris dist chi endroit
> C'on doit plus bone feme amer
> Que haïr malvaise u blasmer.
> Si mosterroie bien raison,
> Car feme a menor oquoison
> Por que ele ait le liu ne l'aise
> De l'estre bone que malvaise,
> S'ele ouevre bien contre nature.
> Bien mosterroie par droiture
> C'on en doit faire gregnor plait
> Que de celi qui le mal fait.
> Se j'ai jehi blasmee Eufeme
> Ne s'en doit irier bone feme.
> Se j'ai Eufeme moult blasmee
> Jo ai Silence plus loëe.           (ll. 6684–98)

This pronouncement of the poet's, that it is harder for a woman to be good than it is for a man, fits in with the feminist reading that women are the victims of circumstance and that if, like Silence, they are given the correct

---
⁹ Thorpe edition, p. 28.
¹⁰ Ibid., p. 32.

*noreture*, they may overcome their natures at least temporarily and be as good as any man. But this does not seem to me to be the central theme to emerge from *Le roman de Silence* even though its central character is a girl brought up as a boy. Indeed, in much of what happens to Silence, notably in her apprenticeship and experience as a minstrel and in her success as a knight in France and England, we tend to lose sight of the fact that she is a woman in disguise. Even her victimisation by the queen is primarily an instance of the Potiphar's wife topos – the fact that the handsome youth whom Eufeme is trying to seduce is really a woman merely adds piquancy. For much of the central part of the romance the fact that Silence is a woman in disguise is of little consequence to the story.

The real interest in *Le roman de Silence* does not lie in the poet's attitude to women, which is in any case somewhat confused by the strains of traditional anti-feminism which creep in. It lies in the values which the poem conveys and promotes at so many points. The blurring of issues involving reward and punishment is one expression of a general ethos in which extremes are shown to be undesirable and in which pragmatic responses take precedence (often with the narrator's implied or explicit approval) over the pursuit of ideals. A striking example of this involves the decision of Cador and Eufemie to have Silence brought up as a boy. Before her birth Cador prays that the child might bring them joy, might come to salvation, might be normal and healthy (ll. 1673–82). This spirit of piety might be expected to include acceptance of the baby's sex as the will of God, but Cador is already working out what steps to take if the child is a girl and therefore unable to inherit. He actually persuades Eufemie to go along with his plan by arguing from the Bible that men and women have much in common: since Eve was taken from Adam's side (ll. 1701–7) and since in marriage two become one flesh (ll. 1711–22) then Eufemie should be of one mind with him in the matter:

> Entr'ome et feme a grant commune,
> Car d'als .ii. est la sustance une.         (ll. 1711–12)

> Le sanc avons (nos) al commun,
> Or aiens le voloir commun.         (ll. 1723–4)

Curiously he does not use the same reasoning to justify on theological grounds bringing a girl-child up as a boy. It is as if he has decided on the scheme that he will embark on if the baby is female and is not going to allow that operational decision to be affected by any abstract considerations at all. This would explain why, although he prays for the baby on several accounts, he does not pray for it to be a boy – for if after his prayer, God responded by making the child a girl, then it would be harder for Cador and Eufemie to persuade themselves that they were doing the right thing by bringing her up as a boy.

In many other details throughout the poem the same idea is reflected that a pragmatic approach is often the best path and that, indeed, there are no absolutes. Although King Ebain promised Cador and Eufemie that they could have the partner of their choice, they hesitate to put their trust in the royal word and (foreshadowing their pragmatic approach at the birth of Silence) even talk of eloping together (ll. 1338–71). The image of wax is introduced to convey the idea that the lovers, being naturally fearful in love, cannot retain their trust in the king's word:

> Escriziés moi ens en le cire
> Letres que om bien puisse lire.
> Faites le cire dont remetre.
> Enne perist donques la lettre?
> Oïl, par Deu! par le calor.
> Nient plus n'a cuers d'amant valor
> De bien retenir s(a) mimorie,
> Que cire encontre fu victorie
> De retenir la lettre escrite.
> Car cho qu'est voirs cho fait mescroire,
> Et tenir fause coze a voire.            (ll. 1169–80)

But the image of wax prefigures the role of the wax seal on the letter from Ebain to the King of France which Eufeme tampers with, and suggests that even the most formal seals of authority are not to be trusted. What is more surprising, it seems that the medieval audience, always requiring reassurance as far as the authority of a story is concerned, cannot even place its confidence wholly in the poet, since he admits in so many words to tampering with his sources!

> Si com l'estorie le nos livre,
> Qu'en latin escrite lizons,
> En romans si le vos disons.
> Je ne di pas que n'i ajoigne
> Avoic le voir sovent mençoigne
> Por le conte miols acesmer            (ll. 1660–5)

In the poet's vision of things, nothing is wholly dependable. Even Nature, who ultimately triumphs over Nurture in the case of Silence, as she always does triumph (ll. 2423–4) is capable of being fickle or careless in her production of human beings, which explains why, in the poet's view, outward appearance does not always mirror inner worth:

> Premierement prent sa matyre.
> Avant tolte ouvre si l'esmie,
> Et moult l'espurge, et esniïe;
> Et quant l'a moult bien esmiié
> Si oste del gros le delié.
> De cel delié si fait sans falle
> Les buens, et del gros la frapalle.

> Mais se il avient que Nature
> Soit corocie, u que n'ait cure
> C'un poi del gros al delié viegne
> Et al mollier avoec se tiegne,
> Cil gros se trait al cuer en oire.
> Et se ne me volés or croire
> Vos le poés par vos prover.
> Ne poés vos sovent trover
> Vil cuer et povre, et riche cors
> Kist sarpelliere par defors?
> Li cors n'est mais fors sarpelliere.        (ll. 1828–45)

The extent of Nature's power in the outworking of human affairs is a timeless topic of debate and one to which Heldris de Cornuälle makes his own contribution, highlighting in the figure of Silence the question of Nature versus Nurture in the establishment of sexual identity.[11] But in the story of Grisandoles which seems to have been the starting-point for his romance, it is the spirit captured by Merlin's sardonic laughter, rather than the tale of a woman disguised as a man, that holds the key to the romance. In Heldris' adaptation of the Grisandoles story Merlin laughs four times[12] as Silence brings him into Ebain's custody, and subsequently explains his laughter in Ebain's court (ll. 6181–552): he laughed at the peasant who had bought some shoes because the peasant was soon to die; he laughed at those begging for alms because buried near them was huge treasure; he laughed at the man lamenting his son's death because the child was really the son of the priest officiating at the burial; and he laughed because he knew that Eufeme's friend the nun was really a man in disguise and that Silence was a woman. Merlin's ability to see beyond untrustworthy appearances resembles closely that of the Hermit in Voltaire's *conte Zadig*,[13] and Heldris' robust, undogmatic and good-humoured scepticism might in some respects be called Voltairian *avant la lettre*. In a world where appearances may be deceptive, judgement can never be absolute. Perceived self-interest and a pragmatic approach to each situation may be the best policy. While *Le roman de Silence* is by no means unique for embodying such attitudes, nevertheless it is noteworthy for reflecting them in such a multiplicity of detail, not least in its presentation of the themes of reward and punishment.

---

[11] See ll. 2257–358, 2497–656.

[12] Merlin laughs only twice in the corresponding episode in *L'Estoire Merlin*. Heldris has taken the two other bursts of sardonic laughter from elsewhere in that work. See Thorpe, pp. 31–2.

[13] In *Zadig* the Hermit sets fire to the home of a kind host because he knows that the man will find treasure beneath the ruins, and he drowns the nephew of a good widow-woman because he knows that if the nephew were to live he would murder both his aunt and Zadig. (Voltaire, *Zadig ou la Destinée*, ed. by Verdun L. Saulnier, Paris: Droz, 1946, ch. XVIII.)

*La tête maléfique dans la littérature médiévale,
étude d'une croyance magique*

## PHILIPPE MÉNARD

Les croyances magiques concernant la tête ne sont pas rares. Depuis longtemps les spécialistes des sociétés primitives, des mondes anciens ou du folklore en ont relevé diverses attestations. Le grand répertoire qu'est le *Motif-Index of Folk Literature* de Stith Thompson mentionne *Magic Head*.[1] L'important *Handwörterbuch des deutschen Aberglaubens* de Bächtold-Stäubli consacre au sujet de longs développements.[2] De nombreuses études ont montré la très large diffusion dans l'espace et le temps des superstitions relatives à la tête.[3] Pour l'histoire des croyances magiques le Moyen Age est toujours une époque-charnière: il hérite des traditions antiques et témoigne d'une activité créatrice originale. A propos de la tête, par exemple, on connaît dans la littérature la place importante de la décapitation, le thème des saints acéphales portant leur tête entre leurs bras ou encore le héros à la tête tranchée qui remet tranquillement sa tête sur le tronc du corps. Les textes arthuriens offrent plusieurs exemples de cette dernière situation, éminemment dramatique.[4] Mais on n'a guère attiré l'attention sur des têtes définitivement

---

[1] Stith Thompson, *Motif-Index of Folk Literature*, Revised and enlarged edition, Copenhagen: Rosenkilde and Bagger, 1955–58 (6 vols.), Vol. II, p. 120 (D 992).
[2] Hanns Bächtold-Stäubli, *Handwörterbuch des deutschen Aberglaubens*, Berlin: De Gruyter, 1927–42 (10 tomes), t.V, pp. 202–15.
[3] Voir Henri Adrien P. de Longpérier, *Oeuvres*, réunies et mises en ordre par Gustave Schlumberger, Paris: E. Leroux, 1883–87 (7 tomes), t. II, *Antiquités grecques, romaines et gauloises*, pp. 311–13, 'Notes sur les têtes de cire placées dans les sépultures antiques à la place des crânes'; P. Sébillot, 'La tête de mort dans les superstitions et les légendes', *L'Homme: Journal illustré des sciences anthropologiques*, III (1886), pp. 33–40; Salomon Reinach, *Cultes, Mythes et Religions*, Paris: E. Leroux, 1908–23, vol. IV, pp. 252–66, 'La tête magique des Templiers'; Adolphe Reinach, 'Les têtes coupées et les trophées en Gaule', *Revue celtique*, XXXIV (1913), pp. 38–60 et 253–86; Waldemar Deonna, 'Orphée et l'oracle de la tête coupée', *Revue des études grecques*, XXXVIII (1925), pp. 44–69; Alexander H. Krappe, 'Un parallèle oriental de la légende de l'empereur Trajan et du pape Grégoire le Grand', *Le Moyen Age*, XXXVI (1926), pp. 85–92, voir pp. 88–90; Roger S. Loomis, 'The Head in the Grail', *Revue celtique*, XLVII (1930), pp. 39–62; Pierre Lambrechts, *L'Exaltation de la tête dans la pensée et dans l'art des Celtes*, Bruges: De Tempel, 1954; Waldemar Deonna, *Le Symbolisme de l'oeil*, Berne: Francke, 1965, pp. 14–20, 'La tête'.
[4] Voir notamment George L. Kittredge, *A Study of Gawain and the Green Knight*, Cambridge (Mass.): Harvard University Press, 1916.

séparées du corps ou bien des têtes sans corps qui ont un redoutable pouvoir magique. Je voudrais rassembler ici un certain nombre de témoignages et tenter de comprendre des inventions curieuses de notre ancienne littérature.

Une branche un peu tardive du *Roman de Renart*, la branche XXIII, composée sans doute dans la première moitié du XIIIe siècle, présente une tête inquiétante, douée d'un pouvoir de révélation, dans une scène de magie qui se passe à Tolède. Renart suit l'enseignement d'un maître ès sciences occultes en cette ville qui passe au Moyen Age pour être la capitale de la magie. Un soir il descend dans une salle souterraine à la suite de son maître. Il trouve là une tête creuse, faite en cuivre. C'est la grande source d'information du maître.

> Une nuit se leva de l'estre,
> Si s'en ala aprés le mestre
> En une voute desouz terre,
> Ou il aloit son savoir querre
> A une grant teste cavee
> Qui estoit de cuivre gitee.
> A cele prenoit ses conseulz
> Les plus privez et les plus seus.[5]

Le maître se plaint de la médiocrité de ses élèves. La tête prend alors la parole et révèle au maître les grands secrets qui permettent de dominer dans les sciences occultes, de connaître les enchantements et les conjurations invincibles.

> Qui bien velt ovrer de cest art
> Venir l'estuet ou tempre ou tart
> Au trou d'une chambre privee.
> Croiz ne soit fete ne nomee!
> Me s'i se velt en nos fier,
> Illeques doit sacrefier
> D'un coc marchois ou d'un noir chat.
> Qui nel puet embler, si l'achat.
> Aprés die sanz autre fable:
> 'Oiez, d'enfer tuit li deable,
> De ceste oevre soiez seignor
> Et si soit fet en vostre honor!'
> La dedenz giet son sacrefice,
> Aprés, s'il velt, de la chambre isse;
> Ja mar fera autre proiere.
> Tot puet faire son majetiere.[6]

Les instructions données sont fort claires. La tête conseille de faire un sacrifice infernal, destiné aux diables. L'opération a lieu au-dessus du trou des

---

[5] Je cite le texte d'après l'édition de N. Fukumoto, N. Harano et S. Suzuki, *Le Roman de Renart (édité d'après les mss. C et M)*, Tokyo: France Tosho, 1983–85, vol. II, p. 360, branche XXIII, vv. 1331–8.

[6] Ibid., branche XXIII, vv. 1353–68.

latrines. Le signe de la croix, emblème du Christ et de la religion chrétienne, est proscrit en paroles et en actions. A lui seul, en effet, il suffirait à chasser les diables. Il empêcherait la tenue de la cérémonie maléfique. Les animaux retenus pour le sacrifice ont un aspect inquiétant. On sait que le chat noir est associé aux sorcières et au diable. Cette mauvaise réputation du chat noir est ancienne. Dans sa bonne étude *Zauberwahn, Inquisition und Hexenprozesse im Mittelalter*, Joseph Hansen en cite un exemple emprunté aux *Otia imperialia* de Gervais de Tilbury, c'est-à-dire antérieur à cette branche du *Roman de Renart*.[7] Quant au *coc marchois*, même si l'adjectif n'est pas relevé dans les dictionnaires, y compris dans le *FEW*, il faut comprendre 'un coc de marais, de marécage'. Il doit s'agir d'un animal proche de la poule d'eau. L'oiseau qui conviendrait le mieux serait la foulque, qui est de couleur noire et qui porte parfois le nom de *coq d'aiwe* ou encore, à cause de sa couleur, *diable de mar* en provençal, *diablo de mar* en espagnol.[8] L'hommage fait aux diables indique que l'on a affaire à de la magie noire. L'officiant invoque les diables. A n'en pas douter, ce sont eux qui opéreront lorsque plus tard le magicien lancera ses incantations.

Robert L. Wagner n'a pas exploité cette scène assez extraordinaire dans son étude *'Sorcier' et 'Magicien', Contribution à l'histoire du vocabulaire de la magie*. Mais on peut appliquer tout à fait à notre passage les remarques suivantes de cet auteur:

> Guillaume d'Auvergne . . . discute bien le problème qui se pose à propos des mots magiques. Sont-ce eux qui par eux-mêmes lient les puissances supra-terrestres ou les Esprits n'obéiraient-ils pas plutôt aux magiciens dans la mesure où ceux-ci leur rendent un culte? Il opine en faveur de cette seconde hypothèse.[9]

Dans le *Roman de Renart* on fait ce sacrifice pour se concilier les puissances infernales. Les mots prononcés indiquent que l'officiant agit pour honorer les démons, les reconnaît comme ses maîtres (le mot de *seignor* est employé) et leur fait hommage de sa personne.

Une fois informé des rites à accomplir, Renart s'empresse de les suivre. Il ne s'embarrasse pas de scrupules. Loin de lui l'idée de faire une grande randonnée afin d'enlever un coq. Il s'empare du coq de la maison et fait le nécessaire dans la *longaigne* (v. 1379). Ensuite il lance des conjurations et des enchantements dont le contenu ne nous est pas précisé.

> Fist ses charmes et ses caraudes,
> Ses conjuremenz et ses laudes.   (vv. 1383-4)

---

[7] Joseph Hansen, *Zauberwahn, Inquisition und Hexenprozesse im Mittelalter und die Entstehung der grossen Hexenverfolgung*, München: R. Oldenbourg, 1900 (Reprint – Aalen: Scientia Verlag, 1983), p. 140. Plus tard Villon fait allusion à cette mauvaise réputation du chat noir dans son *Testament* (vv. 1432-3). On en trouverait facilement d'autres témoignages. Voir par exemple Robert L. Wagner, *'Sorcier' et 'Magicien': Contribution à l'histoire du vocabulaire de la magie*, Paris: E. Droz, 1939, p. 111 (Etienne de Bourbon) et p. 115 (Alain de Lille).

[8] J'emprunte ces informations à Eugène Rolland, *Faune populaire de la France*, Paris: Maisonneuve, 1877-1911 (Reprint 1967), vol. I, p. 366.

[9] Robert L. Wagner, op. cit., p. 110.

D'autres termes sont utilisés, sans qu'on soit informé sur la nature exacte des sortilèges.[10] Mais nous devinons qu'il a acquis un pouvoir surnaturel. Il se déplace aussi vite que le vent (v. 1386). A la cour du roi Noble il fait apparaître des animaux fantastiques, il multiplie les fantasmagories (vv. 1484–2006). Il est répété à plusieurs reprises que ce sont les diables qui agissent réellement derrière ces simulacres (vv. 1509, 1706, 1979). En fait, Renart commande aux diables.

Il fallait s'arrêter un peu sur cette scène de magie pour essayer de comprendre la fonction de la tête dans cet ensemble. L'évocation de l'ensemble de l'opération magique est, d'ailleurs, plus intéressante que la présence de cette tête énigmatique. Revenons maintenant vers la tête magique. Assurément elle joue un rôle mineur, puisqu'elle n'est qu'une informatrice. Toutefois on ne saurait dire qu'elle soit un simple accessoire. Elle se trouve cachée dans les profondeurs de la terre, signe patent qu'elle a une valeur inestimable et qu'elle n'est pas destinée au commun des mortels! Elle détient aussi des secrets extraordinaires. Mieux encore, elle accepte de parler et de faire les révélations décisives. Sans elle, le néophyte n'aurait jamais été initié. Il n'aurait jamais su comment mettre les diables à son service. Il aurait tout ignoré des rites de la cérémonie magique et des paroles à prononcer pour attirer à lui les démons. Cette fois-ci elle révèle à l'instructeur de Renart, au spécialiste de sciences occultes les derniers secrets de son art. Mais il nous est dit que cet enseignant va souvent consulter la tête magique. De ces entretiens cachés il tire l'essentiel de son savoir. Nous voyons donc qu'il s'agit d'une tête savante qui révèle progressivement au disciple les mystères de l'art magique et qui en fait finalement un adepte.

Cette tête magique entre en partie dans la série des têtes extraordinaires qui répondent aux questions des mortels ou qui annoncent l'avenir. Parfois dans les contes c'est une tête de mort qui remplit cette fonction. Le motif de la tête coupée qui parle n'est pas inconnu. Waldemar Deonna a consacré une intéressante étude à ce sujet.[11] Le *Handwörterbuch des deutschen Aberglaubens* donne d'autres témoignages et parle d'une *Kopfmantik*, pratiquée déjà dans l'Antiquité.[12] Les Grecs utilisaient une *képhalaiomantéia*. Pierre Lambrechts a signalé aussi quelques têtes oraculaires dans son ouvrage *L'Exaltation de la tête dans la pensée et dans l'art des Celtes*.[13] On considérait que la tête, siège du principe vital et du savoir, était animée d'une vie propre. Elle pouvait exister indépendamment du corps, parler et prophétiser.

Il existe également des têtes artificielles, fabriquées en cuivre, en bronze,

---

[10] Il est question de *conjures* (v. 1977), d'*ynvocations* (v. 1485), de *forz conjurations* (v. 1486), d'*enchantement* (v. 1488), d'*enchant* (v. 1489). On notera qu'il offre très vite un chat aux diables pour se les concilier (v. 1487).
[11] Waldemar Deonna, op. cit. (1925).
[12] Hanns Bächtold-Stäubli, op. cit., t.V, pp. 204–5.
[13] Pierre Lambrechts, op. cit., p. 109.

etc., dotées de connaissances supérieures et douées du pouvoir de la parole. Les légendes relatives à Virgile au Moyen Age s'en font l'écho. Arturo Graf le relève dans son livre toujours utile *Roma nella memoria e nelle immaginazioni del Medio Evo*.[14] Virgile aurait confectionné une tête magique de cuivre répondant à toutes ses demandes. John W. Spargo cite plusieurs textes attribuant à Virgile l'invention d'une tête qui prophétise.[15] La première attestation apparaîtrait dans l'*Image du Monde*. L'analyse du texte en vers faite par Charles Victor Langlois mentionne la tête parlante qui prédisait l'avenir.[16] On peut dire qu'il s'agit d'un motif de conte: *Oracular artificial head*, mentionné dans le *Motif-Index* de Stith Thompson.[17]

Ici la tête creuse à l'intérieur (*chavee*), moulée en cuivre (*de cuivre gitee*), est une variante particulière de l'*Oracular artificial head*. Elle a sans doute des connaissances surnaturelles, mais elle ne possède pas tous les pouvoirs. Elle sert d'intermédiaire entre l'homme et le monde des diables, un peu comme Salatin dans le *Miracle de Théophile*. Elle est en relation avec le monde des mauvais esprits, sans qu'il soit nécessaire de croire qu'un diable invisible soit caché à l'intérieur et parle par sa bouche.[18] Il est vain de s'interroger sur l'origine de son pouvoir magique. La magie est-elle justiciable de la raison? Par essence l'irrationnel échappe aux explications. La tête magique, dissimulée sous terre, révèle une partie des mystères cachés. Dans la mesure où elle met en contact avec les diables, elle prend un caractère nettement maléfique.

Une tête infiniment plus redoutable apparaît dans l'épisode des lépreux du roman de *Jaufré*. Un enchantement empêche le héros de quitter les lieux, une fois qu'il a tué l'horrible maître de céans, le monstrueux lépreux. Bien que la porte soit ouverte, il ne peut franchir le seuil (vv. 2543–52). Le mot d'*encantamen* est prononcé (v. 2740). Un serviteur du lépreux informe le héros que pour rompre l'enchantement il faut briser une tête de jeune homme placée dans l'embrasure d'une fenêtre. La maison s'écroulera et l'enchantement s'arrêtera (vv. 2748–56). Jaufré est prévenu qu'il doit conserver sur lui son armure pour éviter d'être écrasé lors de l'écroulement de la maison. La scène

---

[14] Arturo Graf, *Roma nella memoria e nelle immaginazioni del Medio Evo*, Torino: E. Loescher, 1882–83, vol. II, p. 255.

[15] John W. Spargo, *Virgil the Necromancer: Studies in Virgilian Legends*, Cambridge (Mass.): Harvard University Press, 1934, pp. 61–6 et 132–4.

[16] Charles V. Langlois, *La Connaissance de la nature et du monde au Moyen Age*, Paris: Hachette, 1911, p. 106. Je n'ai pu consulter les observations complémentaires présentées par Arthur Dickson dans son ouvrage *Valentine and Orson: A Study in Late Medieval Romance*, New York: Columbia University Press, 1929, pp. 191–216.

[17] Stith Thompson, op. cit., vol. II, p. 169 (D 1311.7.1).

[18] On a dit de Gerbert qu'il avait un démon enfermé dans une tête d'or et qu'il le consultait souvent: voir Lynn Thorndike, *A History of Magic and Experimental Science*, New York: Columbia University Press, 1923, vol. I, p. 705. D'autres exemples de têtes qui parlent: ibid., vol. I, p. 662; vol. II, pp. 680 et 825.

se passe comme elle nous a été annoncée, dans un fracas de tempête. Il vaut la peine de regarder le passage de près.

| | |
|---|---:|
| Puis laisa sun elme lusen, | 2770 |
| E es vengutz a la fenestra | |
| E a vista laïns la testa, | |
| Asauta, bela e ben faita. | |
| E aqi eus el la n'a traixa, | 2774 |
| E vas si en u banc pausar, | |
| E puis va sus un colp donar | |
| Qe tuta l'a per mig partida. | |
| E la testa sail sus e crida, | 2778 |
| E sibla e mena tormen, | |
| E par qe tug li elemen | |
| E-l cel e la terra s'ajusta, | |
| E no-i reman peira ni fusta | 2782 |
| Qe l'us ab l'autre no-s combata | |
| E qe sobre Jaufre no bata | |
| E nu-l feira de tal mesura | |
| Qe grans feresa er s'o dura. | 2786 |
| E fes escur e trona e plòu. | |
| E Jaufre esta, qe no-s mòu, | |
| Ans met l'escut sus en la testa. | |
| E casun fóuzers e tempesta. | 2790 |
| E nu-i a trau ni cabrïon, | |
| Teule ni peira ni cairon | |
| Qe nu-l don un colp o un burs. | |
| E-l cels es trebols e escurs, | 2794 |
| E leva-s un'aura tan grans | |
| Qe tot ne porta entrenans | |
| C'a pauc Jaufre no n'a portat | |
| Si non ages Deu reclamat; | 2798 |
| E levet si tal polverieira, | |
| Tal tabust e tal fumadeira | |
| Qe no pogratz lo cel veser, | |
| E prendun peiras a caser | 2802 |
| E lams e fóuzers mot sovent, | |
| E anet s'en ab aqel ven | |
| Tota aqela maldisïun, | |
| Qe no-i remas de la maisun | 2806 |
| Fundamenta ni nuila res | |
| Plus qe s'anc res nu n'i ages. | |
| E Jaufre remas totz cassatz . . .[19] | |

'Puis il lace son heaume brillant et s'approche de la fenêtre. Il voit la tête à l'intérieur, séduisante, belle, bien faite. Aussitôt il la retire de là, il s'asseoit un instant sur un banc, et ensuite il lui porte un coup qui la fend en deux. Aussitôt la tête saute en l'air, crie, siffle et fait un grand vacarme. On dirait que tous les

---

[19] René Lavaud et René Nelli, *Les Troubadours*, Paris: Desclée De Brouwer, 1960–66, vol. I, pp. 15–618, 'Le Roman de *Jaufre*': voir pp. 184–6.

éléments, que le ciel et la terre s'affrontent. Il ne reste pierre ni poutre qui ne combatte l'une contre l'autre, qui ne s'abatte sur Jaufré et ne le frappe de telle sorte que ce sera terrible si cela dure. L'air s'obscurcit, il tonne, il pleut. Jaufré reste sans bouger. Il met son écu sur sa tête. La foudre et l'orage s'abattent. Il n'est poutre, chevron, tuile, pierre ou moellon qui ne l'atteigne et ne le frappe. Le ciel est sombre et obscur. Un vent terrible se lève, si fort qu'il emporte tout devant soi. Il aurait emporté Jaufré, si celui-ci n'avait invoqué Dieu. Un tel nuage de poussière, de particules confuses et de fumée s'élève qu'il est impossible de voir le ciel. Des pierres, des éclairs, la foudre tombent en abondance. Avec ce vent de tempête disparaît tout le maléfice. Il n'est plus rien resté de la maison, ni les fondations ni rien d'autre, comme s'il n'y avait jamais rien eu à cet endroit. Pour sa part, Jaufré est resté là, tout effondré...

On conviendra que cette scène prodigieuse ne manque ni de force ni de cohérence. Le point de départ est la nécessité pour le héros de briser l'enchantement. Cette rupture se fait de manière violente. Pour rompre le sortilège qui pèse sur le lieu, il faut briser la tête magique. On peut parler d'un *Disenchantment by striking*.[20] Un raisonnement par analogie est toujours à la base des comportements magiques. Pour rompre le charme un mouvement violent est indispensable. Le coup d'épée qui tranche la tête en deux symbolise la destruction du pouvoir magique. Il fait plus que 'symboliser', il abat réellement. L'action guerrière qui fracasse la tête supprime l'effigie qui veillait en permanence sur la demeure à la façon d'un radar ou d'un système de protection invisible. On peut supposer que si la tête était placée dans l'embrasure de la fenêtre, c'était pour mieux surveiller la salle et la porte. Tout homme, nous dit le texte, qui commettait un acte hostile à l'intérieur (*qe ren sai forfezes*, v. 2743) ne pouvait plus quitter les lieux. Pour les gens du Moyen Age sans doute des liens invisibles ou un mur d'air empêchaient alors l'agresseur de franchir la porte. On peut penser au verger merveilleux d'*Erec et Enide*, entouré d'une muraille d'air par *nigromance*,[21] ou à un passage du *Perlesvaus* où l'on voit Arthur essayer vainement d'entrer dans une chapelle dont la porte est ouverte.[22] En fracassant la tête, Jaufré détruit irrémédiablement tout le système de détection et de protection. Dès lors la tête magique se fâche, les puissances invisibles se déchaînent. La maison n'est pas soufflée par une explosion, elle est frappée par une tornade qui n'en laisse rien subsister, comme si les diables se ruaient sur elle pour châtier l'insolent qui a osé mettre à mal le délicat mécanisme de surveillance.

On pourrait citer divers exemples où l'on voit une tête maléfique produire des dommages ou des destructions. Waldemar Deonna cite le cas d'une tête de mort à qui un passant lance une pierre et qui se venge aussitôt en rebondissant

---

[20] Stith Thompson, op. cit., vol. II, p. 82 (D 712.3).
[21] *Les Romans de Chrétien de Troyes*: I, *Erec et Enide*, publié par Mario Roques, Paris: H. Champion, 1952, p. 173, v. 5692.
[22] William A. Nitze and T. Atkinson Jenkins, *Le haut livre du Graal: Perlesvaus*, Chicago: University of Chicago Press, 1932–37 (Reprint – New York: Phaeton Press, 1972), vol. I, pp. 286–8.

et en l'aveuglant.[23] On pourrait citer aussi la tête épouvantable, née de l'union d'un mortel avec une morte qui vient d'être enterrée. Cette tête, dont parlent à la fois Gervais de Tilbury et Gautier Map, a le pouvoir de détruire tous ceux qui la regardent, plus efficacement encore que la Gorgone. Quand on la jette finalement au fond de la mer, de terribles tempêtes se produisent à cet endroit-là.[24]

Toutefois la tête magique du *Roman de Jaufré* est assez différente. Il ne s'agit pas du tout d'une tête de mort. On a affaire à un buste. Le texte parle d'une tête de jeune homme (*de tozet* v. 2748). Il n'y a aucun doute sur le sens du mot, comme le montrent bien les nombreux exemples recueillis par Emil Levy.[25] La mention du *tozet* est peut-être un détail sans importance, un mot appelé par la rime.

L'intéressante miniature du ms. B.N., fonds fr. 2164, f. 34 a, reproduite ici, nous donne une idée de la façon dont l'illustrateur comprenait le texte. Pour lui la tête magique est une énorme tête blanche. Il la représente posée sur une longue table recouverte d'une nappe. A ses yeux Jaufré l'a placée là pour la frapper plus commodément. Elle est faite dans une matière blanche et dure. Un capuchon très serré encadre la tête et masque la chevelure. On la voit faire une sorte de grimace au moment où l'épée du héros lui porte un terrible coup. La tête, figée, regarde l'agresseur. Elle est encore immobile. Elle est dépeinte au moment dramatique où l'épée la partage en deux. C'est ainsi qu'un enlumineur du début du XIV$^e$ siècle a imaginé une illustration de la scène. On ne peut pas l'accuser d'avoir mal compris le texte. En représentant une tête monumentale sur une table blanche, il est sensible au caractère fantastique de la scène.

Il apparaît clairement que pour l'illustrateur la tête n'est pas celle d'un ennemi immolé. Même si on sacrifie des enfants dans la maison du monstrueux lépreux (vv. 2662–712), ce n'est pas non plus la tête d'une innocente victime qui y est représentée. Le crâne d'un mort ne pourrait jouer que le rôle d'un fétiche, d'un talisman assurant à son possesseur la force guerrière du disparu.[26] La fonction remplie par la tête magique est tout à fait différente, puisque l'enchantement repose sur elle. C'est la pièce-clé du mécanisme mis en place.

Nous n'avons pas les moyens d'aller beaucoup plus loin dans l'explication de la scène. La tête qui surveille ce qui se passe dans la maison et qui interdit aux ennemis de quitter les lieux fait un choix entre les personnages. Elle

---

[23] Waldemar Deonna, op. cit. (1925), p. 68. Il s'agit d'un passage de l'Anthologie grecque, I, 267.
[24] Voir Gervais de Tilbury, *Otia imperialia*, éd. F. Liebrecht, Hannover, 1856, pp. 11 et 93; Walter Map, *De Nugis curialium*, éd. Montague R. James, Oxford: Clarendon Press, new edn 1983, pp. 366–8. Le texte est mentionné par Salomon Reinach, op. cit., vol. IV, p. 262. Le même auteur cite une histoire semblable, ibid., p. 260.
[25] Emil Levy, *Provenzalisches Supplement-Wörterbuch*, Leipzig: O. R. Reisland, 1894–1924 (Reprint – Hildesheim, 1973), vol. VIII, pp. 337–9, *s.v. tozet*.
[26] Voir Adolphe Reinach, op. cit., pp. 285–6.

n'empêche pas de sortir le serviteur du lépreux, la jeune femme et les enfants. Seul Jaufré se trouve retenu à l'intérieur. Autrement dit, non seulement la tête est au centre du dispositif magique, mais encore elle opère une sélection comme si elle était douée de discernement. Ne parlons pas d'intelligence artificielle (le mot serait déplacé) ni d'automate (le terme serait inexact, car l'on n'a pas affaire à un robot qui bouge). Contentons-nous d'observer que la tête a un pouvoir de commandement et de décision.

Faut-il croire que derrière cette tête séduisante se cache un diable? Ce n'est pas impossible. L'agitation frénétique qui s'empare d'elle, lorsque l'enchantement est brisé, montre qu'elle possède à la fois une certaine vie et une indéniable rage. D'autre part, la tornade destructrice qui accompagne la cessation du sortilège ressemble étrangement aux catastrophes causées par les diables furieux. On croyait au Moyen Age que les diables volaient dans l'air et abattaient furieusement les toitures des maisons, les clochers des églises, les récoltes sur pied. Les tempêtes sont attribuées à l'action des diables. On se souvient que dans la *Queste del Saint Graal*, lorsque le diable, déguisé en femme, s'éloigne de Perceval, la tente du héros se trouve brusquement renversée par une bourrasque, de noirs nuages envahissent les airs, de grands tourbillons secouent la mer sur le passage des mauvais esprits.[27]

Dans le *Roman de Jaufré* le nom du diable n'est pas prononcé. Il n'est pas dit que la tête fonctionne avec l'assistance des esprits infernaux. Tout a l'air de se passer dans un monde moins trouble. Toutefois, il faut se souvenir que la demeure du lépreux est le lieu où sont perpétrés d'horribles forfaits (on y assassine de jeunes enfants). Le dénouement de l'épisode avec cette tempête furieuse où se donnent libre cours les éléments déchaînés, la notation que Jaufré aurait été emporté par la tornade s'il n'avait pas invoqué le nom de Dieu (vv. 2797–8), tout cela donne à la scène un aspect très inquiétant. On a l'impression que si la tête s'agite avec rage, c'est parce qu'un diable est en elle. On est tenté de croire que si la maison s'effondre, c'est parce qu'un diable s'enfuit en brisant tout sur son passage. Si l'on avait le temps de comparer la description avec l'ample évocation de la fin des enchantements à la Douloureuse Garde dans le *Lancelot en prose*,[28] on trouverait des points de rencontre. L'auteur du *Lancelot* met expressément les diables en cause. Ici ils se dissimulent. Mais le dénouement suggère leur présence.

A partir de ces exemples il n'est guère possible de tirer des conclusions générales. Il faudrait beaucoup plus de cas pour qu'on essaie d'y voir clair. D'où vient l'idée d'une tête magique? Arthur Dickson estimait que la tête qui parle ou qui prophétise est une continuation de l'*Oracular idol*. John W. Spargo

---

[27] Voir Albert Pauphilet, *La Queste del Saint Graal, roman du XIII<sup>e</sup> siècle*, Paris: H. Champion, 1923, p. 110.
[28] Voir Alexandre Micha, *Lancelot, roman en prose du XIII<sup>e</sup> siècle*, Genève: Droz, 1978–83, vol. VIII, pp. 416–18.

La tête magique dans le *Roman de Jaufré*, Paris, Bibliothèque Nationale, ms. fr. 2164 (Ms. *A*), f. 34 a

pensait à des automates à air pulsé capables d'émettre des sons.[29] Ces éléments ont certainement joué un rôle, tout particulièrement les statues des dieux antiques ou des idoles auxquelles on prêtait un pouvoir oraculaire. D'autres raisons peuvent être également invoquées, car la tête magique ne se borne pas à répondre aux questions posées. Elle peut révéler des secrets, assurer une protection, disposer d'une véritable puissance surnaturelle, avoir une action faste ou néfaste. Les antiques superstitions sur le savoir et le pouvoir merveilleux d'une tête séparée du corps ont dû exercer une influence. L'existence de reliquaires en forme de chefs, spécialement vénérés par les fidèles, dispensateurs de bienfaits augustes, doit être également prise en compte. Dans le monde chrétien on avait là des signes visibles de la puissance miraculeuse de certaines têtes exceptionnelles. A des titres divers tout cela a contribué à la survivance épisodique de la tête magique dans les textes et les rêves des hommes.

---

[29] Sur ces différentes hypothèses voir John W. Spargo, op. cit., pp. 132–4.

# *Punishments and Rewards of the Questing Knights in* La Queste del Saint Graal

## EITHNE O'SHARKEY

When King Arthur's knights leave the court at Camelot to set out on the quest of the Holy Grail, they are already aware that the object of their search is not of a material kind and that the reward they hope to win is essentially a spiritual one. Gauvain, the King's nephew, following the Grail's miraculous appearance in their midst on the feast of Pentecost, proposes that they should set out at once to discover its mysteries and 'veoir apertement' what is now concealed from their sight. All the Round Table knights are eager to follow Gauvain's example (even though they have to travel far from Camelot), if they can discover the 'secrets' of the Holy Grail and taste daily its delicious food (which they have just enjoyed at the marvellous feast provided by the Holy Vessel). This food has satisfied all their desires; and at least some of them have recognised that, in the banquet, they have received the gift of Divine Grace:

> 'si rendirent graces a Nostre Seignor li plusor d'ax de ce que si grant honor lor avoit fete qu'il les avoit repeuz de la grace dou Saint Vessel . . . et distrent qu'il ne fineroient ja mes d'errer devant qu'il seroient asis a la haute table ou si douce viande estoit toz jors aprestee come cele qu'il avoient iluec eue'.[1]

Just after Galaad's arrival at the court, when he had taken his predestined place at the Round Table, the Siège Périlleux, on which are written the words 'Ci est li sieges Galaad' (p. 8, ll. 12–13), the coming of the Holy Grail had been heralded by a clap of thunder and a brilliant light. Borne by invisible hands, it had entered the hall, offering Grace to all prepared to receive it:

> 'Si furent tantost par laienz tot ausi come s'il fussent enluminé de la grace dou Saint Esperit' (p. 15, ll. 12–13).

King Arthur himself was particularly conscious of the great honour conferred on his court by the presence of the Grail (a favour never before enjoyed by any monarch, except the Roi Méhaignié), although he did not foresee the consequences of this marvellous event. When he realises that all his knights

---

[1] *La Queste del Saint Graal*, edited by Albert Pauphilet, CFMA, Paris: Champion, 1923, p. 15, ll. 31–3 and p.16, ll. 28–31. All subsequent references are to this edition.

are determined to depart on the quest, his joy is turned to grief. The ladies of the court also are anxious to prevent the departure of the knights who, nevertheless, with their elected leader, Galaad, prepare to leave next morning. Then a mysterious old man, in monk's robes, appears among them, saying that he has been sent by the hermit, Nasciens, to warn the knights not to take any lady with them on the journey, and to urge the need for penance and purity of intention and conduct on the part of those who wish to undertake the quest:

> 'ne nus n'i entre qui ne soit confés ou qui n'aille a confesse car nus en si haut servise ne doit entrer devant qu'il soit netoiez et espurgiez de totes vilanies et de toz pechiés mortex. Car ceste Queste n'est mie queste de terriennes choses, ainz doit estre li encerchemenz des grans secrez et des privetez Nostre Seignor et des grans repostailles que li Hauz Mestres mostrera apertement au boneuré chevalier qu'il a esleu a son serjant entres les autres chevaliers terriens, a qui il mostrera les granz merveilles dou Saint Graal, et fera veoir ce que cuers mortex ne porroit penser ne langue d'ome terrien deviser' (p. 19, ll. 16–26).

From this moment the tone is clearly established, for the messenger's solemn warning emphasises that the quest is a spiritual adventure in which only one perfect knight will fully succeed. Moreover,

> 'the call to embark on the Quest is a final call to choose, and the choice is between grace and judgement, between redemption and rejection'.[2]

Most of the questors, however, although they have willingly responded to the challenge and genuinely desire to discover the mysteries of the Holy Grail, pay little attention to the old man's words and apparently disregard his advice concerning the necessity of the sacrament of penance. They seem to be unaware that only the virtuous can hope to find the object of their search, and that punishments await those who, in their attitudes or by their actions, show themselves to be unworthy. Even before the quest begins, however, they have been reminded of the gravity of their undertaking and of the danger of entering 'en si haut servise' in a state of sin.

The first indications of the type of punishment the unworthy knight will meet are to be found in the adventure of King Baudemagus who takes a shield with a red cross, in spite of warnings that it is not intended for him but is reserved for the Best Knight in the world. He is knocked from his horse and seriously wounded by a mysterious White Knight (probably an angelic figure), who tells him:

> 'Et por le pechié que vos i avez m'envoia ça Nostre Sires, por prendre en la venjance selonc le meffet' (p. 29, ll. 17–18).

Because of his greed and presumption, Baudemagus is now unable to continue his quest, but he is left to the care of monks in an abbey, while Galaad departs,

---

[2] Pauline Matarasso, *The Redemption of Chivalry. A Study of the Queste del saint Graal*, Genève: Droz, 1979, p. 185.

bearing the shield. The reference here to sin and to divine retribution, ('venjance'), is unequivocal, and the absolute justice of Baudemagus's punishment is not called into question by anyone.

The next victim of his own imprudence and avarice is a very young knight, Melyant, the son of the King of Denmark, who has just been dubbed by Galaad and reminded by him of the special obligations of his rank. Melyant begs, as a favour, to be allowed to accompany Galaad on the quest, but when they arrive at a crossroads, despite a warning notice and Galaad's advice, the young knight takes a path to the left, leaving his companion. Melyant rides on alone for two days through a forest until he comes to a beautiful meadow where he sees a golden crown on a throne and a number of tables set with rich food, as for a banquet. Greatly attracted by the crown, Melyant snatches it and carries it away, but he meets a knight who commands him to return it as it is not his to possess. The young knight refuses until the stranger strikes him, wounding him and knocking him from his horse, and then rides off with the crown. The wounded Melyant, lying on the ground in great pain, blames himself for not having listened to Galaad's counsel. However, Galaad arrives to rescue him, attacking and putting his enemy to flight (but refraining from killing him):

> 'Et quant cil se sent mehaignié, si torne en fuie car poor a de morir. Et Galaad ne l'enchauce plus, come cil qui n'a talent de fere lui plus de mal que il a eu' (p. 43, ll. 7–10).

His rescuer then carries Melyant to an abbey to be cared for by the monks; and having confessed his sins and received absolution and Holy Communion, the young man tells Galaad that he is now ready to die. However, his wounds can be healed and he is left in the abbey while his companion returns to the quest. One of the monks then explains to Melyant the reason why he has been prevented from continuing the journey in Galaad's company, and the real meaning of his recent experiences. At the crossroads he had turned away from Christ's path of compassion and love, yielding to the temptation of pride. Because he did not appreciate the fact that he had been admitted to the ranks of the 'chevalerie celestiel' (p. 45, l. 23), he had fallen into mortal sin and this had led to the further sin of greed, or concupiscence, resulting in his theft of the golden crown. He had been saved from death only by the Sign of the Cross he had made and the prayer he had said before defending himself against the attack of the enemy knight:

> 'Mes toutes voies por la venjance de ce que tu estoies issuz de son servise te mena Nostre Sire jusques a paor de mort' (p. 46, ll. 4–6).

His punishment by God is of both a physical and a moral kind. He has been deprived of Galaad's companionship and is unable to continue the quest because he lies wounded. But God, in His mercy, on hearing Melyant's cry for help, had sent Galaad to save him from death. Despite his good intentions and religious fervour, the young man had easily succumbed to the first temptations he met on the way. Like so many knights who set out on the quest, he was called to a life of great moral rectitude and religious asceticism, but he failed the test which could have opened to him the path to perfection. Galaad's victory over the enemy (signifying Melyant's sins) resulted from his sanctity and his obedience to God's will in all things. As a King's son, Melyant's pride and ambition might have been understandable, but he was called to follow standards of chivalry which are not worldly. The Good Knight, as he departs, leaves behind a chastened and repentant Melyant who, like King Baudemagus, is thus reminded of his unworthiness to seek the Holy Grail.

Gauvain, like Baudemagus and Melyant, is conscious of Galaad's spiritual and moral superiority and ardently desires his company on the quest. He calls at the abbey from which Galaad has just departed that morning, and is annoyed to find that his search for him has again met with failure:

> 'Diex! fet mesires Gauvains, tant sui meschaanz! Or sui je li plus maleureus chevaliers dou monde, qui vois suivant ce chevalier de si pres et si nel puis ateindre! Certes se Diex donast que je le poïsse trover, ja mes de lui ne departisse, por qu'il amast ma compaignie autant come je feroie la soe' (p. 51, ll. 26–31).

However, one of the monks quietly rebukes Gauvain, assuring him that he is not worthy to accompany Galaad:

> 'Certes, sire, la compaignie de vos deus ne seroit mie covenable. Car vos estes serjanz mauvés et desloiax, et il est chevaliers tiex come il doit estre' (p. 52, ll. 2–4).

Gauvain, surprised that he should be regarded as 'mauvés et desloiax', requests an explanation of the monk's criticism of him, only to be told that he must wait for future events to reveal its meaning. Apparently little troubled by the rebuke and the monk's implicit warning, Gauvain attends mass in the abbey church and is joined there by his brother Gaheriet. As they ride away together, they meet Yvain who complains that he has met no adventures on the quest.

Continuing on their way, they reach the Château des Pucelles, which Galaad has just conquered, liberating the captive maidens and overcoming seven wicked brothers who had committed many crimes. Gauvain and his two companions meet the seven brothers fleeing from the castle and, being attacked by them, kill the brothers, in defending themselves. Later, when Gauvain seeks shelter for the night in a hermitage, the hermit urges him to confess his sins, for he has not been to confession for years. Gauvain makes his confession – although without any manifestation of real sorrow for the actions of his past life – and asks the hermit to explain why he was told at the abbey that he was not fit company for Galaad. The hermit readily tells him why he is so unworthy and merits the title of 'mauvés serjanz et desloiax'. Gauvain has used his knightly rank and his abilities for evil purposes: although his soul belongs to God, he has chosen to serve Satan:

> 'Car vos en avez dou tout esté serjanz a l'anemi, et lessié vostre creator, et mena la plus orde vie et la plus mauvese que onques chevaliers menast' (p. 54, ll. 18–20).

The hermit also informs Gauvain that because of his sinful ways he has killed the seven brothers who otherwise might have repented of their crimes and been reconciled with God. Galaad had conquered them but had not attempted to kill them. The Good Knight is the example, par excellence, of the faithful servant who loyally obeys his Master and who has accomplished the great adventure of the Château des Pucelles in imitation of Christ's Harrowing of Hell, when He was sent by His Father to save mankind. However, Gauvain has still time to turn away from evil and accept God's mercy and pardon if he truly shows contrition for his sins and does penance for them. Gauvain is left in no doubt that he is guilty of homicide, for he has killed many knights without mercy, yet he shows no sign of appreciating the nature of his guilt and he disregards the hermit's advice. He will receive further warnings in the *Queste*, and although he is always curious to learn what they signify, he appears to lack the moral sensitivity and spiritual perception which might have allowed him to respond to the offers of grace and forgiveness. Fundamentally, he is unwilling to repent or to change his conduct. Although he is a courageous knight, anxious to succeed in the quest of the Grail, he displays a complete rejection of the values he must accept if he is to achieve his goal. So, when he leaves the hermitage, he is surprised and disappointed that so few adventures come his way, although he rides about for several months:

> 'des la Pentecoste jusqu'a la Magdaleine' (p. 147, ll. 7–8).

Gauvain meets Lancelot's half-brother, Hector, who has also failed to find adventures and who reports that he has met a number of Round Table knights, riding alone on the quest, like himself, but failing to meet the adventures which they expected. Riding together, Hector and Gauvain then come to a ruined chapel in the forest and go into it to rest for the night. Before lying down to sleep they say their prayers in front of the altar:

> 'come bon crestien doivent fere' (p. 149, l. 3).

Each of the knights has a strange dream. Gauvain in his dream sees a green meadow in which are one hundred and fifty bulls, only three of which are white and beautiful, without spot. These three remain in the meadow while all the others stray from it and do not return for a long time. Some fail to return, and those which eventually reappear are thin and wasted. Hector's dream is of a throne, and he sees Lancelot riding forth by his side, mounted on a great horse. He and Lancelot seem to have set out on a hopeless quest, for Lancelot falls from his horse, is attacked and robbed, and has to continue his journey wearing a ragged garment and riding a donkey. Lancelot also attempts to drink from a splendid fountain from which the water recedes, so he has to return home disappointed. Hector himself seems to arrive at a rich man's house and tries to enter it, to attend a wedding feast, but he is prevented from doing so because of his proud steed, and he too is obliged to depart, filled with grief at his failure.

On awaking, both Gauvain and Hector are anxious to know the meaning of their dreams, but before they can leave the chapel they have a vision of a hand, covered in red samite, which suddenly appears before them, holding a bridle, and of a great candle which is burning brightly. Having passed through the chapel in front of the knights, these objects disappear as mysteriously as they had come. Then a voice is heard, addressing the two companions and telling them that their faith is weak and they are bereft of the three things they have just seen, so they will not achieve the adventures of the Holy Grail.

Gauvain, ready as usual to take the initiative, suggests to Hector that they should look for a hermit who might interpret their dreams and vision. If they follow his advice they may yet have greater success than they have experienced up to this moment. In spite of the prophetic warnings they have been given and the supernatural voice they have heard, Gauvain and Hector do not accept the fact that they are wholly responsible for their lack of success and that the barrier to their progress on the quest is their sinful state and lack of contrition. When they set out next morning to visit an old priest in a hermitage, they are challenged to a fight by a knight who meets them and who wounds Gauvain but is, in turn, mortally wounded by him. At the dying knight's request, they carry him to an abbey where he receives the Last Sacraments with great devotion and tells them, before he dies, that he is Yvain, son of King Urien, who, like them, had set out on the quest but has now been killed as a punishment for his sins. Gauvain is stricken with sorrow and remorse, revealing to Yvain, whom he had not recognised earlier, that he, too, is a knight of the Round Table and he is King Arthur's nephew. Yvain forgives him but prophesies that many of the questing knights will die without discovering what they seek; and he asks that prayers be offered for the salvation of his soul by those who survive. Hector and Gauvain lament his death and after his funeral at the abbey they have a tombstone placed over his grave, with his name inscribed on it and that of the person who killed him.[3] They regard Yvain's death as a great misfortune but continue on their way to the remote hermitage where the venerable hermit, Nasciens, admits that Gauvain needs advice and help, although he is:

'mout sages des terrianes choses' (p. 155, ll. 10–11).

---

[3] On his return from the quest, Lancelot comes to a White Abbey where he sees a splendid tomb, that of Baudemagus, who was killed by Gauvain (p. 261, ll. 23–32). Baudemagus was one of Gauvain's many victims, it would appear.

Nasciens willingly interprets their dreams and vision, explaining the symbolism of what they have seen. The bulls of Gauvain's dream represent the knights of Arthur's court who have fallen into sin, especially the sins of pride and lust, except for the three unspotted animals which represent Perceval, Bohort and Galaad. When the knights set out on the quest they did not go to confession, as they should have done, but followed the paths of wickedness where some of them died and others were killed by their fellow-knights. Even those who were able to return were stained by sin, except the three who will find perfect nourishment from the Grail. Only one of the three successful questors will return in the end to Camelot. However, the final part of Gauvain's dream can still be changed, since future events can be altered in his favour if he chooses to repent.

Hector's dream, too, according to the hermit, foretells failure and disappointment in the quest. The throne he saw represents the Round Table, and what he and Lancelot seek but do not find (because of their unworthiness) are:

'les secrees choses Nostre Seignor' (p. 158, l. 10).

Lancelot's fall from his horse, however, indicates his humiliation and abandonment of pride. He is clothed by Our Lord in a garment of long-suffering and humility and rides a humble animal. The fountain from which he attempt to drink is the Holy Grail:

'ce est la grace del Saint Esperit' (p. 159, l. 2).

He will lose his sight and the power of his limbs for twenty-four days when he sees the Grail, because of his earlier sinful life. But Hector, who is still in a state of mortal sin, will not be permitted to enter the house of the Rich Fisher King to join in the feast, due to his pride. The objects seen by the two companions in their vision in the chapel represent the Christian virtues of charity, abstinence and truth. Because Gauvain and Hector do not practise these virtues but have killed many knights, including some of their fellow-questors, they will not accomplish the Grail adventures. They have already received warnings of the judgment to come: only if they truly repent will they be saved. While the worthy knights will be fed in body and soul by the delicious food of the Holy Grail and be 'repeuz de la grace dou Saint Vessel', those who prefer to serve the Devil will be deprived of this heavenly nourishment. The eucharistic connections of the Grail – already adumbrated in its first appearance at Arthur's court – are here further emphasised by Nasciens's words. Yet Hector and Gauvain ride away, apparently unwilling to admit their guilt and seek forgiveness from God. They meet Galaad in the Forest Gaste where Galaad wounds Gauvain who admits that this is a punishment for his temerity at Camelot when he attempted to draw the sword from the stone before the arrival of the Good Knight. He must now accept the fact that he cannot continue the quest; and Hector's quest, too, comes to an abrupt end when, as his dream had foretold, he is refused entrance to the Grail feast at Corbenic, although Lancelot is seated within, at the King's table, enjoying the marvellous banquet. The Fisher King himself informs Hector that he is unworthy to be accepted as a companion of the questing knights, and Hector is greatly ashamed and distressed as he admits his failure. To the grief of Lancelot, who can do nothing to help him, Hector is chased away from Corbenic: he is like the wedding guest of the Gospels who is ignominiously excluded from the feast because he is not wearing the wedding garment.

There are repeated references in the *Queste* to the sacrament of penance and to the need for true contrition as a condition for the soul's reconciliation with God. The penitential judgment is liberative and aims at healing the wounds of sin; for the confessor functions not only as a judge in the ministry of divine justice, but also as a spiritual physician and teacher who enlightens the penitent about the things necessary for a valid and fruitful reception of the sacrament, encourages him to abandon sin and acquire virtue, and dispenses divine mercy, insisting on the importance of sorrow and of amendment of life. Unlike Baudemagus and Melyant, who accept the punishments inflicted on them and repent, although they cannot follow the quest further, Hector and Gauvain, in their hardness of heart, ignore the need for penance.

Perhaps an even more serious case of the hardened sinner who persists in his folly is that of Bohort's brother, Lionel, who, like the others, is punished by being excluded from the quest. Lionel violently attacks his brother who had not come to his aid when he had been made prisoner and was being beaten by two knights, although Bohort explains the reason (he felt obliged to rescue a maiden first, as she was being carried off by another knight) and asks pardon. When an old hermit interrupts the fight between the brothers, Lionel kills the unarmed old man, and also kills Calogrenant, a Round Table knight, who attempts to intervene to save Bohort's life. Finally, however, a celestial voice commands Bohort to flee and the fight is stopped by a thunderbolt, indicating God's anger at Lionel's wild frenzy and acts of murder. Bohort's patience and charity are contrasted with his brother's violent behaviour, and Lionel is shown to have provoked Divine judgment and retribution.

In contrast, too, to the fate of such unsuccessful questing knights is that of Lancelot who has to suffer a series of set-backs, reproaches and humiliations, but is eventually rewarded by a partial success. He meets many trials and his progress is slow on his way to his goal. Indeed, for Lancelot, the entire quest becomes one of self-discovery, of contrition, penance and purification, before he can achieve what he seeks. His self-discovery begins at Arthur's court when the King asks him to attempt to draw the sword from the stone. This sword is destined for the best knight in the world; and Lancelot replies, somewhat angrily, that he will not make the attempt:

> 'Certes, sire, ne ele n'est moie ne je n'avroie le corage de mettre i main, ne le hardement: car je ne suiz mie dignes ne soffisanz que je la doie prendre' (p. 5, ll. 28–30).

After Galaad's success in this adventure, a maiden on a white palfrey rides up, and addressing Lancelot directly, declares publicly what he has already admitted i.e. that he is no longer the Best Knight in the world:

> 'Vos estiez hier matin li mieldres chevaliers dou monde; et qui lors vos apelast Lancelot le meillor chevalier de toz, il deist voir: car alors l'estiez vos. Mes qui ore le diroit, len le devroit tenir a mençongier car meillor i a de vos, et bien est provee chose par l'aventure de ceste espee a quoi vos n'osastes metre la main' (p. 12, l. 31–p. 13, l. 3).

Lancelot's humility will soon make him aware of his imperfections, for the quest will be for him a spiritual itinerary, a struggle between good and evil, but in the end he will receive a reward commensurate with his moral and spiritual state. Having set out on the quest, he fails to recognise Galaad in the Forest Gaste and attacks him but is repulsed with a blow; and when he tries to pursue him through the forest he is unable to overtake him. Then, riding alone to a chapel near a cross where he decides to rest, he tethers his horse to a tree, hangs his shield on a branch and attempts to enter the chapel, only to find his way barred by an iron railing. Although the chapel appears to be ruined and deserted, Lancelot can see within it a bright light from six candles in a silver candelabra on a richly decorated altar. Full of regret because he is unable to enter the building, he returns to the cross and lies down to rest, still thinking about the Good Knight whom he had been unable to overtake. Lying there, in a kind of trance, he observes the Holy Grail on the silver altar coming from the chapel towards the cross and preceded by the candelabra, carried by unseen hands. He also witnesses the miraculous cure of a sick knight who is carried there on a litter and prays earnestly to be healed. Lancelot, however, is unable to move or respond to these events because of his state of torpor. But he hears the squire who had accompanied the sick knight comment on his lack of reaction in the presence of the Holy Grail:

> 'Par foi, fet li escuiers, ja est aucuns chevaliers qui maint en aucun grant pechié dont il ne se fist onques confés, dont il est par aventure si corpables vers Nostre Seignor que il ne li plaist mie qu'il veist ceste bele aventure' (p. 60, ll. 3–7).

Then the knight and his squire take Lancelot's horse and armour (apparently to punish him for his sins), and the knight swears to go in quest of the Grail's mysteries. When Lancelot is again able to move, the chapel and candelabra are still there, but the Grail has disappeared, and he hears a voice condemning him for having attempted to enter the holy place although he is:

> 'plus durs que pierre, plus amers que fuz, plus nuz et plus despris que figuiers' (p. 61, ll. 16–17).

He is at once overcome with grief and shame and a feeling of despair:

> 'car ce set il bien qu'il est venuz au point qu'il n'avra ja mes honor, puis qu'il a failli a savoir la verité del Saint Graal' (p. 61, ll. 23–5).

For the first time, Lancelot admits that he has failed to perceive spiritual realities because of his sinful state:

> 'Et ce n'est mie de merveille se je ne puis veoir cler: car des lors que je fui primes chevaliers ne fu il hore que je ne fusse coverz de teniebres de pechié mortel, car tout adés ai habité en luxure et en la vilté de cest monde plus que nus autres' (p. 62, ll. 3–7).

This admission, with the specific mention of 'luxure' (his adultery with Arthur's Queen, Guinevere), reveals the extent to which his moral conscience has been awakened, although his spiritual faculties have been seriously impaired. He sets out on foot and reaches a hermitage where he expresses his profound sorrow for sin:

> 'Si s'agenoille en mi le chancel, et bat sa corpe et crie merci a Nostre Seignor des males oevres que il a fetes en cest siecle' (p. 62, ll. 28–30).

The hermit-priest, having finished the mass he has been celebrating, explains to Lancelot how the wounds of sin may be healed by a valid confession of his moral lapses. Lancelot has been like the unprofitable servant in the Gospel who buried his talent. He has been endowed with many gifts by God but has misused them, and he will be completely lost if he does not repent sincerely and change his life:

> 'Sachiez qu'il vos tornera a noient en assez petit de tens, se vos prochainement ne li criez merci en confession veraie et en repentance de cuer et en amendement de vie' (p. 64, ll. 18–20).

If he follows this advice, God will save his soul.

The hermit also explains to Lancelot the meaning of the rebuke he had heard at the deserted chapel, after he had failed to respond to the presence of the Holy Grail:

> 'Mes quant li Sainz Graax vint la ou tu estoies, il te trouva si desgarni qu'il ne trouva en toi ne bone pensee ne bone volonté' (p. 70, ll. 18–20).

Lancelot then admits with shame that his greatest sin has been his adulterous love for Guinevere and that this sin has been his downfall. On promising to lead a chaste life in the future, he confesses his sins and receives absolution from the priest who gives him further advice regarding the heavenly standards he must attempt to reach if he is to continue on the Grail quest:

> 'Bien certes, Lancelot, par noient iriez en ceste Queste, se vos ne vos baez a atenir de toz pechiez mortiex et a retrere vostre cuer des pensees terrianes et des deliz dou monde . . . Car cist services ou vos estes entrez n'apartient de riens as terrianes choses, mes as celestiex' (p. 116, ll. 2–4, 25–7).

Having given him an appropriate penance to perform and provided him with a horse and armour, the hermit bids farewell to his penitent.

The first person Lancelot meets as he rides away from the hermitage is a valet who taunts him, calling him 'desloiax et mescreanz', but he accepts the insult and this further wound to his self-esteem as a fitting penalty for his sins. His humility is certainly remarkable, for it allows him to accept many more disappointments and rebuffs, as well as the aggressive contempt of his inferiors. He has grasped the need for a long and vigorous penance before he can be fully released from his guilt.

Lancelot soon visits a second hermit who helps to confirm him in his resolution to avoid evil and to find a rule of life for the future. As he now understands the spiritual blindness which has resulted from his faults, the hermit reminds him of the great importance of confession and encourages him to replace his vices by the virtues of faith, hope and charity. If he had developed the good qualities with which he was richly endowed, he would not have failed to achieve the Grail adventure in the forest:

> 'Or gardes que tu peusses puis avoir fet, se tu eusses toutes ces vertus sauvees en toi que Nostre Sires i avoit mises. Tu n'eusses mie failli a achever les aventures dou Saint Graal, dont tuit li autre sont ore en peine, ainz en eusse tant mené a fin com nus hons, sanz le Verai Chevalier porroit fere; li oil ne te fussent pas avuglé devant la face ton Seignor, ainz le veisses apertement' (p. 126, ll. 27–33).

In other words, Lancelot might have had a vision of God – the 'secret' of the Holy Grail. If he wishes to feast at the Lord's table, he must wear the wedding garment of grace and virtue. The hermit advises him, as a penance, to wear a hair-shirt (taken from the body of a dead hermit) on his journey and to abstain from meat and wine, also attending as often as possible Church services during his quest.

Following a remarkable dream he has of two knights and seven kings and of a great monarch (God Himself) surrounded by stars, Lancelot pays a visit to a third hermit, to seek further advice. The elder knight in his dream had been dismissed as 'fillastre' rather than 'fil', whereas the younger knight appeared to be transformed into a winged lion and to fly up to heaven. At the hermitage, he attends vespers and again goes to confession before being told the meaning of his dream. He learns from the hermit that the younger of the two knights is his son, Galaad, the person he has been seeking:

> 'ce est li chevaliers que tu quiers' (p. 138, ll. 15–16).

The kings represent Lancelot's ancestors and the elder knight himself. He will be received into paradise in the end if he trusts in God, accepts responsibility for his own salvation, rather than depending on his son's merits, and prays fervently that he may again become a true son of God. Lancelot willingly accepts the humble meal and hard bed provided for him in the hermitage and is now ready for further revelations of a supernatural kind, including a symbolic tournament between earthly and heavenly knights on the quest of the Holy Grail. At his request, a recluse explains the significance of this tournament which is intended to remind him, since he is now following the right path, not to return to his sinful ways. As he rides on his journey, he prays fervently, until he reaches the Eau Marcoise where he meets a strange, black knight who kills his horse. Lancelot accepts this new misfortune without complaint:

'puis qu'il plest a Nostre Seignor' (p. 146, ll. 11–12).

As he waits in this lonely and desolate place, surrounded by high cliffs, the forest and the dark, deep water in front of him, he prays for divine protection. In reality, he has reached the turning-point on his journey – a sort of purgatory from which he is about to be released. He falls asleep and in his sleep hears a voice telling him to take up his arms and enter the first boat he finds. He opens his eyes and sees a bright light which reveals a boat immediately appearing on the dark water. Entering it, he is aware of delicious scents and of such a feeling of joy that he believes he is already:

'en paradis terrestre' (p. 247, l. 10).

Full of happiness and confidence, he falls asleep on board, and on awaking next morning he discovers the body of the saintly maiden, Perceval's sister, whose identity is revealed to him in a document about her life and death. This document also contains information about Galaad and his companions, Perceval and Bohort, and Lancelot is delighted to learn that Bohort and Galaad are together. He prays that he too may rejoin the Good Knight before the end of the quest. The peace and happiness that Lancelot experiences on the boat are increased when an old anchorite from a chapel on a tiny island comes to tell him that if he lives virtuously he will at last reach the house he longs to enter; and as the old man leaves him, he addresses Lancelot as: 'serjanz Jhesucrist' (p. 249, l. 15), indicating that he is no longer to be regarded as a disloyal and unprofitable servant. Moreover, he is about to be rewarded by Galaad's company for a time. The old man asks that Galaad be requested to pray for him.

Lancelot also is nourished during his strange voyage on the boat by heavenly food: 'garni de la grace dou Saint Esperit' (p. 250, l. 1). Filled with hope, he awaits the arrival of his son who spends over six months in Lancelot's company and together they enjoy marvellous adventures when the boat arrives at islands on its mysterious voyage. Galaad's presence is closely linked with the graces bestowed on Lancelot and prepares him for the final stage of his journey. When father and son have to part, a heavenly voice tells them that they will not meet again until the Day of Judgment – a reminder that the just and the unjust will be eternally separated on that day when the questors will receive their ultimate punishment or reward:

> 'ce grant jor espoantable que Nostre Sires rendra a chascun ce qu'il avra deservi: et ce sera au jor del Juise' (p. 252, ll. 19–20).

After Galaad's departure, the boat takes Lancelot to the Grail Castle of Corbenic where he again betrays some of his human weaknesses, such as a certain lack of faith, and an impulsiveness which may, of course, be a form of reaction against his earlier lethargy when the Holy Grail passed in front of him outside the deserted chapel in the forest. At the gates of Corbenic Lancelot fears two lions which seem to guard the entrance and he draws his sword which is at once knocked from his grasp by a fiery hand, while a voice condemns him for his lack of faith. In the castle, he ignores a prohibition, again uttered by a voice from heaven, to enter a room where he can see the Holy Grail resting on a silver table at which a priest is celebrating mass. At the consecration, when Lancelot perceives the figures of the Three Divine Persons being raised up in the celebrant's hands in the host, for the elevation, he attempts to approach the altar to support the burden the priest seems to raise, but he is immediately struck by a burning wind which sears his face, and he falls to the ground, senseless. His punishment suggests the danger for ordinary mortals to approach sacred things too closely. Lancelot is carried away by unseen hands and lies in a trance-like state for twenty-four days, to the amazement of the people of Corbenic who assume that this is a sign of divine retribution (p. 256, ll. 30–31).

There is, indeed, some ambiguity about his situation, as it appears to represent at once punishment and reward. When he at last awakes from his ecstatic sleep, Lancelot explains that he has enjoyed a vision of heavenly things:

> 'que ma langue nel porroit mie descovrir, ne mes cuers meismes nel porroit penser' (p. 258, ll. 7–8).

He believes, however, that his vision of the mysteries of the supernatural world could have been more complete had it not been for his former sinful state. His appreciation of the Grail's 'secrets' has been hampered by the twenty-four years of his life devoted to sin. Even when he is told that his quest is now over and he need no longer wear his hair-shirt, Lancelot continues to wear it, beneath a pure linen robe, as a sign of contrition. He enjoys the hospitality of the Fisher King for four days and on the fifth day the Holy Grail reappears, as it had done at Camelot, filling all the tables with delicious food.

The wheel has come full circle for Lancelot who has achieved what he set out to find so many months earlier. He must now return to Arthur's court where he is welcomed with great joy after such a long absence. But other knights who have returned without success in the quest are ashamed of their failure:

'Et cil qui revenu estoient n'avoient riens fet en la Queste, dont ils ont grant honte' (p. 262, ll. 17–18).

For the three Good Knights who respond wholeheartedly to the call to sanctity – represented by the quest – there is no question of divine punishment, although Perceval and Bohort are tested by various temptations on the journey. It is interesting to note that in the *Queste* Perceval does not bear the burden of guilt for his mother's death or for the unasked question during the Grail procession (as he does in so many other versions of the Grail legend), and his aunt, the recluse, does not condemn him for leaving his mother to seek adventure. He is shown to be a young man of great faith (p. 95, ll. 13–14), and she tells him that he is one of the 'elect' knights who will achieve the quest. Like the Israelites of old, he is fed by the manna which represents divine grace and is a pledge of his eternal salvation. His aunt, however, warns him especially to guard his virginity, and she also reminds him that many unworthy knights were struck dead for their rashness in sitting in the Siège Périlleux. After he has resisted various temptations, Perceval's great reward is a visit from Christ Himself, in the guise of a priest, wearing vestments and a crown of white samite: this heavenly visitor comes to him in a boat draped in white samite to give him spiritual consolation and to explain to Perceval the significance of certain visions he has had (of a serpent, a lion, etc.). He also tells him that the temptations were a means of testing his worthiness to follow the Grail quest. But later, when Perceval is again tempted by the Devil, in the form of a beautiful maiden, and almost yields to her attractions, he wounds himself in the thigh with his sword, as a punishment for his weakness. But when he prays for help, he is again visited by the divine Comforter whose presence heals his wound, and he is strengthened by the grace of the Holy Spirit. Perceval recognises his visitor as the Saviour and makes an act of Faith, declaring that he believes Him to be:

'li Pains vis qui descent des ciex' (p. 115, ll. 11–12).

Like Perceval, Bohort has to conquer certain weaknesses, and an old priest advises him to live an ascetic life, not enjoying any other food except bread and water until he feasts at the table of the Holy Grail. Bohort accepts the advice he is given, goes to confession, receives Holy Communion, and wears a white shirt as a sign of penitence. After many difficult encounters, he meets Perceval and they rejoin Galaad (who, throughout the *Queste*, has been as much the sought-after as the seeker). As they advance together on the last stages of their journey of discovery, the eucharistic theme dominates in their final adventures, largely replacing the earlier emphasis on the sacrament of penance, so that the theology of the entire romance can be seen to move from the purgatorial way to illumination and union. Gradually, as the quest draws to an end, justice and retribution are overshadowed by the eucharistic visions which are part of the Grail revelations promised to the successful questors.

Alone among the Round Table knights, Galaad is not subjected to any temptation or trial, since, as the Perfect Knight, he is so ready to obey God's will and to accomplish his own predestined role that he becomes: 'essentially the tool of providence'.[4] He is the chosen leader and a type of the Redeemer, yet he seems at times a complex human figure, not always understanding the actions he is called upon to perform, although led by angelic messengers and constantly sustained by divine grace. When wielding the Sword of David, Galaad becomes an instrument of God's vengeance on the wicked, yet he also heals the sick, liberates captives, saves Symeu from damnation (p. 264) and re-establishes, as it were, the moral law throughout Logres. He recognises that God has used him to punish evil-doers (since God alone is the Judge of sinners):

'la vanjance n'en est pas nostre a prendre, mes a Celui qui atent tant que li pechierres se connoisse' (p. 231, ll. 1–3).

Nevertheless, his very presence brings joy and healing to those who live in hope of his coming, like King Mordrain who welcomes him as the:

'serjant Dieu, verais chevaliers' (p. 262, l. 30).

The three Good Knights receive special favours, including the grace of final perseverance, but Galaad alone receives the additional gift of being confirmed in grace (i.e. of being sinless in this life), so that for him alone is reserved the supreme revelation of the Grail's 'mysteries'. The Grail appears to the knights at three masses, and they are granted extraordinary visions of supernatural things. The first of these masses takes place in a hermitage to which they are led by a White Stag, accompanied by four lions. The mass of the Holy Spirit is being celebrated and at the moment of consecration the Stag is seen to be transformed into the figure of a man, seated on the altar, while the lions are changed into the symbols of the four Evangelists. The knights also hear a celestial voice speaking of the dogmas of the Incarnation, the Virgin Birth and the Resurrection, and after the mass is over, the priest explains to them that they have been specially privileged, since:

'vos estes cil a qui Nostre Sires a mostrez ses secrez et ses repostailles' (p. 235, ll. 30–31).

Their response is to weep with joy:

'et rendrent graces a Nostre Seignor de ce qu'il lor a ceste chose mostree apertement' (p. 236, ll. 22–4).

---

[4] P. Matarasso, op. cit., p. 68.

At Corbenic they again are present at mass, this time accompanied by nine other chosen knights. The celebrant on this occasion is Josephus, the first Christian bishop, who had been consecrated by Our Lord in the celestial city of Sarras. At the most solemn moment of the liturgy, the figure of a child with a fiery countenance (signifying the presence of the Holy Spirit) is seen coming from heaven, and in the Host the form of a man. The attitude of Galaad and his companions to these marvellous happenings is in sharp contrast to Lancelot's reaction to his Trinitarian vision in the Grail Castle. They display the greatest reverence as they are told by Josephus that they are about to receive the highest reward possible – Holy Communion from the hand of Christ:

> 'le plus haut loier que onques chevalier receussent' (p. 269, l. 31).

As the twelve apostles first received the Eucharist at the Last Supper, so the knights are to be given the celestial food which they have desired so much. Then Christ replaces Josephus and addresses those present as:

> 'Mi chevalier et mi serjant et mi loial fil, qui en mortel vie estes devenu esperitel, qui m'avez tant quis que je ne me puis plus vers vos celer, il covient que vos veoiz partie de mes repostailles et de mes secrez . . . Or tenez et recevez la haute viande que vos avez si lonc tens desiree, et por quoi vos estes tant travaillez' (p. 270, ll. 5–9, 14–16).

Just as in the code of chivalry fame and true love must be merited by suffering and effort, so, in the *Queste*, the love of God requires a single-minded devotion, and this devotion is now recompensed. The three Good Knights, with their companions, are made aware of the Real Presence in an extraordinary way and perceive 'la vraie semblance' (p. 16, ll. 17–18) which they have been seeking in their quest of the Grail.

The supreme revelation, however, is reserved for Galaad in Sarras,[5] after he has been made king, following a year's imprisonment by the unjust King Escorant (perhaps a figure of Antichrist). Galaad and his two friends have accompanied the Grail to Sarras and been sustained by its food during their imprisonment. They build a Spiritual Palace as a shrine for the Holy Vessel, and Josephus again appears from heaven, surrounded by angels, to celebrate the mass of Our Lady. At the consecration, Josephus invites Galaad to look into the chalice (which is the Grail) and the Good Knight thanks God for permitting him to see at last what he has longed for yet what is beyond the power of man to comprehend or describe:

> 'car ore voi ge tot apertement ce que langue ne porroit descrire ne cuer penser' (p. 278, ll. 4–5).

[5] Sarras is the Celestial City, described by St Paul:

> 'What you have come to is Mount Sion and the city of the living God, the heavenly Jerusalem, to God Himself, the Supreme Judge, and been placed with spirits of the just who have been made perfect: and to Jesus, the mediator of the New Testament' (*Hebrews*, 12:18–19, 22–4).

Galaad's vision is of a purely spiritual nature: forms and symbols are no longer necessary, for this is the '*visio dei*', the reward of the Blessed in heaven. After receiving Holy Communion and saying farewell to Bohort and Perceval (with a message of greeting to his father), he no longer wishes to survive such an experience and dies in front of the altar. At once, the Holy Grail, with the lance, is removed by a hand from heaven and disappears forever from the world.

The knowledge revealed to the questors who reach their goal is not of an intellectual kind but is a form of illumination and, in Galaad's case,

> 'analogous to the Beatific Vision'.[6]

It is:

> 'la vision qui reste ineffable, la connaissance qui est donnée à l'amour et non à la seule intelligence'.[7]

---

[6] F. W. Locke, *The Quest for the Holy Grail*, Stanford, California: Stanford University Press, 1960, p. 101.

[7] *La Quête du Graal*. Edition présentée et établie par Albert Béguin et Yves Bonnefoy, Paris: Seuil, 1965, p. 36. cf. also, Fanni Bogdanow, 'An Interpretation of the Meaning and Purpose of the Vulgate *Queste del Saint Graal*', in *The Changing Face of Arthurian Romance*, Cambridge: D. S. Brewer, The Boydell Press, 1986, p. 32.

## Reward and Punishment in Chrétien's Erec and Related Texts

### D. D. R. OWEN

Like most romance plots, that of the Erec legend could be envisaged as a series of acts, rarely gratuitous but each having either a positive or a negative value and hence inviting some form of reward or punishment for its perpetrator or working less directly for or against the interests of the main characters. For the hero the positive eventually outweighs the negative to produce the characteristic happy ending. Thus Erec might be seen as performing a service for which he is indirectly rewarded with a bride of surpassing beauty. His recreance as a married knight demands a period of atonement or self-punishment, from which he emerges with his chivalric merit re-established, to be rewarded in actual and symbolic terms by his coronation as a model king. Within this overall scheme, individual episodes could be construed as embodying the reward/punishment principle. As a generalisation, however, it conceals many subtle variations; and this clearly appears when one considers the different versions of the story as found in the Welsh *Gereint vab Erbin*, Chrétien's *Erec et Enide* and Hartmann's *Erec*.[1]

In following our theme through these texts, we shall find in the presentation of what are basically the same events striking differences suggestive of dissimilar authorial outlooks as well as different attitudes to the narrative art. Some of the evidence presented could serve in the debate on the relationships between the works. Without myself using it for this purpose, I may say in passing that none of it shakes my belief in a source common to *Gereint* and Chrétien's *Erec* or leads me to suppose that Hartmann must have known such a source. I should add that my discussion of elements, by proceeding from the Welsh version to Chrétien and then to Hartmann, may convey the impression that Chrétien has transformed relatively simple features by the application of

---

[1] For *Gereint* see *Llyfr Gwyn Rhydderch*, ed. by Gwenogvryn Evans, Pwllheli, 1907, reprinted with introduction by R. M. Jones, Cardiff, 1973, pp. 193–226; I have used the translations by Gwyn Jones and Thomas Jones, London: Everyman, 1949, and by Jeffrey Gantz, London: Penguin Books, 1976. Christian von Troyes, *Erec und Enide*, ed. by Wendelin Foerster, Halle: Niemeyer (*Christian von Troyes Sämtliche Werke*, III), 1890. Hartmann von Aue, *Erec*, ed. and translated by Thomas Cramer, Frankfurt am Main: Fischer, 1972.

sophisticated narrative techniques which Hartmann, in his rehandling of the material, has in some cases subverted. I am aware that this confers on Chrétien a privileged position by concentrating on his skills and doing less than justice to the different but real merits of the other works. These, however, I must leave to others to assess without myself pretending to offer overall value-judgements.

*The sparrow-hawk contest*

In all three texts the hero rides off in pursuit of a knight to take vengeance on him for having allowed his dwarf to strike him after insulting the Queen by similarly attacking her maiden. The gentleman who gives the hero lodging tells of the forthcoming challenge for the sparrow-hawk.

In *Gereint* any challenger must attend with the lady he loves best in order to joust for the hawk with its present 'holder'. Edern, the offensive knight, has won it for two years; and a third success would entitle him to be known as the Knight of the Sparrow-hawk. Gereint says Enid should take the bird, since she is more beautiful, finer and nobler than Edern's lady. In a fluctuating combat it is only when Gereint's host reminds him of the dwarf's outrage that he vanquishes Edern. Once the latter begs for mercy, Gereint declares himself satisfied; but Edern must go to make amends to the Queen. So the contest has been essentially a test of strength between two knights; and for the victor it has also been the means of exacting punishment for an affront.

Chrétien describes the contest rather differently. The challenger must claim the hawk on behalf of a lady on the grounds that she is not only virtuous but also the most beautiful of all. The combat is engaged after Yder and Erec have each declared his own companion's beauty to be supreme, the bystanders having already given their verdict in favour of Enide. When the knights rest, exhausted, in mid-fight, Erec's spirits are revived by his awareness of Enide's love and beauty; and only then is his anger rekindled by thoughts of revenge. On getting the upper hand, Erec would have cut off Yder's head, had he not pleaded for mercy. As it is, he must go to surrender to the Queen; and this he does, paying tribute to Enide's surpassing beauty. When Enide is back with Erec in her father's home, we see her happily feeding the hawk on her wrist; and later, on the ride to Arthur's court, she plays with the bird, the only precious thing she took with her.

Central to Chrétien's art is his selection and dexterous manipulation of themes, which he develops throughout his romances.[2] In *Erec* an outstanding example is that of physical beauty, exemplified in the hero himself and even in

---

[2] Cf. my comments in 'Theme and Variations: Sexual Aggression in Chrétien de Troyes', *FMLS*, XXI (1985), pp. 376–86.

Count Galoain, but above all, associated with the motifs of silence and dress, in the person of the radiant Enide.[3] Before the sparrow-hawk contest, Chrétien had already begun his exploitation of the beauty theme in the scene at the home of the vavasour. Now he continues and intensifies it by making of what in *Gereint* was a test of chivalric prowess a clearly defined beauty contest, with the symbolic prize being retained by the maiden: in the Welsh there was no indication of its destination.

Hartmann preserves the nature of the duel as a beauty contest, though not with quite the same insistence as in Chrétien. Indeed he rather detracts from its validity as a fair competition by showing that Ider had won the hawk for the past two years by sheer intimidation, though it was generally held that there were many ladies fairer than his own. So when Erec tells him that he holds the bird unjustly and that it is his intention to show by combat that Enite is more beautiful than his own *vriundîn*, the demonstration will be of only her relative and not her absolute beauty. The emphasis is thus slightly shifted from Enite's beauty to Erec's prowess; and rather more stress on the idea of revenge[4] has the same effect, notably when Erec's vigour is restored during the fight first by his thoughts of vengeance and only then by the sight of Enite. Hartmann, one might think, is more interested in the flow of his narrative than in the meticulous development of themes. One had already suspected this when he unnecessarily put direct speech into Enite's mouth (l. 322), flawing the presentation of her as pure vision as well as lessening the impact of her later fateful words, the first we hear her utter in Chrétien's romance. Then, by omitting the mention of Enite's toying with her sparrow-hawk on the ride, he robs a scene focusing on the silent contemplation of beauty of the prize for and very symbol of that beauty.

It could be argued that whereas Chrétien concentrated on the reward aspect of the episode it was revenge and punishment that more interested Hartmann and received from him some degree of thematic development. Feeling, perhaps, that the dwarf had escaped his just deserts, he made the victorious Erec threaten to lop off his hand before having him soundly drubbed by two servants. His master, though, is generously treated in all three texts. In *Gereint* Edern tells his story to the Queen and then to Arthur, who suggests that she should pardon him and that thereafter, should he recover from his wounds, the men of the court might decide what amends he must make. In the event Gereint himself forgives him and takes him with him to his own land. In Chrétien's *Erec* Guenevere tells Yder he will get off lightly, but it is the King who asks her to release him on condition that he join his court.

---

[3] Cf. Glyn S. Burgess, 'The Theme of Beauty in Chrétien's *Philomena* and *Erec et Enide*', in *An Arthurian Tapestry: Essays in Memory of Lewis Thorpe*, ed. by Kenneth Varty, Glasgow: French Department, 1981, pp. 114–28. See also his *Chrétien de Troyes: Erec et Enide*, London: Grant & Cutler (Critical Guides to French Texts), 1984.

[4] See ll. 136, 491, 928–34, 1037–8, 1130–5.

More appropriately, perhaps, Hartmann accepts Chrétien's resolution of the affair, but with the Queen as the sole arbiter. The outcome in each case might be thought eminently civilised.[5]

*The reward of the stag*

An examination of this episode yields conclusions similar to those prompted by the sparrow-hawk adventure: what in the Welsh was little more than a *fait divers* is harnessed by Chrétien to a leading theme with an enhanced symbolic function, which is retained by Hartmann with its focus slightly less sharp.

In *Gereint* the hunting of the white stag is a single, chance occurrence. At Gwalchmei's suggestion, its head is to be presented by the man who takes it to either his own or a companion's beloved. When Arthur is the successful huntsman, his courtiers bicker as to who should be the recipient of the head; and the Queen suggests a postponement of the decision until Gereint's return.

Chrétien presents the hunt as a custom which is to be worthily revived. Moreover, like the sparrow-hawk combat, it is associated with a test of beauty since, as Gauvain points out, the stag's slayer must kiss the fairest maiden at court. That, says Gauvain, could lead to trouble, as indeed it does when the King takes the stag. He seeks advice; but at Guenevere's suggestion, the choice is put off to await Erec's return.

Hartmann's opening is missing; but later developments show that it must have been similar to Chrétien's. He too makes the Queen request the postponement of the kiss, though not (as implied in the Welsh and French versions) to defuse a difficult situation, but simply because she would like Erec to be there when it is bestowed. Not only is this motivation rather weak, but it also has the effect of playing down the idea of competition for the kiss. Indeed at this point Hartmann states that the duty of the King now is to kiss whichever of the maidens he chooses: the 'beauty contest' aspect appears only later in the surviving text.

In the Welsh, the Queen proposes that the stag's head be bestowed on Enid, since she is the maiden of the greatest renown. The court approves, Arthur complies, and Enid's fame is thereby increased. One finds here some slight competitive element, though it is unrelated to the girl's beauty. Chrétien, however, has Guenevere suggest that Arthur should give Enide the kiss since she is the fairest maiden not only at the court but in the whole world. Arthur's reaction is to put the proposal to his lords, calling in a

---

[5] It is interesting to find Chrétien providing a sharp contrast in *Cligés* where, under the influence of the epic and surely with this episode in mind, he made a vengeful Arthur insist that the reluctant Guenevere hand over prisoners for execution.

stuffily legalistic fashion for any objections to be made known, for it is his duty to safeguard justice and the right. Needless to say, his motion gains unanimous support, and with due ceremony he bestows the kiss. In contrast Hartmann's Arthur, thinking it time to exercise his right, promptly gives the kiss to Enite on account of her surpassing beauty, there being no objections.

Once again, then, Chrétien has manipulated what one may suppose to have been a straightforward narrative element in his source in order to make it serve as reinforcement for the principal theme of the first part of his romance, that of Enide's unrivalled beauty. By investing the reward of the kiss with such pomp and circumstance and having the King confirm with his barons the justice of his act, he comes close to giving it the blessing of divine approval, just as the combat for the sparrow-hawk had taken on the appearance of an 'unofficial' *iudicium Dei*. Nothing of this is present in *Gereint*, and even Hartmann's version lacks the rigorous consistency of the French.[6]

## The second quest

Many scholarly pages have treated the nature of and motivation for the hero's ill-tempered ride with his wife in search of adventure, the so-called 'second quest'. I shall follow the pair through to their reconciliation in an attempt to determine what part, if any, is played by the idea of punishment in this period of estrangement. Once more we shall discover significant differences in our three texts.

In the Welsh story, Gereint, after his marriage, runs out of worthy opponents and lets his chivalry lapse. His father asks Enid if she is responsible; and in bed one morning she bewails this possibility in words which Gereint hears. The thought strikes him that she is in love with someone else; and he reacts by ordering her to don her worst dress to go riding: she will soon discover if he has lost his strength, as she seems to believe, and if she will find pleasure in infidelity. Gereint's motives seem uncomplicated: he wishes to punish Enid for doubting his prowess and for contemplating infidelity; and part of her penance is to wear her worst dress as a sign of shame.

---

[6] An interesting variation on the stag hunt theme is found in Guillaume le Clerc's *Fergus*, which contains a good deal of burlesque and depends for much of its humour on a previous knowledge of Chrétien's romances and the *Perceval* Continuations. As in the *Second Continuation*, Perceval is the hero of the hunt, which is initiated by Arthur, who offers a gold cup to the taker of the white stag. After a long chase, Perceval's hound catches and drowns the quarry, whereupon Perceval proudly sounds the kill on his horn. Having been rewarded with the cup by Arthur, he at once hands it over to Gauvain. One reflects with amusement that the custom in *Erec* was for the taker of the stag to honour with the 'prize' the most beautiful maiden at court. That Gauvain should be the recipient now prompts a smile, especially in view of his own taste for feminine beauty; and that Guillaume should have had this irony in mind is suggested by the fact that elsewhere in his romance we find Gauvain playing a quasi-female role, not least when Fergus is seen lavishing on him more affection than on his newly won bride.

As they ride, she must keep well ahead of him and not speak or turn back. Having sighted four robber knights, she thinks Gereint may well kill her if she disobeys him. When she does in fact speak, he shows no gratitude but asserts that she would like to see him dead (reminding us of his suspicions of her unfaithfulness). She must take charge of the horses of the vanquished knights and will be punished if she speaks again. Two further marauding bands are encountered, with similar consequences: Enid gives her husband a warning which he scorns, saying she may yet repent it. His anger leaves him indifferent to the trouble she has in managing the twelve captured horses, which he orders her to guard throughout the night while he sleeps. On their arrival in the town of an amorous earl, Gereint tells Enid to keep apart from him in their lodging; and when she informs him of the earl's intentions, he shows his usual anger. She still has to ride ahead after the earl is defeated. The noble dwarf Gwiffred Petit, after his combat with Gereint, offers the couple hospitality, touched in particular by Enid's wretched state; but Gereint rejects the prospect of rest and recuperation. When, shortly afterwards, they are discovered and detained by Arthur and his retinue, the King asks Enid the reason for this journey; and she replies that she does not know. When it is resumed, she is instructed to ride ahead and keep her distance as before. So Gereint's harsh attitude remains constant until the very moment of reconciliation at the earl Limwris' castle, when he regains consciousness and is struck by pity at Enid's wretched appearance. Then he realises that the right is on her side; and, with his suspicions allayed, his unjustified punishment of his wife is at an end.

In Gereint's eyes Enid appears as the sole offender: there is no indication of his knowing that the complaints concerning his recreance originated with his men and his father. His own conscience, one assumes, was clear, since he had secured his reputation and no longer found opponents worthy of his mettle in the lists. Moreover, suspecting Enid of infidelity, he has a double motive for inflicting on her what can only be thought of as the punishment of the ride. His behaviour towards her appears to become only marginally less harsh before his sudden realisation of her innocence. As for Enid herself, we gain little insight into her secret thoughts: she seems merely the puzzled victim of circumstances.

Matters in Chrétien's *Erec* are far more complex. Erec becomes recreant through love alone and not, so far as we are told, because of a lack of worthy opposition on the tournament circuit. When Enide hears general criticism of his behaviour, she is distressed, but dares not tell him of it, because he would be quick to take offence (ll. 2469–72). Indeed, she blames herself for bringing shame on him. When Erec is wakened by her lament, or at least by the words 'Con mar i fus!' (l. 2507), he asks her the reason; but in her alarm she dissembles. Up to this point he has addressed her tenderly; and as if to advise us that Erec harbours no thoughts of her infidelity, Chrétien makes him say: 'Por moi fu dit, non por autrui' (l. 2522). After her prevarication, however, his tone becomes harsh. She confesses the reason for her grief, adding that he must answer the criticism by regaining his former reputation. Erec appears to agree:

> 'Dame', fet il, 'droit an eüstes,
> Et cil qui m'an blasment ont droit.' (ll. 2576-7)

When he then tells her to prepare to go riding, she concludes that she is to be banished for her presumption in uttering *la parole*. Erec refuses to tell his father the purpose of his journey, but does beg him to love and cherish Enide and give her half his land, should she return alone.

Chrétien never clarifies Erec's motives for us, though near the end of the romance he playfully claims to have done so (ll. 6478-82). However, at this point there seems to be no question of punishment in Erec's mind: his request to his father shows that he still loves Enide; and he has, after all, conceded to her that she was right. He orders her to wear her finest dress; and when he tells her to ride ahead and keep quiet, he adds that she will be quite safe (l. 2775). But this is not how Enide sees things: Erec, she laments, has conceived a hatred for her. As she is immersed in these thoughts, she sees three robber knights approaching and warns her husband. She shall be pardoned this once, says Erec, but not again. When a second band of marauders appears, Erec sees them but pretends not to, whereupon Enide calls another warning. Once more Erec forgives her, but declares that he hates her all the more for this unwanted service. As we now know that there is an element of dissembling in his behaviour, we are less inclined to believe his words. He seems to be wanting to see Enide's reactions, to test her feelings for him, perhaps, but hardly to punish her. Indeed, he again shows for her a consideration foreign to Gereint when night falls and he orders her to sleep while he keeps watch. Her objection that it is he who needs the rest pleases him: 'Erec l'otroie, et bel li fu' (l. 3095). Enide, though, continues to blame herself for her *parole*, and muses that she has not suffered half what she deserves.

I shall return to the Galoain episode; but we may notice now that we are not shown Erec telling Enide to keep her distance in their lodging, though the amorous count does find them sitting apart (they are not at table). When Enide discloses the count's plot, she is not rebuked, but Erec recognises her loyalty:

> Or ot Erec que bien se prueve
> Vers lui sa fame leaument. (ll. 3486-7)

Later, however, her warning of the count's approach does bring a threat of punishment – 'unless I change my mind', says Erec (l. 3570). The cloud over their relationship seems less dark, though still not so in Enide's mind. When, after a battle with her conscience, she warns Erec of Guivret's proximity, he again makes a show of threatening her,

> Mes n'a talant que mal li face;
> Qu'il aparçoit et conoist bien
> Qu'ele l'aimme sor tote rien,
> Et il li tant que plus ne puet. (ll. 3767-9)

If Chrétien has been testing Enide in some way (and it seems that he has), he has no further reason to do so. During their encounter with Arthur and his company we are given no indication of any overt tension remaining between them: they sleep in adjacent beds (Erec being gravely wounded); and when they resume their ride, Chrétien does not say that Enide proceeds ahead. She, however, is still far from easy in her mind, as is obvious when, thinking Erec dead, she heaps the blame on herself, declaring in her lament that she is guilty of his murder through her *parole* and wishing to expiate her crime through suicide. The Limors adventure, though, sees the cloud finally dispersed for both of them. As Erec carries Enide away on his horse, he tells her he has put her completely to the proof (not punished her), loves her now more than ever and is certain of her own perfect love. He will be hers to command, as before;

> 'Et se vos rien m'avez mesdite,
> Je le vos pardoing et claim quite
> Del forfet et de la parole.' (ll. 4927-9)

So if Enide has ever wronged him (and Erec leaves it as only a possibility), it has been solely in her speech.

Hartmann follows Chrétien's account of Erec's recreance in its general outline, but adds vivid details. It is for fear of losing him that Enite does not tell him of the criticism he is incurring. Her prevarication and eventual explanation are handled more briefly, but we are told that she informs Erec of the situation only on condition that he would not be angry with her. His subsequent conduct is poor evidence of his keeping his promise; and when Enite trustingly explains matters, his response, 'der ist genuoc getân' (l. 3052), is very cryptic. His treatment of his wife is in fact harsher than in Chrétien. He makes no provision for her should she return alone and gives her no reassurance regarding her safety on the ride. His warnings to her must be obeyed on pain of death ('bî dem lîbe', l. 3095 etc.); and rebuking her after his fight with the first robber band, he says she will suffer for her typically feminine disobedience. When Enite begs his forgiveness, he agrees to let her go unpunished ('ungerochen', l. 3267) just this once, though without letting her off scot free, since she must look after the captured horses as a servant ('knehte', l. 3275). All this is repeated after the second encounter with marauders. Then, at the beginning of the episode of the amorous count, an almost vindictive note intrudes when, after Erec has presented one horse to the count's squire, Hartmann assures us that he would have given them all but for the fact that it would have made Enite's life easier. Erec, indeed, refuses the squire's kind offer to relieve her of the burden of leading them. One notes too that Hartmann has omitted the scene of the overnight bivouac, which Chrétien used not only to show Enide's selfless service to her husband but also to introduce a further hint of Erec's enduring consideration for her.

When the couple are lodging in the count's town, it is clear in Hartmann but not in Chrétien that Erec has placed his wife away from him as they sit at table. When asked the reason by the count, Erec replies with a surly: 'herre, mîn gemüete stât alsô' (l. 3745). Later he orders their beds to be set apart too, and Hartmann comments on the wrath that has brought him to this strange conduct. During their escape from the castle, Erec reproves Enite for having warned him of the count's designs (in Chrétien it is only for alerting him to the approach of their pursuers) and again says she will pay with her life for further disobedience.

After a lacuna at the beginning of the Guivreiz episode come the lines:

> dô er den strît niuwen vant,
> dô wart im aber ir triuwe erkant.     (ll. 4318–19)

This is the point at which Chrétien tells us that Erec recognises the extent of Enide's love and of his own. It was after her disclosure of the count's plot that we were told he had evidence of her loyalty. Hartmann, it seems, is reluctant at this stage to give any hint of tenderness on Erec's part: on the other hand, we find no further suggestion of tension between him and Enite; and although they are separated when they are lodged in Arthur's camp, this is not at Erec's request. It is true that in her lament on thinking Erec dead Enite does speak as though they are estranged for some reason unknown to her, though her 'klagenden sûft' (l. 5951) had brought matters to a head. At Limors, however, Erec takes her by the hand; and as they ride away their reconciliation is complete. We learn, though not directly from Erec, the reason for his behaviour:

> ez was durch versuochen getân
> ob si im wære ein rehtez wîp.     (ll. 6781–2)

He has now assayed her as gold in a furnace and found her loyal and constant, possessing 'triuwe unde stæte' (l. 6789). He kisses her and asks her forgiveness for their estrangement and the tribulations of the journey. She does pardon him at once, but admits she could have borne it no longer.

In Hartmann's version we find rather less psychological shading than with Chrétien. Yet he touchingly develops Enite's exemplary love and *triuwe* despite her apparent puzzlement over Erec's treatment of her: his motive, Hartmann assures us, was to test Enite's qualities as a wife. Her fidelity is fully established, not that Erec ever seems to have doubted it; but there is no suggestion that, like Chrétien's hero, he is consciously putting to the test the depth of her love. A grimmer character than his French counterpart, he shows none of the latter's consideration for his wife; and his threats do not have the ring of mere pretence. On the contrary, having apparently promised not to be angry with her, he shows himself intent on her punishment and almost vindictive in its pursuit. In this he is a more transparent character than Chrétien's Erec, with the result that his relations with Enite appear more straightforward. Whereas with Chrétien we feel that throughout the ride the couple's relationship, though strained on the surface, is persisting at a deeper level, with hints of concealed tenderness on Erec's part, with Hartmann we sense that a gulf has opened between them, to be bridged only at the final reconciliation.

Reviewing the handling of the 'second quest' in our three texts, we again find significant differences in treatment. *Gereint* presents a simple tale of male vanity and suspicion leading to an unjustified punishment and the final realisation of the innocent truth. Gereint's suspicions of Enid's infidelity are reflected in the worst clothes he makes her wear. Chrétien, typically, is less straightforward, leaving his public with a situation open to various interpretations. For me his choice of Enide's finest dress for the ride shows the theme of her beauty still uppermost in his mind. On learning that there is talk of his being ensnared by his wife, Erec accepts the justice of the belief and determines to prove to himself as well as others that he can maintain his prowess with Enide at her most radiant, the source of his temptation, constantly in view. He perhaps feels that through his lapse from chivalry he may have forfeited his right to her love and that he must therefore put that too to the proof. Yet he is examining himself more than her. For him the whole experience has been salutary; and far from pardoning Enide for her disclosure, he should have thanked her. He has certainly entertained no thoughts of punishing her, though she herself misconstrued his purpose.

If this was in fact Chrétien's view of things, it was not Hartmann's. I see his Erec as a knight whose vanity is, initially at least, bruised as much as his conscience, and who vents his spleen by punishing Enite for a fault of which she is only vaguely aware. Eventually, realising he has behaved unjustly, he apologises with some unconvincing talk of having tested her loyalty. If one sees his conduct in this light, and since in the Joie de la Cort episode he will show an awareness of past failings remedied, one may conclude that, whereas Chrétien's hero was prompt to perceive and acknowledge his own fault, in the German work the lesson was learnt only after a period of trials and self-discovery. In this section, too, Hartmann has diverged from his model by showing less concern than Chrétien for a studious exploitation of the beauty theme. On the other hand, he exhibits a more evident moral awareness than the French poet, and as a result the motivation of his principal characters is more exemplary and less individualistic or, indeed, enigmatic.

## The amorous lord

Having treated some aspects of this episode in the last section, I shall look here at the behaviour and fate of the lord himself, and in particular consider the extent to which each text treats his defeat by the hero as punishment for his treachery.

In *Gereint* the earl shows courtesy towards the travellers. Then seeing, as he remarks to Gereint, that he and his companion are estranged, he proposes privately to Enid that she remain with him. When she refuses, he obliquely threatens to kill Gereint; and this secures her feigned agreement. There is an element of treachery here, but it is not stressed; and the vanquished earl's plea for mercy is readily granted. His defeat is not depicted explicitly as a punishment for his disreputable conduct.

Count Galoain, in the French romance, appears initially as a generous person. Then, although Erec and Enide are not obviously estranged, he seems genuinely to pity Enide for her lowly condition and the fact that she is not enjoying her husband's affection. However, when she rejects his advances as very wrongful, he becomes aggressive and threatens to kill Erec before her very eyes. At the end of the episode, Erec, having felled him from his horse, immediately rides off. Galoain's men want to give chase, but he forbids them to do so. His own action, he says, was criminal:

> 'Bien m'an devoit maus avenir.
> Sor moi an est venuz li maus.
> Que fel feisoie et desleaus
> Et traïtres et forsenez!'     (ll. 3648–51)

He accepts his defeat, then, as a fully merited punishment for his villainy.

Without condoning the count's behaviour, Hartmann does provide him with some partial excuses. In fact he will never admit his guilt; nor will he be pardoned by Erec. Hartmann insists that it was wicked of him to think of taking Enite from Erec; yet before he was robbed of his reason by love, 'we have heard' that he was a good and righteous man. He receives from Erec an evasive answer when he asks if Enite is his wife. Then, in conversation with her, he sympathises with her over her situation and says of Erec: 'er hât iuch zeinem knehte' (l. 3773). In reply to his offer of marriage, Enite claims to be unworthy: she is better suited to her companion ('geselle', l. 3811), since neither of them is rich. After the count has threatened to take her by force, though without threatening Erec's life, she states that she had been abducted from her family, only to be kept as his wife in this wretched state: may God reward anyone who frees her from it! Having taken an equivocal oath of loyalty (without specifying to whom), she proposes to steal Erec's sword during the night, so that the count may take her in the morning. When he arrives with that intention only to find them both gone, he blames himself for having overslept, adding that whoever thinks merely of his own comfort deserves to lose his honour in disgrace. Having come up with the fugitives, he threatens to slay Erec as an abductor (he would hang him were he not a knight) unless he release Enite, whom he says he will then return to her family. However laudable this may sound, when he is gravely wounded by Erec, Hartmann comments: 'sô genôz er sîner untriuwen' (l. 4257).

In each of our texts the lord has his good qualities, but they are negated by his lust. *Gereint* as usual offers the simplest version. There is no dwelling on moral issues, on crime and punishment: the earl's plot is foiled, and he is vanquished and pardoned. The conduct of Galoain, in Chrétien's romance, is the most despicable, since there is no obvious rift between the two travellers, whom he knows to be husband and wife. He is spared, but not explicitly pardoned, by Erec. However, he himself recognises his crime for what it is, and in an act of contrition accepts his defeat as rightful punishment. Enide's beauty, he says, fired him with love and inspired his treachery. Thus Chrétien continues to develop his leading theme by making beauty alone generate the action. Hartmann, by contrast, while accepting lust engendered by beauty as the prime motivator and never disguising the criminality of the count's intentions, does considerably add to the mitigating circumstances, especially with Enite's tale of abduction, her hint that God will reward her rescuer, and her equivocal oath. Although Hartmann does say, almost as an afterthought, that the count paid for his treachery, he seems at least as interested in the continuing rift between Erec and Enite. Especially intriguing is the count's declaration that sloth quite properly brings disgrace. We think back to Erec's recreance and wonder if we should see here a hint that Hartmann sees him too as suffering his rightful deserts, and the 'second quest' as being a punishment for him as well as Enite.

*The Joie de la Cort*

To claim that this adventure offers examples of reward and punishment is to stretch one's definitions a little. In *Gereint* it represents a test of valour; and the blowing of the horn signals the end of the earl's 'enchanted games', which he would in any case have abolished had Gereint made the request. For the heroes of Chrétien's and Hartmann's romances to sound the horn means that they have won supreme chivalric honour and brought joy to the whole court—a reward of sorts for them; but can it be construed as a punishment not for the king, who is benevolent enough, but for the knight and his companion who have dwelt so long in the garden? If there is punishment, there must be guilt: who bears the guilt for instituting this grim trial?

Chrétien supplies explanations by both Mabonagrain and his *amie*. Mabonagrain tells of their childhood love and of how the girl asked of him an unspecified boon, the so-called *don contraignant*. He solemnly pledged that he would grant it. When he was knighted, she demanded that he should not leave the garden until he was overcome in combat. His oath bound him to meet all challengers, and his honour forbade him to spare his efforts. Now he will be liberated ('desprisoné', l. 6146) once Erec has blown the horn, which he urges him to do without delay. His *amie*'s account is subtly different: they loved as children and formed mutual wishes and pacts until he swore he would bring her here; and this he did, secretly, to their great satisfaction. Now, however, she makes a show of bitter sorrow, thinking that her lover would not be with her so much, because he would want to leave the garden. Their stories, then, are discrepant. The fact that Mabonagrain seems anxious to be out of the garden, coupled with the initial *don contraignant*, places the balance of responsibility with the girl. But if we think of her present misery as a punishment, then it is quickly over, since both she and Mabonagrain soon participate in the Joy.

A sign that Hartmann's hero has learnt his lesson comes when Erec solemnly criticises Mabonagrin for wishing to shut himself off from society, tied to his 'wip' (l. 9421). Mabonagrin says it was not his choice to live like this; but all his life he would have had to remain thus, had God not delivered him. He tells how he came there with the girl following his willing granting of the boon she asked. Erec's victory has brought shame upon him, but harmlessly, since it has released him from this bond and its cares: now he can go wherever he likes. It has restored joy to the court, because it was his loss that had caused the unhappiness there. His companion, though, was distressed at not being able to remain there with him; but her spirits too were soon raised by Enite.

In neither the French nor the German text is there any insistence on punishment. With Chrétien even the question of guilt is ambiguously handled. As with the 'second quest' the two people concerned see their situation in different lights, and we are given an insight into both the male and the female point of view. Although we are inclined to blame the girl for their clearly reprehensible arrangement, the shattering of her dream of an eternal private paradise is nevertheless as much a disillusionment as a punishment. Hartmann, by omitting her explanation, has again neglected an opportunity to probe a little deeper into feminine psychology, and in this case has sided more positively with the male character.

We have seen in this limited study how the same basic story elements can receive the imprint of widely differing authorial outlooks on such social imperatives as merit and guilt, reward and punishment. The Welshman responsible for *Gereint* was more interested in events than in their psychological, ethical or sociological implications. Chrétien appears as a self-conscious literary craftsman, selecting certain elements of his story to develop as themes: in this case the idea of physical beauty has provided a constant, unifying thread. At the same time he reveals something of his own character, marked by a magnanimity that stems from a true understanding of the dilemmas of his characters. Surprisingly advanced for his day in his grasp of feminine psychology, he has explored the way in which events may be viewed differently by the two sexes. Hartmann shows other interests, other virtues. While following Chrétien in the main developments of the story, he has appeared less concerned with the manipulation of themes, blurring at times the sharp focus of his model. A less tolerant individual, one might suppose, or at least more dedicated to the exposition and illustration of moral principles,[7] he seems to have had a particular relish for punishment and a less sensitive appreciation than Chrétien of some of the finer points of human and especially feminine motivation. Each work has its particular merits; and these a comparative study may help to define and sometimes even disclose, thereby bringing its own ample reward.[8]

---

[7] For a recent discussion of the moral and Christian dimension of Hartmann's adaptation see René Pérennec, *Recherches sur le roman arthurien en vers en Allemagne aux XII$^e$ et XIII$^e$ siècles*, Göppingen: Kümmerle (Göppinger Arbeiten zur Germanistik), 1984, Vol. I, Ch. II. See also the comparative study in Hartmann von Aue, *Erec*, übersetzt und erläutert von Wolfgang Mohr, Göppingen: Kümmerle (Göppinger Arbeiten zur Germanistik), 1980.

[8] I acknowledge with gratitude the advice on Hartmann's *Erec* given me by my colleagues Dr J. R. Ashcroft and Dr W. H. Jackson. For my conclusions, however, I bear the sole responsibility.

## *Le Châtiment et la Mise à l'Épreuve du Jeune Lancelot*

### MICHEL ROUSSE

L'éducation des enfants est un domaine où les notions de châtiment et de récompense trouvent à s'appliquer de façon privilégiée. J'ai donc voulu relire à la lumière de ce thème les pages que le *Lancelot en prose* consacre à la jeunesse du héros auprès de la Dame du Lac, en particulier le chapitre IX,[1] qui a déjà attiré maintes fois l'attention et suscité des commentaires d'une pertinence et d'une sagacité exemplaires.[2] Au centre de cet épisode figure en effet le châtiment que le maître veut infliger à Lancelot en lui donnant d'abord un terrible soufflet, puis en frappant d'un bâton le lévrier qu'il avait reçu en cadeau. Ce châtiment provoque la révolte de l'enfant et va l'amener de plus à remettre en question le principe même de l'éducation par un maître.

L'importance de cet épisode est soulignée dans l'écriture même du roman. Car il marque un tournant dans la façon dont l'auteur désigne son héros.

Lorsque débute le roman, l'auteur nous dit en effet que le fils du roi Ban a reçu le nom de Galaad en baptême, et que Lancelot est son 'sournon'. Mais il s'agit du chapitre liminaire qui met en place la dénomination et la situation des différents personnages. Lorsqu'ensuite l'action s'engage, le nom de Lancelot est rarement utilisé. Jusqu'à l'épisode de sa révolte contre son maître, il est presque constamment désigné par l'appellation 'l'enfant'. C'est ainsi qu'il est mentionné lorsque le roi Ban quitte son château assiégé pour tenter de gagner la cour du roi Arthur: un écuyer porte 'l'enfant' devant lui dans un berceau (p. 10) et quand le cheval du roi Ban revient seul, l'écuyer 'met l'enfant a terre' (p. 25) pour aller voir ce qui est advenu à son maître; mais dans cet épisode, Lancelot n'existe encore que par son rapport au roi, son

---

[1] *Lancelot. Roman en prose du XIII<sup>e</sup> siècle*, édition critique par Alexandre Micha, tome VII, Paris-Genève: Droz, 1980, pp. 70–86. Dans la suite de cet article, les références données à la fin des citations renvoient aux pages de cette édition.

[2] Citons en particulier les articles suivants: Alfred Adler, 'The education of Lancelot: Grammar – Gramarye', *BBSIA*, IX (1957), pp. 101–7. Jean Frappier, 'L'institution de Lancelot', in *Mélanges Hoepffner*, Paris: Les Belles Lettres, 1949, pp. 269–78. Micheline de Combarieu, 'Le *Lancelot* comme roman d'apprentissage. Enfance, démesure et chevalerie', in *Approches du 'Lancelot en prose'*, Etudes recueillies par Jean Dufournet, Paris: Champion, 1984, pp. 101–36.

père, ou à la reine, sa mère; et c'est cette relation qui le désigne le plus souvent: l'action se déroule en dehors de lui et concerne essentiellement ses parents; il est le 'fils' dont la dépendance est appuyée de la présence d'un adjectif possessif. 'Et de mon cheitif fil, sire vous remenbre qui est si jones orphenins . . .' (p. 25), prie le roi Ban sur le point de mourir. La présence de Lancelot dans la narration est ainsi constamment liée aux actions et propos de ses parents royaux. L'auteur a su tirer un effet singulièrement aigu de cet emploi dans la scène centrale où se joue le sort de Lancelot. La reine, accourue sur le corps de son époux mort, songe soudain à son fils ('si li remembre de son fil', p. 27), et le paragraphe 7, qui décrit sa peur à la pensée de son fils qu'elle a laissé seul devant les chevaux, est scandé par le retour de cette appellation, jusqu'à ce qu'elle le voie entre les bras d'une demoiselle: 'si voit son fil hors del bercheul tout desliié et voit une damoisele qui le tenoit tout nu en son giron . . .' (p. 27). Il est encore 'son fils'; dans sa perception de la scène, elle le dissocie de la demoiselle qui le tient. Mais lorsque, après avoir décrit comment la demoiselle se comporte tendrement avec lui, l'auteur émet un commentaire sur la scène, Lancelot y apparaît comme détaché de son entourage familial, prenant les dimensions d'une destinée à l'échelle du monde: 'et ele n'avoit mie tort car che estoit *li plus biaus enfes de tout le monde.*'

Au début du paragraphe suivant, la mère, s'adressant à la demoiselle, lui dit: 'Bele douce amie, pour Dieu, laisiés *l'enfant* . . .'. Déjà dans les mots qu'elle emploie s'inscrit la réalité du nouveau destin de Lancelot; il ne lui appartient déjà plus et ses paroles semblent montrer qu'elle en a comme le pressentiment. Dès lors, l'histoire propre de Lancelot est enclenchée et la demoiselle 'se lieve atout *l'enfant* qu'ele tenoit entre ses bras . .' Au début du paragraphe 9, une phrase résume, dans la double désignation de Lancelot, le drame qui vient de se jouer: 'Quant la roine voit *son fil* dedens le lac, si se pasme; et quant ele est revenue de paumisons, si ne voit ne *l'enfant* ne la demoisele.' (p. 28). Elle a perdu son fils, elle peut bien dire désormais: 'Voirement sui je la roine as grans dolors.' (p. 29).

Lorsque l'auteur, après avoir interrompu, selon un procédé qui lui est cher, le récit de cette action, le reprend, il donne à Lancelot son nom, sans quoi le lecteur ne s'y retrouverait plus: 'Or dist li contes que la damoisele qui Lanselot emporta el lac . . .' (p. 38). Cependant il frustre encore notre attente: nous attendions de savoir ce qu'il allait advenir de Lancelot, il nous raconte la naissance de Merlin et ses amours avec Niniene, et ne revient qu'ensuite à Lancelot qu'il devra donc nommer à nouveau par son nom: 'Chele qui l'endormi et seela si fu chele damoisele qui Lancelot porta dedens le lac' (p. 43). Soucieux de ménager notre curiosité, il ne nous décrit la vie de Lancelot dans le lac qu'au chapitre IX, vingt cinq pages plus loin. Le nom propre revient tout naturellement en tête de ce chapitre 'Chi endroit dist li contes que quant Lancelos ot esté en la garde à la damoisele . . .' (p. 71). Mais au long des 22 paragraphes qui racontent son éducation, Lancelot n'est jamais appelé autrement que 'l'enfant' (pp. 71–86). Le nom propre en ce début du roman est donc utilisé uniquement comme un repère qui aide le lecteur à situer les divers récits que l'auteur prend plaisir à entrelacer.

Or, après le récit des événements qui marquent sa formation, Lancelot n'est plus jamais appelé 'l'enfant'. Lorsqu'il réapparaît à nouveau dans le récit, à propos du séjour de Lyonel et de Bohort chez la dame du lac, son nom est répété quatre fois dans le même paragraphe (pp. 173–4), et le paragraphe suivant s'ouvre par cette phrase où le nom propre se trouve repris deux fois à un mot d'intervalle: 'Toutes les choses qu'il [Lyonel] avoit dites a Lancelot conta Lancelos a sa dame . . .' (p. 175). Désormais Lancelot n'est plus 'l'enfant'; le texte dit et redit le nom de ce Lancelot dont il se plaira par la suite, après son passage à la cour d'Arthur, à varier les dénominations en fonction des aventures qu'il poursuivra. Mais, à ce point de son entreprise, il s'applique en le désignant de son nom propre à convoquer à l'existence le héros qui, par sa précocité et la force de sa personnalité, a quitté pour toujours les domaines relativement anonymes et indifférenciés de l'enfance. Le pronom personnel le représente parfois, renvoyant donc au nom précédemment énoncé. L'auteur semble, en agissant ainsi, avoir le souci de tout relier à ce nom, quitte à s'exposer à des formulations un peu embarrassées: 'Et la dame le prent entre ses bras, si li baise les iex et la bouche moult doucement. Et quant Lambegue voit la merveille que la dame faisoit *de chelui laiens*, si se merveille moult qui il puet estre' (p. 189). L'interrogation de Lambègue est aussi celle du lecteur: en prenant soin de ne jamais le nommer autrement que par son nom propre ou par un pronom y renvoyant, l'auteur fait de son personnage un être unique, indéfinissable selon les catégories des noms communs, impossible à réduire à autre chose qu'à lui-même. Cet enfant n'en est plus un; il est Lancelot; l'épisode où il rejette son maître est un moment capital de son évolution. En un sens, il conquiert là pour un premier temps son nom propre. Ce n'est que lorsqu'il arrive à l'âge où il souhaite devenir chevalier que son destin va devenir commun: il sera 'le valet' jusqu'à ce que la reine Guenièvre lui fasse parvenir une épée: 'et dist que ore est il chevaliers, Dieu merchi et sa dame, et por che l'a apelé li contes vallés dusques chi' (p. 298). Tout se passe comme si l'épisode de son affrontement avec son maître marquait l'accomplissement de sa personnalité dans ce monde à part où la dame du lac l'a entraîné. Lorsqu'il quittera ce monde pour venir à la cour d'Arthur et affronter les aventures, il lui faudra à nouveau conquérir sa personnalité et son nom.

Le chapitre consacré à l'éducation de Lancelot marque donc une étape décisive dans son évolution. Le début décrit les modalités de cette éducation et fait le portrait physique et moral du héros, 'li plus biax enfes del monde' (p. 71); mais le paragraphe 8 introduit le récit d'une série d'événements à la suite desquels, comme nous venons de le voir, Lancelot n'est plus un 'enfant' et a conquis dans l'écriture l'identité de son nom propre.

Ces événements ne sont pas de simples anecdotes. La manière même dont l'auteur en engage la narration appelle notre attention: 'Il avint un jour que il chaçoit un chevrecel' (p. 75). Le verbe utilisé en tête de ce récit appartient à la famille d'un mot-clef des romans arthuriens: dans l'existence de l'enfant, c'est l'aventure qui fait soudain irruption. Elle fera des événements un avènement,[3] et conduira de l'enfant à Lancelot. Dans les lais de Marie de France, dans les romans de Chrétien de Troyes, dans *La Queste del saint Graal*, l'aventure est révélation d'un autre monde. Mais elle est aussi et peut-être essentiellement un de ces événements exceptionnels qui 'vous font descendre dans une couche plus profonde de votre existence, où votre destinée s'accomplit' comme la définit Reto Bezzola,[4] en des termes qui conviennent tout à fait à cet épisode qui révèle le héros à lui-même.

Et pour que ne subsiste aucun doute dans l'esprit du lecteur quant au sens qu'il entend donner à l'enchaînement d'événements qu'il s'apprête à raconter, à l'emploi significatif du verbe *avenir* il ajoute d'autres éléments qui servent traditionnellement à caractériser l'aventure. L'aventure surgit en effet ici, comme en bien des récits, lors d'une chasse au chevreuil.[5] Elle comporte de plus la part de risque préliminaire destinée à assurer au héros qui l'assume sans hésiter la parcelle de mérite qui légitime son élection: dans cette chasse qui se prolonge et qui finit par épuiser ses compagnons, Lancelot va se retrouver finalement seul. Et si, en une péripétie symbolique de ce qui va constituer le sens de cette aventure, il ne se retourne même pas lorsque son maître, qui l'a suivi un temps, tombe ('ne onques li enfes nel regarda', p. 75), c'est qu'il est tout entier pris par cette poursuite de lui-même qu'il ne peut que mener seul.

L'épisode se construit ensuite selon un double mouvement: d'abord un temps d'action puis un temps de réflexion. Chacun de ces deux temps se dédouble à son tour: – rencontre d' 'un moult biaus varlés de prime barbe' (p. 75), et ensuite d'un 'vavassour' (p. 78); – discussion sur ce qui s'est passé lors de ces deux rencontres, d'abord avec son maître, ensuite avec la dame.

Lors de chacune des rencontres, il est à remarquer que Lancelot se trouve apparemment en position d'infériorité; c'est un enfant qui, au cours d'une partie de chasse, a perdu le reste de ses compagnons, et qui se trouve confronté à des hommes faits qui vont à leurs occupations. Dans chaque cas, Lancelot

---

[3] J. Le Goff écrit excellemment dans sa préface à *L'Aventure chevaleresque. Idéal et réalité dans le roman courtois* d'Erich Kohler, traduit de l'allemand par Eliare Kaufholz, Paris: Gallimard, 1974: 'Le héros courtois est plus à la recherche d'un avènement que d'un événement' (p. XVI).

[4] *Les Origines et la formation de la littérature courtoise en Occident*, Paris: Champion, 1963, III, t. I, p. 303.

[5] On peut remarquer que le plus souvent il s'agit d'une chasse au cerf. Remplacer le cerf par un chevreuil relève peut-être d'une volonté délibérée de l'auteur qui souligne par là que cette aventure constitue le premier degré dans l'accès à ce monde de l'aventure, adapté aux forces physiques et à la condition de l'enfant qu'est encore Lancelot.

trouve une solution au problème qui préoccupait son interlocuteur, en donnant au premier son cheval, en offrant au second le chevreuil qu'il vient de tuer. Ces rencontres peuvent paraître constituer les éléments d'une épreuve initiatique. Le héros en sort vainqueur, non point par sa force physique ou grâce aux privilèges attachés à une fonction sociale, mais par sa seule générosité et noblesse de coeur.

Si l'auteur ne s'était soucié que de créer des occasions où le héros puisse manifester cette générosité naturelle, l'épisode aurait pu en rester là. Son dessein est manifestement autre. Ces deux rencontres ne sont que l'amorce de l'essentiel: à travers l'épanouissement d'une personnalité qui en vient à l'affirmation de soi, l'exposé discret mais ferme des conceptions de l'auteur sur l'éducation. Aussi est-ce l'examen de ce deuxième temps de l'épisode qui va retenir notre attention.

La conclusion qui ressort de cet épisode est que le but de l'éducation est d'amener l'enfant à assumer la responsabilité de ses actes. La réduplication de la scène où Lancelot est amené à donner un bien qu'il possède a pour but de montrer qu'il ne s'agit pas d'un effet de hasard, mais d'une disposition profonde. Par le fait de l'aventure, il s'est trouvé placé deux fois devant une situation où il était seul pour prendre une décision. Il y a montré que la largesse était en lui comme naturellement inscrite, et qu'il avait la capacité de se déterminer lui-même. Le maître lui dénie cette liberté et prétend lui imposer sa façon de juger des choses. A ses yeux, la faute de Lancelot n'est pas d'avoir donné le cheval et la venaison, mais de l'avoir fait sans son 'congé' (p. 81). Et dans la discussion qui s'instaure entre eux, il se révèle clairement que toute l'éducation est fondée sur la menace et la coercition: 'Lors se trait avant li maistre et le manache moult' (p. 81), et, après des paroles d'intimidation, il va jusqu'à le frapper: 'Lors hauche le paume, si li doune tel flat qu'il l'abat del ronchi a terre' (p. 82). L'éducation telle que la comprend le maître consiste donc à imposer sa manière de juger à l'enfant qui lui est confié. Ce dernier se forme une morale en s'en remettant aux décisions du maître et en s'y conformant: c'est une morale de l'imitation qui ne laisse aucune initiative au sujet et qui ne fait aucune place au raisonnement.

Or Lancelot a essayé de se justifier et de raisonner. A vrai dire cette justification est entachée d'un certain mépris, il s'adapte à son interlocuteur et prend des arguments dont la référence n'est pas sienne. A son maître, il répond en alléguant la valeur marchande du lévrier et en avançant qu'elle est supérieure à celle du cheval qu'il a donné. Mais ce n'est qu'un raisonnement de circonstance, qui n'a rien à voir avec les véritables motifs de son acte, et devant la dame il ne le reprendra pas. Mais même cette argumentation *ad hominem* ne trouve pas d'écho auprès de son interlocuteur. Le premier principe de l'éducation procurée par le maître est que l'opinion du maître ne se discute pas. Le développement de la scène fait apparaître un second principe qui découle du premier: les coups donnés en châtiment d'une conduite jugée incorrecte tiennent lieu de toute explication ou raisonnement, ils doivent suffire à ramener l'enfant dans la voie de l'obéissance. Or le maître constate que, malgré la violence du coup reçu en punition, Lancelot ne se soumet pas et 'parole encore contre se volenté' (p. 82). Il s'en prend alors au lévrier et provoque ainsi la révolte de Lancelot.

La scène est audacieuse, car Lancelot pousse cette rébellion jusqu'à rouer de coups son maître. Quelles que soient les raisons que l'on puisse invoquer pour souligner que la situation est exceptionnelle, il n'en reste pas moins que décrire un enfant qui non seulement ne se soumet pas à son maître et conteste son autorité, mais encore n'hésite pas à le frapper et à le blesser, avait de quoi choquer nombre d'esprits en ce début du XIII$^e$ siècle.

Le sens profond de cette scène est dévoilé par la scène où Lancelot se présente devant la dame. A l'inverse de ce qu'avait fait le maître, la dame, tout en feignant d'être mécontente, interroge Lancelot sur les raisons de ses actes: 'Por coi avés vous fait tel outrage . . .?' (p. 83); si elle feint de juger ses actes comme inadmissibles, elle se garde bien de prononcer des paroles qui abaisseraient Lancelot; elle l'interpelle en l'appelant 'Fiex de roi', et l'emploi même du terme 'outrage' garde une mesure et, à certains égards, une objectivité, qui contrastent avec le caractère infamant du mot 'folie' que le maître avait utilisé. De la sorte, Lancelot est conduit à raisonner, à justifier ses actes et à en prendre l'entière responsabilité. Il doit les assumer lui-même et expliquer ses motivations. Malgré la colère feinte de la dame, il reste ferme dans sa détermination, et pas plus qu'il ne s'était laissé influencer par les menaces et les coups, il ne modifie sa façon de voir par crainte de mécontenter la dame pour laquelle il a une très grande affection (comme le souligne le début de cette scène où Lancelot s'apprête à mener son lévrier à la dame pour le lui faire admirer et partager avec elle son plaisir). Entre la dame et lui, s'engage une discussion où il est amené à approfondir sa pensée et à mesurer les conséquences les plus graves de sa façon d'agir. Au contraire du maître qui avait condamné sans s'informer et sans écouter les raisons de Lancelot, la dame interroge et s'enquiert; loin d'essayer de l'emporter par des menaces ou des châtiments, elle permet à Lancelot de s'exprimer et l'amène ainsi à affirmer son indépendance et sa personnalité dans la réponse pleine de dignité, de détermination (elle est scandée par la répétition du verbe *vouloir* quatre fois utilisé en deux phrases consécutives) et de vigueur (elle se termine sur une imprécation revendiquant hautement la justesse de ce qu'il a fait) qui nous est présentée au paragraphe 21 (p. 85).

Les leçons de cet épisode sont multiples. Bornons-nous à dégager comment se trouve ici exposé, à la fois dans les faits et dans les idées, un idéal pédagogique.

Comme nous l'avons déjà reconnu, l'éducation ne peut se fonder sur l'emploi du châtiment, c'est-à-dire en dernier ressort sur la supériorité physique du maître, car l'enfant peut se révéler aussi fort que le maître. De plus, la confrontation du maître et de Lancelot fait ressortir que l'éducation n'est pas affaire d'autorité abstraite: l'élève répond selon le modèle que lui propose son maître. Il avance une justification qui ne rend pas compte des véritables motifs de sa façon d'agir mais des préoccupations de son interlocuteur; au courroux du maître ('Maistre, ore ne vous courrechiés...', p. 81) fait suite le courroux de l'enfant ('Lors fu li enfes moult coureciés', p. 82); les coups du maître ont leur reflet dans les coups donnés par Lancelot. Les principes d'une telle éducation ont des conséquences néfastes. La façon de procéder de la dame se révèle autrement efficace et féconde: point de menace, mais des questions et une écoute attentive. Le texte a souligné que Lancelot revenait au lac 'tous coureciés' (p. 83), il y trouve la dame qui 'semblant fait d'estre courechie moult durement' (ibid.); dans cette manifestation extérieure d'un 'courroux' qu'elle n'éprouve pas réside sa force: en réalité elle n'est que tendresse pour Lancelot. En prenant cette attitude, elle peut exiger des explications de Lancelot: d'une certaine façon, elle se refuse à lui manifester sa tendresse afin qu'il éprouve sa solitude et assume jusqu'au bout, seul, sans l'éventuel secours d'une affection indulgente, la responsabilité de ses actes. De plus, la pression affective qu'une attitude différente aurait pu opérer sur Lancelot n'aurait peut-être pas été moins à blâmer que les menaces du maître.

Enfin ce 'courroux' qu'elle feint alimente et entretient le 'courroux' de Lancelot:

'Et nepourquant d'estre *courechie* fait grant samblant. Et quant il voit che, si s'en part de devant li moult *iriés* et manache moult chelui qui si l'a vers lui *courouchie*' (p. 84).

Nous touchons-là une des idées les plus étonnantes de l'auteur du *Lancelot*. Avant l'éclat de colère qui amène le héros à frapper son maître et à rejeter son autorité, il a insisté à deux reprises sur ces accès de colère de Lancelot. Lorsqu'il en trace le portrait physique, il décrit longuement les changements que la colère apporte à son visage:

'Mais quant il fu iriés a chertes, che sambloit carbon espris et estoit avis que parmi le pomel des joes li sailloient goutes de sanc toutes vermeilles; et fronchoit del neis en sa grant ire autresi com uns chevaus et estregnoit les dens ensemble si que il croissoient moult durement, et iert avis que l'alaine qui de sa bouche issoit fust toute vermelle, et lors parloit si fierement que che sambloit estre une buisine, et quanqu'il tenoit as dens et as mains tout depechoit. Au daarain ne li menbroit en sa grant ire fors de che dont il iert ireus...' (p. 72).

Il reprend ce thème lorsqu'il fait le portrait moral de son héros: 'Mais quant il se courechoit d'aucune chose que l'en li eust mesfaite, n'estoit lors pas legiere chose de lui apaier' (pp. 74–5).

Il est clair qu'il a voulu donner une signification à la colère de Lancelot. Micheline de Combarieu a analysé avec beaucoup de pertinence 'l'alliance de "folie" et de "mesure" qui fait la richesse et l'intérêt du personnage de

Lancelot', et elle a montré comment 'pour le *Lancelot*, l'enfant participe de deux principes contraires, faiblesse et violence'.[6]

Nous rendons 'irié' et 'courouchié' par des mots de la famille de colère, mais telle que cette émotion nous est décrite en Lancelot, il s'agit d'une véritable transformation de l'être qui tient à la fois de l'indignation et de la colère, mais qui porte aussi en soi quelque chose de surnaturel. La description de ses manifestations physiques nous en apporte un témoignage incontestable. Derrière les 'colères' de Lancelot, il y a les colères des prophètes dans la Bible; de plus, la dominante vermeille sur sa face (l'adjectif est deux fois mentionné) associe l'apparence de Lancelot sous l'emprise de la colère à celle des anges que les miniatures ou les spectacles théâtraux signalaient par un visage coloré en rouge. Il en ressort que la colère ainsi entendue est la manifestation d'une énergie et d'une qualité d'âme hors pair, proche du divin. C'est un soubresaut des forces pures de l'être qui refuse de se plier à ce qui peut paraître inéluctable.

A cette colère il faut opposer les pleurs. Devant les obstacles, devant le mal, devant l'impossible, dans les situations les plus désespérées, les pleurs sont un mauvais choix. Lancelot en fait reproche au 'valet' qu'il voit se lamenter des 'mesqueances' qui lui adviennent: 'Comment, fait il, estes vous gentiex hom et puis si plorés! Por mesqueance qu'il avigne, se chou n'est d'ami que vous aiés perdu ou de honte qui fait vous soit que vous ne poés amender, nus haus cuers ne se doit esmaier de perte qu'il puisse recovrer!' (p. 76).[7]

Il aura la même réaction devant les larmes qui montent aux yeux de Lyonel lorsque Leonce de Paerne évoque la terre dont il a été déshérité par Claudas: 'Lors saut avant Lancelos qui sa malvaise chiere vit, si l'en pesa moult, puis li a dit: Fi, biax cousins, ne plorés ja por paour de terre avoir . . .' (p. 193); l'exclamation 'Fi' dit assez combien Lancelot désapprouve ces larmes qui lui paraissent indignes d'un gentilhomme, ainsi qu'il le confiera ensuite à la dame du lac: '. . . je ne sai combien je sui gentiex hom de lignage. Mais par la foi que je doi vous, je ne me deigneroie pas esmaier de che dont je l'ai veu plorer' (p. 195).

La colère de Lancelot est l'autre face de ce refus des larmes vaines. Elle est sursaut devant l'inadmissible. Elle entraîne inévitablement l'excès. Et c'est un autre aspect de la pédagogie prônée par l'auteur du *Lancelot*: l' 'outrage', la démesure n'est pas toujours condamnable. Il est des situations auxquelles il faut réagir avec une vigueur sans concession à la morale conformiste du juste milieu, et c'est la force merveilleuse de l'enfance, sa grâce propre, que d'être capable de telles réactions. Le but de l'éducation n'est pas d'acquérir le sens de la mesure et du compromis qui caractérise souvent l'âge adulte, il faut viser avant tout à développer la noblesse du coeur.

---

[6] Micheline de Combarieu, art. cit., p. 131 et p. 110.
[7] Pour se passage nous adoptons une ponctuation différente de celle de l'édition d'Alexandre Micha.

Lancelot rejette désormais tout maître,[8] car sa présence relève d'une morale néfaste, une morale de la sanction et de la répression: '... cuers d'omme ne puet a grant honour venir qui trop longement est sous maistre ne sous maistresse, car il le covient souvent trambler ...' (p. 85). Une telle morale engendre la crainte là où il faut savoir oser: 'Mal dehait ait fiex de roi, s'il n'ose la soie chose douner hardiement' (ibid.). L'éducation doit donc savoir accepter les élans et les violences de l'enfant lorsqu'il sont fondés sur de bonnes prédispositions. Mais l'apprentissage de la morale se fera non par affirmation, non par recours à l'autorité, mais par l'interrogation, le dialogue qui permet à l'enfant de réfléchir à la valeur des actions qu'il a entreprises. Cette morale allie l'élan naturel et le recours à la réflexion et à la raison. Est-ce que cela n'est pas incompatible avec les préceptes de la morale chrétienne? Il est en tout cas curieux de constater qu'ils sont totalement absents de cette éducation. Mais Lancelot n'est pas le chevalier élu pour les hautes aventures du Graal. Ce destin est réservé à Galaad son fils qui précisément jusqu'à l'âge de quinze ans sera éduqué dans une abbaye.[9]

---

[8] Il n'est pas sans intérêt de constater que Niniene elle-même avait rejeté son maître Merlin et l'avait 'enserré'.
[9] *Lancelot*, ed. cit. tome VI, p. 243.

# The Troubadour's Vassalage — An Axiology of Courtly Love

## ARIÉ SERPER

Our title takes us back to Ovid, who inspired many a troubadour: Folquet de Marselha is said to borrow at least fifteen passages from the Master of Love. Arnaut Daniel and Bernart de Ventadorn certainly read the *Metamorphoses*; Rigaut de Berbezilh writes:

> C'Ovidis dis el libre que no men . . .,[1]

Ovid says so in the book that does not lie.

The book referred to is the *Ars amatoria*, but the *Amores* are also often quoted and imitated. Andreas Capellanus and Brother Matfre Ermengaud also quoted and imitated Ovid, the former in *De reprobatione amoris*, the latter in 716 verses of 'Remedis per escantir [*sc.* "to put out"] folia d'aymador' that conclude his *Breviari d'Amor*.

It is not without interest to note that the twelfth century is not only the age of the renewal of mystical love, but also that of a new conception of human love. We have, of course, to distinguish between the love of the Goliards, in which one discovers a revolt against religious law, a claim in favour of the senses, and courtly love, which is not courteous love although it may be adorned with nobility of worship.

This dramatic conception of love, where one unveils not only the creative generosity but also the sacrifice of the Cross, is specifically Christian. As Bernart Alanhan de Narbona has it:

> Verays Dieus, on ver'amors nays, . .[2]

True God in whom real love is born, . . .

---

[1] 'Tuit demandon qu'es devengud' Amors' (P.C. 421,10), ed. Alberto Varvaro, *Rigaut de Berbezilh: Liriche*, Bari: Adriatica Editrice, 1960, pp. 198–214, No. IX, l. 29. See also Mauro Braccini, *Rigaut de Barbezieux: Le Canzoni, Testo e commento*, Florence: Leo S. Olschki, 1960, pp. 73–9, No. IX, l. 29. This troubadour's poems were first edited by Joseph Anglade and Camille Chabaneau, 'Les Chansons du troubadour Rigaut de Barbezieux', *Revue des Langues Romanes*, LX (1918–20), pp. 201–310 (see pp. 283–6, No. X).

[2] 'No puesc mudar qu'ieu non diga' (P.C. 53,1), ed. Carl Appel, *Provenzalische Inedita aus Pariser Handschriften*, Leipzig: Fues, 1890, pp. 21–2, l. 37.

However, a comparison may be drawn between the love of man for woman and the love of the soul for God. In fact, courtly poets do exalt the Lady, who is considered a goddess. Rigaut de Berbezilh prostrates himself in front of the one whom he admires above all:

> Tot atressi    con la clartatz del dia
> apodera totas altras clartatz,
> apodera, domna, vostra beltatz
> e la valors e·l pretz e·ill cortessia
> – al mieu semblan – totas celas del mon . . .[3]

Just as the brightness of the day exceeds all other brightness, so do your beauty, your valour and merit and courtesy outshine – methinks – those of all the world. . . .

This admiration seems nevertheless to contain a certain Platonism. Here we have no priority of creative love. The Lady is content to exist, ornate in her valour; she, therefore, in a passive way, incites one to love. She does not initiate love, nor does she sow it in the lover's soul. This lover is elevated towards her by an *eros* that addresses itself to physical and spiritual beauty and which offers itself to all. The personal dialogue of love begins after the man's first steps, and the response – or reward – comes from the Lady, a reward humbly solicited and courageously won.

Love is sometimes unilateral, when the Lady does not answer her lover's worship; there can be no *joi* without hope of reward. What then is *joi*? It would seem to be the rhythm of the world pervading a soul, universal love vibrating in a heart. Arnaut de Maruelh sings:

> Si cum li peis an en l'aiga lor vida
> l'ai eu en joi e totz temps la·i aurai, . .[4]

Just as the life of fish is in water, so mine is in joy and I shall always have it there, . . .

This cosmic joy is the poet's reward when he loves and is loved. He then experiences enjoyment, *gaug*, which is the reward of *joi*.

Nevertheless, it has to be admitted that, in spite of the somewhat Platonic content of courtly love, it is too concrete not to encourage a measure of freedom. Even if the loved one is something of an idol, this idol is a person capable of loving in its turn. The lover's heart has chosen the beloved: but it is a choice made in all liberty, expressing itself through a chivalrous pledge, as in Bernart de Ventadorn:

> Domna, vostre sui e serai,
> del vostre servizi garnitz.

---

[3] P.C. 421,9: ed. Alberto Varvaro, op. cit., pp. 186–98, No. VIII, ll. 1–5; cf. Mauro Braccini, op. cit., pp. 68–72, No. VIII, ll. 1–5.

[4] P.C. 30,22: ed. Ronald C. Johnston, *Les Poésies lyriques du troubadour Arnaut de Mareuil, publiées avec une introduction, une traduction, des notes et un glossaire*, Paris: Droz, 1935, pp. 43–9, No. VIII, ll. 1–2.

> Vostr'om sui juratz e plevitz
> e vostre m'era des abans.

Lady, I am yours and will be, ready for your service. I am your man, sworn and pledged, and yours I was before.[5]

Love can have impediments: there subsists nevertheless an irrevocable choice. For, even with no reward in sight, the lover gives of himself and that is what matters. Incidentally, courtly love will be accompanied by acts of prowess, produced by the poet's heart:

> Non es meravelha s'eu chan
> mels de nul autre chantador,
> que plus me tra·l cors vas amor
> e melhs sui faitz a so coman.

It is no wonder that I sing better than any other singer, for my heart draws me more toward love and I am better suited to its command.[6]

Should the Lady not be present or should she refuse, the lover will, by way of punishment, be banished to the land of exile. Since courtly love knows temptations and its law is faithfulness, it transcends the preliminary pleasures. As Guilhem de Montanhagol states:

> qar amors non es peccatz,
> anz es vertutz qe·ls malvatz
> fai bons e·ll bo·n son meillor,
> e met hom'en via
> de ben far tot dia.[7]

For love is not sin but rather virtue that renders the evil good and the good better and sets all men on the road to good actions for ever.

This particular kind of love, exalted by the force of *joi*, discovers its internal consistency and its legitimacy in its own uprightness. That is the reward which the Countess of Die expects from the man she loves:

> Ab joi et ab joven m'apais
> e jois e jovens m'apaia,
> que mos amics es lo plus gais,
> per qu'ieu sui coindet' e guaia;
> e pois ieu li sui veraia, . .[8]

In joy and youth do I delight; joy and youth delight me, for my friend is the happiest of men. And so I am gracious and happy, for I am faithful to him. . . .

---

[5] 'Pel doutz chan que·l rossinhols fai' (P.C. 70,33), ed. Stephen G. Nichols, Jr, John A. Galm *et al.*, *The Songs of Bernart de Ventadorn*, Chapel Hill: University of North Carolina Press, 1962, pp. 138–40, No. XXXIII, ll. 29–32.

[6] Bernart de Ventadorn (P.C. 70,31), ed. S. G. Nichols, Jr, ibid., pp. 132–4, No. XXXI, ll. 1–4.

[7] 'Ar ab lo coinde pascor' (P.C. 225,2), ed. Peter T. Ricketts, *Les Poésies de Guilhem de Montanhagol, troubadour provençal du XIII<sup>e</sup> siècle*, Toronto: Pontifical Institute of Mediaeval Studies, 1964, pp. 121–4, No. XII, ll. 13–17.

[8] (P.C. 46,1), ed. Oscar Schultz[-Gora], *Die provenzalischen Dichterinnen: Biographien und Texte*, Leipzig: G. Fock, 1888, pp. 17–18, No. 2:1, ll. 1–5.

This is 'pure love' or *fin'amor*, love extending towards the chosen person, awaiting a total reward. He who applies himself to it is saved. Jaufre Rudel declares:

> Qu'*anc no fuy tan lunhatz* d'amor
> Qu'er non sia sals e gueritz.
> Plus savis hom de mi mespren,
> Per qu'ieu sai ben az escïen
> Qu'anc fin'amor home no trays.

For never was I so distanced from (by) love/ that now I may not be safe and healed./ A wiser man than I makes mistakes (a wiser man makes mistakes about me),/ for I know well by my own knowledge/ that refined love never betrayed (led [. .]) a man.[9]

The lover possesses the immediate, profound and existential *intelligence* of the beloved one's valour. He therefore desires her, as does Albertet de Sestaro for example:

> Dezirier n'ai, q'anc hom no l'ac major;

Desire I have of her greater than any man before.[10]

What Albertet de Sestaro says is repeated by most courtly poets. They desire the happiness of a union beyond flesh, the reward of love won by an amorous joust. The Countess of Die, who sang 'Ab joi et ab jovens m'apais', declares:

> anz vos am mais non fetz Seguis Valenssa,
> e platz mi mout quez eu d'amar vos venssa,
> lo mieus amics, car etz lo plus valens;[11]

I love you more than Seguin loved Valensa, and it pleases me greatly that I should vanquish you by love, oh, my friend, for you are the most valiant of men.

Courtly love, too, attains perfection in reciprocity, as in the well-known stanza of Guilhem de Peitieu:

> La nostr'amor va enaissi
> com la brancha de l'albespi,
> qu'esta sobre l'arbr'en treman
> la nuoit, ab la ploi' ez al gel,
> tro l'endeman, que·l sols s'espan
> per la fueilla vert el ramel.[12]

---

[9] 'Belhs m'es l'estius e·l temps floritz' (P.C. 262,1), ed. Rupert T. Pickens, *The Songs of Jaufré Rudel*, Toronto: Pontifical Institute of Mediaeval Studies, 1978, pp. 144–9, No. IV, ll. 31–5.

[10] 'Bon chantar fai al gent temps de pascor' (P.C. 16,8), ed. Jean Boutière, 'Les poésies du troubadour Albertet', *Studi Medievali*, X (1937), pp. 1–129; see pp. 53–5, No. VII, l. 9.

[11] 'A chantar m'er de so qu'ieu non volria' (P.C. 46,2), ed. O. Schultz[-Gora], op. cit., p. 18, No. 2:2, ll. 11–13. *Seguin et Valenssa* seems to have been an epic, much appreciated in the times of the troubadours. See Sernin Santy, *La Comtesse de Die: Sa vie, ses oeuvres complètes, les fêtes données en son honneur, avec tous les documents*, Paris: Picard 1893, p. 49, n. 1. Cf. Camille Chabaneau (ed.), *Poésies inédites des troubadours du Périgord*, Paris: Maisonneuve, 1885, p. 6.

[12] 'Ab la dolchor del temps novel' (P.C. 183,1), ed. Nicolò Pasero, *Guglielmo IX: Poesie*, Modena: S.T.E.M.-Mucchi, 1973, pp. 241–66, No. X, ll. 13–18. Pasero's emendation of *treman* (Ms. a¹, p. 499) to *creman* has been rejected in line 15.

Our love is like the hawthorn branch, which is on the tree, trembling at night, in rain and frost until the morrow, when the sun spreads amid green leaves on the bough.

There is the cosmic joy, rewarding the two lovers, surpassing them:

> totz lo jois del mon es nostre,
> dompna, s'amdui nos amam.[13]

All the joy in the world is ours, my Lady, if we both love one another.

Any capriciousness on the part of the lady is considered destructive. The lover is punished and cannot live without her. Thus, the same Guilhem de Peitieu contrasts the Lady's 'jolly welcome, her lovely and pleasant look', which restores health to the ill, with her rage, which renders the wise mad and makes a churl out of the most courteous of men:

> E deu hom mai cent ans durar
> qui·l joi de s'amor pot sazir.[14]

Over one hundred years shall live the man who can possess the joy of his love.

The lover is indifferent to everything but being loved:

> Si·m vol midons s'amor donar,
> pres soi del penr' e del grazir
> e del celar e del blandir
> e de sos plazers dir e far . . .[15]

If my Lady wishes to grant me her love, I am all ready to accept it and render grace, to conceal (*i.e.* be discreet) and tell her gentle words, to say and do her pleasure. . . .

Courtly love aspires to reciprocity. Being granted the possibility of courtship is part of this aspiration. So Bernart de Ventadorn has lost himself in the eyes of his Lady, just like the beautiful Narcissus in the spring:

> Miralhs, pus me mirei en te,
> m'an mort li sospir de preon
> c'aissi·m perdei con perdet se
> lo bels Narcisus en la fon.

Mirror, since I saw myself reflected in you, deep sighs have been killing me. I have destroyed myself just as the beautiful Narcissus destroyed himself in the fountain.[16]

---

[13] 'Farai chansoneta nueva' (P.C. 183,6), ed. N. Pasero, ibid., pp. 297–308, No. (VIII), ll. 27–8.
[14] 'Molt jauzens, mi prenc en amar' (P.C. 183,8), ed. N. Pasero, ibid., pp. 213–40, No. IX, ll. 23–4. In line 23 the reading *sent tans* of Ms. E, followed by Pasero except for orthography, has been rejected in favour of the reading of Ms. C.
[15] Ibid., ll. 37–40.
[16] 'Can vei la lauzeta mover' (P.C. 70, 43), ed. S. G. Nichols, Jr, op. cit., pp. 166–8, No. XLIII, ll. 21–4.

But this loss is no more an act of annihilation than is the rancour of the man whose friend the Countess of Die is, after the awful ending of a rewardless love:

> tant me rancur de lui cui sui amia, . . .
> . . . . . .
> e membre vos cals fo·l comenssamens
> de nostr'amor! ja Dompnedieus non vuoilla
> qu'en ma colpa sia·l departimens.[17]

Even if all the lover's desires are not fulfilled, love is not without reward for him, and this reward consists precisely in the 'elevation' of his soul.

To sum up all these considerations, one might assert that everything must be sacrificed to the joy of love, that joy depends on reciprocity, but that love itself is dependent neither upon reward nor on punishment.

---

[17] Countess of Die, 'A chantar m'er de so qu'ieu non volria' (P.C. 46,2), ed. O. Schultz[-Gora], op. cit., p. 18, No. 2:2, ll. 2, 20–2.

## Sin and Retribution, and the Hope of Salvation, in Rutebeuf's Lyrical Works[1]

### RICHARD SPENCER

Discussing Rutebeuf's lyrical works, Jean Frappier notes that the poet rarely uses courtly versification and that his poems are not musically linked. This leads him to pose the question as to how far Rutebeuf's works can be called lyrical, and to this he replies as follows:

> Son lyrisme s'exprime jusque dans ses pièces satiriques dont le caractère subjectif, dû à la franchise de ses convictions, n'est pas niable; il en est de même dans ses effusions religieuses, dans ses louanges de Notre-Dame, dans ses pièces (y compris celle de Théophile) à Notre-Dame, la seule dame qu'il ait chantée.[2]

Frappier adds that the most markedly lyrical of the works are the 'Poésies personnelles' (*i.e.* what Faral and Bastin call 'Poèmes de l'infortune'). For the purpose of this study I have taken as lyrical all the works which are not narrative or dramatic, and have excluded as primary sources the three hagiographical pieces (*La Vie de Sainte Marie l'Egyptienne*, *La Vie de Sainte Elysabel* and *Le Sacristain et la Femme au Chevalier*) together with *Le Miracle de Théophile* and *La Voie de Paradis*.

As far as possible I have respected the autonomy of each poem and tried to observe the chronology so admirably established by the editors. To follow a single chronological line has not, however, proved practicable because of the nature of the works and the intriguing questions they provoke. The poems directed against the Mendicants must be treated apart from those in support of the crusades. I regret that my subject and the space available require concentration on the content rather than on the form and style of the poems.

Rutebeuf's religious beliefs are not unorthodox, though perhaps a little one-sided. He accepts the essence of the Creed, the Incarnation, Crucifixion and Redemption, and the doctrine of original sin. The need for repentance, the struggle to merit salvation, the Last Judgment and Hell-fire are never far

---

[1] For references to the text of Rutebeuf I have used the excellent edition by Faral and Bastin (hereinafter F/B): Edmond Faral et Julia Bastin, *Oeuvres complètes de Rutebeuf*, Paris: Picard, 1959–60, 2 vols.
[2] Jean Frappier, *La poésie lyrique en France aux XII<sup>e</sup> et XIII<sup>e</sup> siècles*, Paris: CDU, 1963, pp. 224–5.

from his thoughts. He has thus from the first much in common with the missionary friars.

In *Le Dit des Cordeliers*, an early work written presumably before his move to the capital, Rutebeuf is already concerned with what he sees as the corrupt worldliness among parish clergy, a corruption sharply contrasted to the saintly attitudes of the Franciscans, 'la gent que je miex prise' (l. 16). Their wholehearted commitment to poverty and their mortification of the flesh he finds admirable:

> ... chacuns a mis
> Son cors a grant martire contre les anemis
> Qui sont, plus de cent foiz le jor, a nos tramis.     (ll. 2–4)

They are, he tells us, a body of healers come into the town to fight against the prevailing 'pechié et grant ordure' (l. 73), hinting that thereby they demonstrate greater heroism than their cloistered counterparts.

At that time Rutebeuf undoubtedly saw himself as the ally of these uncloistered monks with their particular interest in the poor. Some years later, when attacking the Jacobins, and later the Cordeliers, he invariably condemns their attitude to the poor and to money, the material symbol of worldliness. Implicitly his critique of the Mendicants raises the question of how the Church can function within a society by definition sinful. Rutebeuf himself, as can be seen also in several of his hagiographical works, was fascinated by the notion of *contemptus mundi*, the retreat from the world and its distractions. Zozimas the monk of *La Vie de Sainte Marie l'Egyptienne*, renowned for saintliness, fears he may be overcome by pride in his own virtue, and moves into the desert to join a more austere community. Théophile fails to avoid such a fault and has to be rescued by a miracle. To renounce the world, to strip oneself of possessions, must be for most people only an ideal. Nevertheless, throughout his career Rutebeuf uses it as a yard-stick for evaluating not only the role of the mendicant friars, but of the Church in general. The same conviction also lies behind his approach to the crusades.

It is in the measure that the Jacobins and other Mendicants appear to depart from the austerity of monastic discipline and cease to work exclusively among the poor that they fall foul of Rutebeuf. They were at their inception a new type of organisation, being both monastic and also functioning within society. Some, like the Dominicans and Franciscans, dated from well before Rutebeuf himself; others he had seen created in his lifetime; all were favourably viewed by Pope and King. It was perhaps the very success of the older Orders in fields other than social welfare, namely in teaching, acting as Papal agents, and penetrating into most of the Church's activities, which aroused his suspicion that they did not have the interest of the poor at heart. So far from representing a renewal of religion, they became in his eyes no better than the rest of the Church, whose integration with a sinful society he deplored. The Mendicants were in fact especially dangerous for being ostensibly new, dynamic and holy. Long established, the Orders are sinister; newly created, they are ludicrous.[3]

A number of poems dating from the period of the University Quarrel are aimed in various ways against the mendicant Orders, though not always exclusively. *La Discorde de l'Université et des Jacobins* is an open attack on that Order for its persistence over the matter of Chairs, an attack which, though revealing the writer's familiarity with the dispute, also shows the flimsiness and triviality of the charges he levels against the friars. He condemns for instance their hypocrisy for preaching against 'corouz et ire' (l. 12) yet insisting on their right to teach:

> Or guerroient por une escole
> Ou il vuelent a force lire.  (ll. 15–16)

Here the whole point depends on the sophistry of *guerroient*. Rutebeuf charges the friars with *orgueil* (personified as 'Orguex', l. 21), whose meaning in the context is conveniently elastic, indicating perhaps ingratitude, a desire to dominate and a general propensity to evil. But this allegation, vague though it is, is based upon a misrepresentation of the original aims of the Jacobins:

> Quant Jacobin vindrent el monde,
> S'entrerent chiés Humilité.  (ll. 17–18)[4]

The poet writes for an audience of the converted, not to analyse but to vituperate.

In other pieces the poet uses quasi-allegorical abstractions to blur the contours of his attack still further. In *Du Pharisien* the figure of 'Ypocrisie' (l. 7), risen (by curious logic) from humble (*i.e.* righteous) station to mastery of the world thanks to her influence and accumulated wealth, can be interpreted to indicate the friars and also the social corruption which makes them predominant. Her proliferating followers, we are told, being forerunners of the Antichrist, make war on traditional values like

> ... Verité,
> Pitié et Foi et Charité
> Et Larguece et Humilité  (ll. 64–6)

and find few to challenge them, from which it follows that they are guilty of

---

[3] See F/B, Vol. I, pp. 49–51.

[4] The Dominicans were from the start an Order of preachers and teachers. They aimed, it is true, to own no property, and to live in apostolic poverty. Yet, as W. A. Hinnebusch makes clear, expansion of the organisation, the establishment of priories, as well as the conditions imposed by the Papacy, modified this broad commitment to poverty and produced divisions of labour: 'It was one thing to apply stringent poverty to itinerant preaching; it was quite another to extend it to the entire scope of religious life' (William A. Hinnebusch, *The History of the Dominican Order. Origins and Growth to 1500*, New York: Alba House, 1965, Vol. I, p. 147). Hinnebusch notes too that by 1275 the practice of poverty was 'weakly' observed (ibid., pp. 162–3).

numerous offences – lying, arrogance, avarice and heresy among them. These failings remain, as they must in this type of writing, quite nebulous. Clearly the aim is to discredit the Mendicants.

In a similar way the *Complainte de Guillaume* represents an attempt to rob the opposition of credibility. Here the poet speaks through the personage of 'sainte Yglise' (l. 4), symbolising the authentic Church, who laments her own weakness and the persecution of her innocent members, both of which may be ascribed to the infiltration of hypocrites and the victory of vice over virtue. Familiar abstractions, 'Ypocrisie', 'Vaine Gloire', 'Tricherie', 'Faus Samblant' and, above all, 'Envie, Qui tout enflame' (ll. 76–9) dominate the contemporary scene, says 'sainte Yglise'. The friars, says the sub-text, are not what they seem: they aim in reality at wealth and power, but they are a part of a wider pattern of corruption.

A persistent accusation in these polemics is that corporately the friars are money-orientated. Rutebeuf often complains that these Orders have the right to administer the sacraments. It is logical therefore to accuse them, as in *Des Règles*, of deliberately seeking wealthy death-bed conversions with absolute indifference to the fate of the souls concerned, a sweeping charge which could with equal justification have been laid against the secular clergy, whose interests, the poet assures us without irony, are adversely affected by such activities! The same, rather disordered compilation does not disdain even more trivial smears about alleged relations between friars and Béguines, or about the evangelising style of the Mendicants as a sure sign of hypocrisy.

Despite the unscrupulousness of his propaganda, however, the poet remains aware that his assault on the friars is implicitly a critique of the Church and society in which they flourish. In *Des Règles* he holds the upper ranks of the clergy responsible for the success of these Orders, a theme given major importance in his *Dit de Sainte Eglise*, where, as in the *Complainte de Guillaume*, it is the decadence of true religion, the sad fate of the authentic Church, which explains the popularity of these saintly hypocrites. People are deceived by appearances, accept the habit as a proof of holiness, fear to 'connoistre le voir' (l. 18), while theologians and canon-lawyers, afraid for their livelihood, fail to controvert the new doctrines invented by the friars. For not upholding 'Droiture et raison et mesure' (l. 84) prelates are doomed to Hell-fire.

The sins attributed to the Mendicants are corporate, vague but plausible enough to satisfy some sections of the *gent menue*, and though the writer constantly harps on a small number of themes, he knows how to vary their presentation. His persistence is surprising, and all the more so when one considers how few allies he can count upon. As time goes by, the scope of his strictures extends, and he assumes increasingly the role of a voice crying in the wilderness, lacking sympathy for the dominant forces of Church and State. Gradually the allegorical abstractions reflect this growing isolation, and he begins to use more systematically the traditional categories of vice and virtue, first of all ranged in battle order, then more ambitiously presented as allegory. In *Le Dit d'Hypocrisie*, still concerned with the mendicant Orders, he gives equal prominence to general allegations of ecclesiastical corruption stemming from Rome, where 'Avarice est de la cort dame' (l. 177) in league with 'Covoitise' (l. 184). 'Ypocrisie', symbolising the Mendicants and their supporters, is described as ruling the Church, and though Rutebeuf presents the new Pope as a man after his own heart, his remarks about the political influence in France of the friars suggest that he had little hope of change.[5] More clearly here than before he projects the view of the friars as emissaries of a Papacy he mistrusts.

*La Bataille des Vices contre les Vertus* introduces irony as a variation in the now customary polemic, with praise for 'Humilitez' grown so powerful that 'Orguex' has left the field. In this way it is suggested that, so far from ministering to the needs of the poor, the friars have become an instrument of coercion at the disposal of an interfering Papacy and a compliant monarch. The same pattern of vice and virtue in *Des Jacobins* characterises the contemporary world as governed by material appetites, whilst those who should possess humility, *viz*. the leaders of Church and State, are ruled instead by its opposite. As for the Jacobins, they are roundly charged with ignoring the poor and with having become bankers (*changeor*, l. 32), preaching austerity and practising self-indulgence, apparently saintly, in reality acting as dictators. This poem, which Faral and Bastin date from about 1263–65, seems to mark the high point of Rutebeuf's hostility to the Mendicants.[6] In their different ways *Les Ordres de Paris*, *La Chanson des Ordres* and *Des Béguines* use a more relaxed approach. Wit, concision and derision, and the exploitation of lyrical resources achieve much more in the direction of discrediting the multiplicity of begging Orders and their royal patron than did the vituperation of the earlier pieces. Rutebeuf's aim in all these is to query their saintliness and their *raison d'être*.

In all the polemical anti-Mendicant poems the line of attack is broadly consistent: the main charge is about money and the fate of the poor, the second about hypocrisy, to which is linked *Orgueil*, the arrogance of power. As we have seen, the poet is not over-scrupulous in his approach, and his allegations are often vague and sweeping. Yet these Orders were called upon to fulfil a great diversity of tasks and as corporate bodies often had to assume contradictory roles. There was a difference, no doubt, between what Rutebeuf considered necessary and what they were able to provide. He wanted an organisation to minister to the poor: that was for him the essence of the Church's role. It should be on the side of the poor and could not also serve the interests of the rich and powerful, especially those of the *nouveaux riches*. When

---
[5] *Le Dit d'Hypocrisie*, ll. 291–302.
[6] See F/B, Vol. I, pp. 313–14.

he sees Mendicants acting as Papal agents, installed in the royal palace and involved in the Inquisition, his reaction is one of disapproval. His particular animus against the Dominicans and later the Franciscans is probably explained by their political prominence. The argument over university chairs is, as far as Rutebeuf is concerned, part of this wider appraisal of the Mendicants.

Our analysis also suggests that in opposing the begging Orders the poet was not attempting to protect the interests of the secular clergy.[7] Perhaps on occasion, for tactical purposes, he may have sought their support. His general stance is to criticise the Church for the same 'sins' as he ascribes to the friars.

If we accept by and large the chronology proposed by Faral and Bastin, the poet's relative loss of interest in the Mendicants can be assumed to result from increasing involvement (c. 1262) with crusading. Both campaigns are in a sense lost causes in the short run: the friars thrive despite his eloquence, the crusades interest fewer and fewer people. Not that he abandons his distaste for the mendicant Orders. It is simply subsumed into wider concerns with Church and society, concerns already perceptible in *Le Dit d'Hypocrisie* and in *La Voie de Paradis*, where the picture of general decadence serves both to explain the prevailing indifference to the fate of the Latin kingdom and to justify the poet's commitment thereto.

His most comprehensive statement on society is found in *L'Etat du Monde*, which from the start deals with money relations and the fate of the poor.[8] This is not for Rutebeuf a mere matter of original sin. In addition to that 'historical' state of things, he speaks of more recent social changes for the worse, with mercenary attitudes predominant and a general atmosphere of 'dog eat dog'; and his comments on various social groupings are intended to support that contention. He looks first at the clergy, the estate responsible in theory for the spiritual health of society. Of the cloistered Orders, Benedictines and Cistercians, richly endowed with property and movable wealth, 'toz sont sers

---

[7] Cf. F/B, Vol. I, pp. 51–2: 'Ceux qu'il plaint, ce sont les humbles prêtres des paroisses, pauvres ceux-là'. Jean-Charles Payen considers this attack on the Mendicants as expressing 'le corporatisme des séculiers . . .' ('Littérature et chrétienté sous le règne de saint Louis: équilibres et malaises', in *Septième Centenaire de la mort de saint Louis*, Actes des Colloques de Royaumont et de Paris (21–27 mai, 1970), édition préparée par Louis Carolus-Barré et Maurice Roche, Paris: 'Les Belles Lettres', 1976, pp. 331–44, see p. 336). Omer Jodogne takes a similar view ('L'anticléricalisme de Rutebeuf', *Lettres Romanes*, XXIII (1969), pp. 219–44, see p. 236). It would be logical to sympathise with priests who practise austerity. *Des Règles* shows 'Povre provoire' (l. 139) intimidated by the friars. The main thrust of the poet's thinking is, however, to see the whole Church as in the grip of corruption. Cf. also two further articles in *Septième Centenaire* above: Yves Congar, 'L'Eglise et l'Etat sous le règne de saint Louis', pp. 257–71; and Michel-Marie Dufeil, 'Le roi Louis dans la querelle des mendiants et des séculiers (Université de Paris, 1254–70)', pp. 281–9.

[8] '. . . nule gent n'est més maniere/ De l'autrui porfit porchacier,/ Se son preu n'i cuide chacier./ Chascuns devient oisel de proie:/ Nus ne vit més se il ne proie.' (*L'Etat du Monde*, ll. 6–10).

a Covoitise', he asserts in his usual downright fashion (l. 20). The proof of their fault is their involvement in commerce:

> Toz jors vuelent sanz doner prendre,
> Toz jors achatent sanz riens vendre;
> Ils tolent, l'en ne lor tolt rien.        (ll. 21–3)

The absurdity of his formulation here no doubt arises from his anxiety to present the monks as being above all accumulators, hoarders, not distributors, of wealth. According to him, not only are they corporately uncharitable, but in order to pursue mercenary activities they have ceased to teach the faith, and among them

> Cil qui plus set de l'art du siecle,
> C'est le meillor, selonc lor riegle.        (ll. 29–30)

Less surprisingly, the begging Orders, warring among themselves in their money-grubbing, are also beset by covetousness: they love one another as misers do, he quips, and since they contrive to trick one another, they merit the title of super-swindlers.

On the secular clergy, his comments are no more original and no less exaggerated. No mention is made in this instance of parish clergy or of the prelates, but, like Villon two centuries later, the poet refers to 'plusor chanoine' (l. 49), the middle elements of the hierarchy, who plunder Church funds meant for the poor and carry out religious duties, if ever, only for mercenary gain. He puts special stress on their alleged indifference to the poor:

> Quant chascuns a chape forree
> Et de deniers la grant borsee,
> Les plains coffres, la plaine huche,
> Ne li chaut qui por Dieu le huche ...        (ll. 59–62)

Clerics specialising in law, troublemakers in their own interests, feather their nests but are not intent on justice, he says. Taking the Church as a whole, says Rutebeuf,

> Briefment, tuit clerc, fors escoler,
> Vuelent Avarisce acoler.        (ll. 89–90)

If the Church is blamed for its sinfulness, the laity fare little better, for 'Covoitise' (l. 95) is the salient fault of 'Provost et bailli et maieur' (l. 93), representatives of the civil power, the first having bought their office in order to recoup their outlay with interest, the second eager to placate their masters, and none of them committed to justice.

Merchants, more than any other group engaged in money transactions, are a particular target.[9] They practise usury:

> Si vendent a terme, et usure
> Vient tantost et termoierie
> Qui sont de privee mesnie;
> Lors est li termes achatez
> Et plus cher venduz li chatez.      (ll. 130–34)

Even the 'genz menues' (l. 135) are condemned for seeking good pay for minimal work and defending their rights.[10]

Rutebeuf next turns to the feudal classes whom he finds to be poor specimens as against the heroes of yesteryear – they reflect directly the current social crisis. Old chivalric values have gone by the board and knights 'vivent de rapine' (l. 154), while even princes and prelates are money-orientated. Woe betide the poor who approach them, for Charity is dead. This is, in short, a society 'de toz biens [. . .] estrangiez' (l. 174).

Poems such as this are frequently viewed, and in effect dismissed, as belonging to a literary tradition or exploiting a known topos (*laudatio temporis acti*). They also have to be understood, especially in the case of Rutebeuf, as expressions of the poet's own reaction to contemporary society. It would be a mistake to obfuscate his concern for the plight of the poor. He speaks not simply as a *jongleur* seeking a hand-out but as a citizen and committed Christian. If he distorts, exaggerates, amplifies abuses, it is the better to convey his invariable cry that French society is not ruled by the injunction 'Love thy neighbour!'. That is precisely the starting-point of his argument in *Les Plaies du Monde*. To answer his own query about the absence of love by explaining that people's hearts are full of bitterness, cruelty and envy, seems at first to be absurd, but Rutebeuf goes on to identify poverty as the source of all these undesirable traits. Even within families

> Qui auques a si est amez,
> Et qui n'a riens s'est fols clamez.      (ll. 21–2)

Poverty is feared by all, for to be poor is to be shunned. Therefore each one clings desperately to what he has. In such a situation of general insecurity the poor cannot help the poor. This 'plaie', this social problem, needs to be tackled, and implicitly the responsibility is placed upon the rich, who alone by charity could alleviate it.

The second problem is essentially gross materialism of the sort highlighted

---

[9] At least, if they are successful. *La Nouvelle Complainte d'Outremer* dilates on their sinful, usurious practices (ll. 281–326).

[10] Jean Frappier, op. cit., p. 220, sees Rutebeuf as 'porte-parole de la "menue gent" '. His persistent defence of the poor is undeniable: much depends on the definition of 'menue gent'. *Le Dit de Sainte Eglise* exonerates them from responsibility for the Mendicant ascendancy on the ground of their credulous ignorance and blinkered preoccupations (ll. 97–105).

in *L'Etat du Monde*. With the exception of the students (not yet involved in the economy) all the clergy are alleged to be 'd'avarisce vergié' (l. 38), and the poet draws, after Gautier de Coinci, a 'worst case' picture of the eventual futility of enslavement to wealth.[11]

Thirdly, there is the problem of the 'chevalerie' (l. 105), the warrior estate from which, says the poet, spring 'Tout sens, tout bien et toute honor' (l. 111) – an interesting judgment considering his harsh view of the clergy. The problem is that the feudal classes are not what they were, and he turns as before to the myths of a heroic past. Today the world has changed, and

> ... uns leus blans [money ?] a toz mengiez
> Les chevaliers loiaus et preus:
> Por ce n'est més li siecles preus.         (ll. 118–20)[12]

In these two poems, the message of which can be confirmed in his other works,[13] if money itself is not the source of sin, certainly attachment to wealth is condemned, as is the existence of unrelieved poverty. In *L'Etat du Monde* there is mention of 'le soufissant vivre' (l. 52) with which clerics should be content, and no doubt this orthodox idea is taken into account by Rutebeuf despite his absolute approach. It is probable that what he condemns is really over-fondness for wealth, for in practice a line must be drawn between avarice and largesse. He is not a radical social reformer, though some of his strictures belong to a tradition destined much later to bear radical fruits. We must remember, too, that he writes within the less than 'open' society of thirteenth-century France. He calls into question for those with ears to hear the prevailing balance between poverty and wealth.

In his crusade poetry Rutebeuf always starts with the conviction that the Holy War for the conquest of God's own country and at God's behest is unquestionably right.[14] A dissident viewpoint is to be found in only one of the eleven pieces devoted to this question, *La Disputaison du Croisé et du Décroisé*, a dialogue designed to combat dissidence. Notwithstanding his harsh condemnation elsewhere of the Papal curia and of the mendicant Orders, the poet

---

[11] *L'Etat du Monde*, ll. 47–8. Cf. *Les Plaies du Monde*, ll. 35–88; *La Chanson de Pouille*, ll. 41–8. A similar picture of avarice is found in *Le Testament de l'âne* (F/B, Vol. II, pp. 283 ff., especially ll. 20–32).

[12] Cf. *La Voie de Paradis*, ll. 603–56.

[13] In addition to the critique expressed in *La Complainte d'Outremer* and *La Nouvelle Complainte d'Outremer*, see *Le Dit d'Hypocrisie*, ll. 177–92, and *Complainte de Guillaume*, ll. 70–95. The theme is prominent in *La Voie de Paradis*, ll. 507ff., especially ll. 633–760, as also in *La Vie de Sainte Marie l'Egyptienne (passim)*.

[14] 'Deus vult' in the early period was already a commonplace of crusade preaching. In Robert of Rheims' account of Urban II's appeal at Clermont, 1095, the Pope is reported as endorsing this slogan: 'May that call be to you in military affairs a battle-cry summoning you to war, because it is brought from God' (see Louise and Jonathan Riley-Smith, *The Crusades: Idea and Reality 1095–1274*, London: Arnold, 1981, p. 44). For Humbert of Romans' argument for the same slogan, justifying recapture of the 'Land of Promise', see ibid., pp. 103–17.

never fails to support the principle of crusading and any specific expedition passing for such, whether or not the King agrees. Apulia, Tunis, Constantinople and Acre are all one to Rutebeuf.

Being mandatory, the crusade cannot in his opinion be ignored by any Christian without sin being involved. On the other hand, there are indulgences offered to those taking part, and total remission of sins is promised as a reward to those who die in the campaign. Rutebeuf, rather more generous than the Popes, usually suggests that all participants win entry into Paradise.[15]

Although these are occasional pieces, responding to a particular event such as the fall of Constantinople to the schismatic Greeks, a threat to Acre or a new turn in the struggle between Pope and Emperor, the basic appeal varies little. It is a call for support on religious grounds, directed towards certain social categories and almost invariably exploiting the spiritual advantages which the indulgences offer.

In *Le Dit de Pouille*, written about 1265,[16] the poet sets himself the task of winning support for the 'crusade' in southern Italy, the aim of which is to put the Papal nominee Charles d'Anjou on the throne of Sicily in place of Manfred. Hence, no doubt, the reverential tone in which the poem begins but which is promptly followed by a call to back the 'roi de Cezile, que Dieux puisse avancier!' (l. 6), linked to the notion of personal spiritual credit to be won. The poet mentions the pretender's links with the French monarchy and naïvely argues that his high standing is proof of Charles' disinterested search for salvation: he risks his life to save his soul. The current attitude of the French crown is not mentioned.

Personal salvation is the keynote of what follows. The argument remains on a religious level, not apparently aimed at any one social grouping. The Holy War is a precious opportunity, not of picking up land or booty, but of winning the prize of Paradise. The argument, skilfully presented as ever, is familiar enough: human life is short; once dead, we cannot influence our eventual fate. 'Dieux done paradix a touz ses bienvoillans,' says Rutebeuf (l. 21), meaning those who join Charles' war, and woe betide the rest. An allusion to the *Chanson d'Aspremont* cleverly presents Anjou as in the epic line, a new Charlemagne resisting Saracen invaders – an impudent misrepresentation or at best a misapprehension:

> Trop at contre le roi d'Yaumons et d'Agoulans;
> Il at non li rois Charles, or li faut des Rollans.     (ll. 23–4)

---

[15] Cf. Carl Erdmann, *The Origin of the Idea of Crusade*, trans. by Marshall W. Baldwin and Walter Goffart, Princeton UP, 1977, pp. 343–4: 'The relevant canon of the Council of Clermont set out the indulgence in the canonically correct form; without reference to the forgiveness of sins, it spoke only of the remission of penance, that is, of ecclesiastical penalties. But the world took no account of this distinction [. . .]. What predominated was the general belief that the crusade procured forgiveness of sins and the soul's salvation'.

[16] See F/B, Vol. I, pp. 435–6.

A reference to the martyrdom of St Andrew hints at the kind of sacrifice demanded, and it is argued that to die 'naturally' (without some indulgence under one's belt) is to risk damnation, for salvation is otherwise hard to achieve and demands ceaseless struggle for merit. Failing help from 'Dieux' and 'la douce Dame' (l. 35) the outlook is bleak. There is, finally, a special appeal to sinners ('Picheour', l. 37), who are urged to seek, instead of the mere 'penitance' (l. 39) to be acquired from a pilgrimage to Rome, the more generous terms available to crusaders.

In conclusion, the poem sums up the crusade as a way to 'eschueir le feu qui tout adés emprant' (l. 42) and the folly of non-participation. Less theoretically, it congratulates not the King himself but his brother Alphonse for giving help to the cause, and it prays for success in what would seem a fitting ending. An additional stanza, however, far less gracious than the rest, demands that the prelates pay over the tithe-money without delay.[17]

Rutebeuf's idea of salvation is determined by his view of the Divinity, in which the Trinity has little prominence; nor is much stress laid on the possibility of grace, except that available from the Virgin Mary. God appears as above all the inflexible judge of the *Dies irae*, and salvation is something of a lottery with prizes few and far between.

The poet is not unaware of the inertia which crusading propaganda must combat. He himself is passionately committed, but he notes the inefficacy of crusade preaching and its offers of indulgences, and more than one of the poems ends on a note of despair at the general indifference. *La Complainte d'Outremer*, for instance, harks back to the heroic First Crusade in lamenting the lack of fighting spirit,

> Ne jone homme ne ancien
> N'ont por Dieu cure de combatre,      (ll. 154–5)

at the time when new perils threaten the Latin kingdom. Rutebeuf sees, or affects to see, no possibility of help reaching Geoffroi de Sergines:

> Quar com plus en sermoneroie,
> Et plus l'afere empireroie.
> Cis siecles faut: . . .      (ll. 171–3)

Similar lamentations are expressed also in *La Nouvelle Complainte d'Outremer* (ll. 327–56).

The apparently irrelevant passages in these poems, dwelling on the corruption of the clergy or the sinfulness of the merchants, are not simply reversions to the wider theme of social decadence. They must also be understood as a recognition by the poet of the need for financial support for

---

[17] Cf. *La Chanson de Pouille*, ll. 41–8; *La Nouvelle Complainte d'Outremer*, ll. 197–220.

hiring mercenaries or, as he himself puts it when he addresses rich prelates in *La Nouvelle Complainte d'Outremer*:

> Mais vos poeiz entor vos prendre
> Asseiz de povres gentilz homes
> Qui ne mainnent soumiers ne soumes, . .
> ........................
> A cex doneiz de votre avoir, . . (ll. 210–15)

In the same poem there is a lengthy warning to other clergy living comfortably 'Dou patrimoinne au Crucefi' (l. 223) about the long-term implications of hoarding wealth.

'Riche borjois d'autrui sustance' (l. 281) who do not look after the poor are condemned for their way of making money and similarly advised that they will not be able to control their fortune from beyond the grave. The poet's aversion to the merchant class is obvious here as elsewhere.

The crusade, a good action, stands therefore in contrast to the corruption on the home front. Those who do the fighting remain above criticism simply because they participate. The poet is interested not in the battles but in persuading warriors to take part. In the last analysis all but one of the crusade pieces are intended to win support from the feudal classes, the knights in particular. The upper ranks of the social hierarchy contain men of power and influence who must be pressed to implement Papal policy. That is the main aim of *La Complainte de Constantinople*, which summons the King to reverse his policy, favouring the knights not the Mendicants. *La Voie de Tunes* celebrates, not without hyperbole, an impressive list of princes and barons committed to the crusade, with the King at their head, and calls on other ranks – 'Vauvaseur, bacheleir' (l. 85) – to follow this example and not to believe 'pris ne honeur' (l. 86) can be won elsewhere.

These lesser elements, as Rutebeuf well understands, are essential to the success of the enterprise, and he makes special efforts to interest them not simply as Christians but as warriors possessed of the more secular ideology of chivalry. He makes it clear that failure to engage in the war means dishonour. Even the tournament, which Jean Renart[18] still regards earlier in the century as a noble occupation, is regularly condemned by Rutebeuf as irresponsible, notably in *La Nouvelle Complainte d'Outremer*:

> Tournoiëur, vos qui aleiz
> En yver, et vos enjaleiz,
> Querre places a tournoier,
> Vos ne poeiz mieux foloier. (ll. 115–18)[19]

In *La Chanson de Pouille* the comte de Blois is urged to join the war as a worthwhile contribution after so long frequenting tournaments.

---

[18] Jehan Renart, *Le Lai de l'Ombre*, ed. by John Orr, Edinburgh UP, 1948, p. 3, ll. 80–87.
[19] Cf. *La Complainte d'Outremer*, ll. 135–48.

Barons are warned in *La Nouvelle Complainte d'Outremer* that their honour is at stake in Palestine; dishonour awaits those who stand by while 'la Terre absolue' (l. 109) falls into enemy hands:

> Saveiz vos honte si aperte
> Com de soffrir si laide perde? (ll. 113–14)

Knights or squires not participating readily incur the charge of cowardice: 'Ja coars n'enterra en paradyx celestre,' states *La Voie de Tunes* (l. 93). A lengthy development in *La Nouvelle Complainte d'Outremer* goes further, portraying the alleged social irresponsibility and domestication of young nobles, and for good measure linking indifference to the war with the socially demeaning occupation of trading. Rutebeuf pictures young squires riding roughshod over poorer neighbours but taking their cattle to market like peasants. 'Toute gentilesce effaciez,' he tells them (l. 163), and calls for nobler standards:

> Mais se vos amissiez honeur
> Et doutissiez la deshoneur
> Et amissiez votre lignage,
> Vos fussiez et proudome et sage. (ll. 173–6)

The same poem provides a further vignette identifying those who stay behind as 'Chevaliers de plaiz et d'axises' (l. 245), comfortable country gentlemen addicted to hunting and drinking, corrupt judges and cowards to boot.

The *décroisé*, for once allowed a voice, questions the assertion that only in the Holy War can knights win salvation.[20] Why not by living righteously and peacefully at home among friends and family, he asks. His questions are never satisfactorily answered (that would contradict the writer's aim), but he is assured that what keeps him at home is wickedness and a desire for creature comforts, in other words cowardice.

Adherence to the chivalric code is thus projected as demanding participation in this great *aventure*. That is also the message of the eulogies for fallen crusaders, which give the poet a chance to praise even more positively the feudal qualities he admires. In *La Complainte de Monseigneur Geoffroi de Sergines*, the King's liegeman, a special hero for Rutebeuf, is carefully presented as a 'preudon' (l. 82), a warrior symbolising both Christian and chivalric values. He is characterised by contrast both to those who mortify the flesh in the cloister through *contemptus mundi* and to the 'recreants' intent on worldly satisfactions. Geoffroi is no mere warrior hero, however, for in civil life he is also exemplary, 'Douz et cortois et debonere' (l. 68), and just, charitable and respectful of true worth,

> Ne fu mesliz ne mesdisanz
> Ne vanterres ne despisanz, (ll. 87–8)

as well as loyal to the Crown – a paragon worthy, then, of the accolade of 'preudon'.

---

[20] *La Disputaison du Croisé et du Décroisé*, especially ll. 153–68.

Eudes de Nevers is another hero who typifies the qualities of knighthood in a *complainte* that bears his name.[21] Rutebeuf sees him as a born leader, eager to be dubbed at the earliest possible moment, imbued with the spirit of adventure:

> Puis ne fu voie ne sentiers
> Ou il n'alast mout volentiers
> Se hon s'i pot aventureir.  (ll. 28–30)

He, too, says the poet, had the makings of an upright citizen, an honest judge, helpful to the good, hard on the wicked. Eudes' sacrifice of his property, his privileges and his life is exemplary, but it represents a heavy blow to the Holy Land. This 'Terre plainne de noblesce, De charitei et de largesce' (ll. 49–50) would not be so devoid of defenders, the poet declares,

> Se morte ne fust gentilesce
> Et vaselages et proesce, . .  (ll. 52–3)

In other words, the feudal classes have abandoned chivalric values, values which sprang from their role as warriors and social leaders, but which wither in the purely domestic context.

There are two other eulogies of high-ranking nobles, whose deaths, following the disastrous Tunis expedition, are not the pretext for a crusading appeal. Thibaut de Navarre[22] is shown as uncorrupted by his great wealth, upright, devout and fully committed both personally and financially to the crusade. Rutebeuf is at pains to portray him as a man of charity, not in any respect 'orguilleuz' (l. 72) but on the contrary:

> Fontainne estoit de cortoisie;
> Toz biens i ert sanz vilonie.  (ll. 117–18)

Similarly, qualities such as 'pitié', 'charitei' and 'amistié' characterise Alphonse de Poitiers,[23] whose largesse is that of an Alexander. He is dubbed 'preudons' in his turn:

> Ne fist pas honte a son boen pere,
> Ainz montra bien que preudons iere
> De foi, de semblant, de meniere.  (ll. 114–16)

The notion of the 'preudomme' is also given some importance in *Le Dit d'Aristote*, a sort of 'Miroir de prince' which draws heavily upon the Latin *Alexandreis* of Gautier de Châtillon.[24] The *Dit* is a conservative document which highlights sections of the original, recommending reliance in general on

---

[21] *La Complainte du comte Eudes de Nevers.*
[22] *La Complainte du roi de Navarre.*
[23] *La Complainte du comte de Poitiers*, ll. 89–90.
[24] See F/B, Vol. I, p. 560.

the old nobility, while favouring other promotions which meet certain criteria. These are indicated in terms of certain values; the truly noble person is one who

>     ... fausetei et traïson
>     Heit et eschue, et honeur ainme. (ll. 40–41)

The man of virtue is distinguished by his attitude to money, for he gives generously and wholeheartedly. Everyone is revealed by his actions. The ruler must learn to distinguish the good from the evil. Largesse is the mark of the 'preudomme':

>     Seule noblesce franche et sage
>     Emplit de tout bien le corage
>     Dou preudoume loiaul et fin;
>     Ses biens le moinne a boenne fin. (ll. 69–72)

A correct attitude towards money (i.e. Humility, Charity, Pity, Largesse, etc.) is what Rutebeuf considers essential in a ruler. These are the very qualities the absence of which, as we have shown, the poet regularly condemns.

Whether opposing the friars or popularising the crusaders, he sees himself as in battle against a sinful world. In reality his fight is, however, a political one. In support of crusading he uses religious categories to discredit all who for any reason hold back. His critique of the Church, equally political, uses similar means of expression. He attacks his opponents corporately in terms of vices for which individual damnation will be awarded to them after their death, at the Last Judgment.[25] The King could, as he is enjoined to do, send help to Sergines, or the Pope might withdraw his objections to Guillaume de Saint-Amour. If some such change does happen, then credit will accrue in Heaven for the individual concerned: if not, the Last Judgment will be a harrowing one. The appeal to this remote tribunal is a convenient way of dividing society into sheep and goats. Those who agree with Rutebeuf are reasonably sure of salvation: those he disapproves of will suffer in the end.

Rutebeuf has not been well served by the critics. Labelled 'jongleur', he has too often emerged as a paid propagandist from whose work no 'coherent ideology' can be deduced. It is not his personal convictions, argues Dr Regalado,[26] but those of a faction, which inform his verse against the Mendicants, while for the same scholar, the crusade poems are 'part of a propagandizing campaign made by the papacy ...'.[27] To back papal policy over crusading yet oppose it in the matter of the Mendicants is certainly a

---

[25] Cf. *La Complainte de Guillaume*, ll. 156–70; *Dit de Guillaume de Saint-Amour*, ll. 7–8; *Dit de Sainte Eglise*, ll. 70–72; *Complainte de Constantinople*, ll. 34–6 and 169–80; *Voie de Tunes*, ll. 129–32, etc.
[26] Nancy Freeman Regalado, *Poetic patterns in Rutebeuf: a study in non-courtly poetic modes of the thirteenth century*, New Haven/London: Yale UP, 1970, p. 4.
[27] Ibid., p. 40.

contradiction, but is it insoluble? Jean-Charles Payen,[28] touching on the same problem, explained the one element in terms of 'une pensée conservatrice qu'inquiète le prestige croissant de ces communautés novatrices dans tous les domaines . . .', and sought to query the other on the ground that Rutebeuf's 'doctrine en la matière est incertaine, ambiguë et contradictoire'. Payen's justification for the latter remark seems to be that in two of the poems the writer 'oublie son sujet initial et se contente de décrire la société de son temps et de cultiver la *laudatio temporis acti*'. Given that Rutebeuf's attitudes, on the one hand to the Mendicants, on the other to the crusades, were consistent and enduring, it seems unlikely that in either case his own convictions were not engaged. If he was able to live with the contradiction, it was presumably because in his own mind it was either non-existent or justifiable. There is a further point to be made regarding what I have called the poet's 'critique' of the contemporary world. Both the scholars mentioned tend to classify this as 'moralistic' writing of a traditional kind and thereby in effect exclude it from any possible discussion of Rutebeuf's own *Weltanschauung*. Such a procedure is methodologically dubious. The critic must look at the whole corpus of the writer and not confuse diachronic and synchronic approaches. The social critique lies behind both the crusade poems and the attacks on the mendicant Orders.

Payen is right in considering Rutebeuf a conservative thinker, as is Dr Regalado when she envisages him as looking back to an 'idealized past age'.[29] Rutebeuf, in my view, supports crusading because he seeks a renewal of the feudal order, a return to traditional values. The crusades, being an activity primarily for warriors, are seen by him not only as a vehicle for the salvation of individuals, but as a means of encouraging the old values, cultivating heroism and suppressing unacceptable mercenary attitudes. 'On aurait tort', writes Payen, 'de voir en Rutebeuf un contestataire . . .'.[30] I would not entirely agree. He is no revolutionary, nourishes no notions about radical social change of a modern type, yet in his insistence upon the problem of poverty and his critique of the Church there is an implied call for change. He seeks a change of heart coming from the top of the feudal hierarchy, a spiritual and therefore political renewal which will bring old feudal and Christian values to the fore, restore the Church to its early austerity and bring new hope to the poor.

---

[28] Jean-Charles Payen, op. cit., pp. 336–7. Harry H. Lucas, reviewing the F/B edition (*French Studies*, XV (1961), pp. 157–9), explains Rutebeuf's apparent contradictions in terms of his attachment to Guillaume de Saint-Amour and Geoffroi de Sergines: 'This attachment to a great crusader and to the great champion of the University – themselves of eastern origin – may suffice to explain his enthusiasm for the crusades and for the cause of the University on the one hand, and his hatred for the Friars, their enemies, on the other. Given this, his attitude to king, clergy and all classes of society becomes intelligible' (p. 158).

[29] Nancy Freeman Regalado, op. cit., p. 16.

[30] Jean-Charles Payen, op. cit., p. 336.

## Punishment and Reward in Christine de Pizan's Lyric Poetry

### CHARITY CANNON WILLARD

Kenneth Varty's valuable introduction to his anthology of Christine de Pizan's poetry, together with Pierre Le Gentil's perceptive essay, 'Christine de Pisan, poète méconnu',[1] provide a good, overall view of the extensive body of lyric poetry which marked the initial state of Christine's literary career. Although her poetry was, in general, available to modern readers before her prose works,[2] it has been somewhat neglected in recent years because it has been considered lacking in originality, merely following the models of such poets as Guillaume de Machaut and Eustache Deschamps.

It is, of course, true that she shows many common traits with these poets and others of the late fourteenth and early fifteenth century – she undoubtedly owed a great deal to Deschamps' *Art de Dictier* and was perhaps inspired by the *Cent Ballades* collected by Jean le Seneschal[3] in composing her own *Cent Balades*, her first poetic effort – but there are other aspects which merit further consideration. These would certainly include her constant experimentation with new arrangements of verse within the fixed verse forms she practised, often giving the impression that she was quite carried away by her discovery of her own facility. Another would be the sort of preview of themes that she would develop later at greater length in her narrative poetry or prose. She herself spoke in her autobiographical *Avision* of having found through practice the form of expression most congenial to her,[4] but the introduction of these themes which she would develop later gives her poetry certain traits which distinguish it from earlier courtly poetry. Among these is her quite personal understanding of the punishments and rewards encountered in life.

---

[1] *Ballades, Rondeaux and Virelais*, ed. Kenneth Varty, Leicester University Press, 1965; Pierre Le Gentil in *Mélanges d'histoire littéraire offerts à Daniel Mornet*, Paris: Nizet, 1961, pp. 1–10.
[2] *Oeuvres poétiques de Christine de Pisan*, ed. Maurice Roy, SATF, Paris: F. Didot, 1886–96, 3 vols.
[3] *Les Cent Ballades, poème du XIV<sup>e</sup> siècle composé par Jean le Seneschal*, ed. Gaston Raynaud, SATF, Paris: F. Didot, 1905.
[4] Et comme de plus en plus alast croiscent le bien de ma congnoiscence adonc fus je aise quant joz trouve le stile a moy naturel me delittant en leurs soubtilles couvertures et belles matieres mucees soubz fictions delictables et morales . . .', *L'Avision-Christine*, ed. Sister Mary Louise Towner, Washington, DC: Catholic University of America, 1932, p. 163.

As she started writing poetry to console herself for the death of her husband and to distract her mind from the all too real tribulations of widowhood, it is scarcely surprising that in these first poems punishments should outweigh rewards. It is, moreover, this poetry of widowhood, some of her most original work, which calls attention to her dual system of regarding these punishments and rewards.

By temperament, Christine does not seem to have been especially devout, but she did not deviate from the basic religious ideas of the day. She obviously had a conventional concept of Heaven and Hell, possibly influenced by her reading of Dante's *Divine Comedy*, for she was one of the first in France to speak of his writings. But in addition, she was obsessed by the idea of Fortune, the goddess with her wheel who controlled individual human fates. Her inspiration may have been admiration for the *De Consolatione* of Boethius, which she mentions throughout her works, but first of all in Ballade XCVII of the *Cent Balades*:

> De commun cours chascun a trop plus chiers
> De Fortune les biens, que de Nature;
> Mais c'est a tort, car ilz sont si legiers
> Qu'on n'en devroit a nul fuer avoir cure.
>     Boëce en fait mension
> En son livre de Consolacion, . . .[5]

Indeed, the influence of Fortune on human affairs is an idea which occurs repeatedly from the earliest of the ballades to the long allegorical poem entitled *La Mutacion de Fortune*. It is understandable that she was not prepared to blame her husband's untimely death on God's will, so it was convenient for her to vent her rage and her sorrow on the instability of Fortune. This she does in Ballade X, which follows immediately the one in which she marks five years of widowhood:

> Se Fortune a ma mort jurée,
> Et du tout tasche a moy destruire,
> Or soye si maleürée,
> Qu'il faille qu'en dueil vive et muire, . . .[6]

This is followed by 'Seulete suy', perhaps the most famous of all Christine's ballades, but the idea of Fortune's quality of punishment is taken up immediately following:

> Qui trop se fie es grans biens de Fortune,
> En verité, il est deceü; . . .[7]

This ambivalence with regard to pagan Fortune and Christian destiny may seem initially surprising, although it might be understandable in one of Italian

---

[5] Roy, op. cit., Vol. I, p. 97, No. XCVII, ll. 1–6.
[6] Ibid., p. 11, No. X, ll. 1–4.
[7] Ibid., p. 13, No. XII, ll. 1–2.

birth who early in her career as a writer was involved with Parisian intellectuals who were already in contact with Italian humanistic influences. The relationship of Fortune, predestination and Free Will was of interest to such as these. A striking illustration of this concern, and one quite possibly known to Christine, was to be seen in certain copies of the French translation of St Augustine's *De Civitate Dei* made by Raoul de Presles for Charles V. At the beginning of Book V in Paris, B.N. Ms. fr. 25 (fol. 161), for instance, a miniature shows on the left Fortune and her wheel personifying Fate and on the right God representing Divine Will.[8] Both forces are evident from the beginning of Christine's poetry. Thus in the second of her *Cent Balades* she speaks of the Roman custom of rewarding a victorious warrior with a laurel crown, but in Ballade XVI she calls attention to the need for patience to await a reward in Heaven:

> Chascun vray cuer se doit enamourer
> De la vraye celestiel lumiere,
> Et du seul Dieu que l'en doit aourer.
> C'est nostre fin et joye derreniere;[9]

One particular aspect of Fortune in the Middle Ages, as Howard R. Patch pointed out many years ago,[10] was her association with the God of Love. She was generally thought to be unfavourable to at least one of a pair of lovers. Christine saw this as the case in her own widowhood, for she says:

> Et tant a fait Fortune, Dieu lui mire!
> Qu'elle a changié en vie doloreuse
> Mes jeux, mes ris, et ce m'a fait eslire
> Dueil pour soulas, et vie trop greveuse.[11]

Indeed, the punishment brought on by the God of Love provided the inspiration for much of Christine's love poetry, which comprises the major portion of her lyric verse. A number of these poems are arranged in cycles which describe the progress of love affairs, sometimes from a young woman's point of view, although in one case from the man's, and in still another there is a dialogue between the pair. But as Kenneth Varty has pointed out,[12] Christine was a poet of love's ending rather than its happier beginning, so these tales inevitably end in misfortune.

---

[8] Alexandre de Laborde, *Les manuscrits à peintures de la Cité de Dieu*, É. Rahir: Paris, 1909, Vol. II, p. 318; see also BN Ms. fr. 6272 and former Cheltenham Ms. fr. 4359, both of which date from the early years of the fifteenth century. For the background, see G. Ouy, 'Paris, l'un des principaux foyers de l'humanisme en Europe au début du XV$^e$ siècle', *Bulletin de la Société de l'histoire de Paris et de l'Ile-de-France*, 1970, pp. 71–98.
[9] Roy, op. cit., Vol. I, p. 17, No. XVI, ll. 17–20.
[10] Howard R. Patch, *The Goddess Fortuna in Medieval Literature*, Cambridge (Mass.): Harvard University Press, 1927 (Reprinted New York: Octagon Books, 1967), pp. 90–8.
[11] Roy, op. cit., Vol. I, p. 19, No. XVIII, ll. 8–12.
[12] Kenneth Varty, op. cit., p. xxvii.

Needless to say, Christine was following in these cycles the traditions of courtly love, in which the affair is both illicit and secret. The essential point she wanted to make, however, was not in accord with her models; there is little happiness in such love, especially for the woman, and sometimes even for the man. This theme continued to interest her as she progressed to longer works, as can be seen in her *Livre du Duc des Vrais Amants* and again in her final poetic cycle, the *Cent Balades d'Amant et de Dame*.[13] She discussed the pitfalls of such love in even greater detail in her *Livre des Trois Vertus*, her book of advice to women of all classes of society. A revival of interest in the traditions of courtly love marked the society which surrounded Charles VI and his pleasure-loving queen, Isabeau de Bavière. These were also cultivated at the court of Louis d'Orléans, which Christine frequented at the time she was writing this poetry and at the *cour amoureuse* founded in Paris in 1401: but Christine questioned the motives of many courtiers who pretended to praise women and love while really following quite different objectives. This form of social hypocrisy was the object of her scorn in her first long poem, *L'Epistre au Dieu d'Amours*,[14] but is also evident in a number of her shorter poems. Her complaints, mingled with rather pointed social satire, leave little doubt that she was reporting contemporary life as she observed it.

The first of her love cycles opens immediately after her initial group inspired by her widowhood. The first of this new group (XXI) records a young woman's confession of having fallen in love; she sings the praises of her lover rejoicing that love has shown her this favour. Her euphoria is short-lived, however, for her lover is soon called away to fight in the Holy Roman Empire, and in any case their meetings are already threatened by gossips who are spying on them, a problem which always seems to menace Christine's lovers. Before her lover leaves her, she grants him the favour he has been begging, and they swear eternal fidelity, but she never sees him again. Finally, ill from despair (XLIII), she renounces her love, admitting that if she could have foreseen the outcome, she would have conducted herself more prudently. Her chagrin is compounded by jealousy because of the rumour that her faithless lover is paying attention to another woman. Two years have passed between their meeting and her final renunciation of her love, saying:

> Je ne te vueil plus servir,
> Amours, a Dieu te comand.
> Tu me veulz trop asservir,
> Et paier mauvaisement;
> Pour loier me rends tourment.
> C'est fort chose a soustenir:
> Je ne m'i vueil plus tenir.[15]

---

[13] Roy, op. cit., Vol. III, pp. 59–208; pp. 209–317.
[14] Ibid., Vol. II, pp. 1–27.
[15] Ibid., Vol. I, p. 49, No. XLVIII, ll. 1–7.

Another love affair, this one told in rondeaux (XIV–XLII), turns out badly for the lover. After an initial period of happiness, the lovers quarrel and the lady will have nothing to do with her admirer, who is then left to console himself with memories of past happiness. In spite of two brief reconciliations, their final separation is inevitable, for the lady's husband returns home after an absence and there is no possibility of further meetings. Once more the lover is left alone to lament his misfortune:

>Or est mon cuer rentré en double peine
>Quant le mary, ma dame, est revenu,
>Qui du païs s'est hors long temps tenu.
>
>Helas! j'ay eu du tout en mon demaine
>Joye et plaisir et soulaz maintenu,
>Or est mon cuer rentré en double peine.
>
>Il me touldra, Dieux lui doint male estraine,
>Tout mon deduit, car souvent et menu
>J'estoye d'elle au giste retenu,
>Or est mon cuer rentré en double peine.[16]

This theme of the lover abandoned by a married lady with a jealous husband would be developed in the *Livre du Duc des Vrais Amants* in which an inexperienced young man falls in love with a married cousin. There is no outcome for this attraction possible except sorrow for both of them, in spite of their desire to be faithful to each other.

A second love cycle in the *Cent Balades* (LXV–LXXXVIII) takes the form of a dialogue between the two lovers. The lady in this case seems more mature than the young girl in the first, and she responds more readily to the man's advances. But the development of their love is again inhibited by prying gossips and a jealous husband. Once more it is the woman who seems to have the power to make her lover suffer. She reviles him, for instance, when he stays away too long, although she eventually forgives him. In the course of time, however, the gossips are so malevolent that he is obliged to go away for a time to avoid the revelation of their love and a subsequent scandal. In the final poem of this cycle it is once more the lover, who has been faithful to his lady for ten years, who complains of the loneliness which is his recompense:

>Ha! ma dame, je me doy bien doloir,
>Quant il convient que hors du païs saille
>Ou vous estes, m'amour et mon vouloir;
>Ne pouoir n'ay que d'aultre riens me chaille;
>Tout autre amour je ne prise une maille;
>De vous venoit tout mon avancement.
>Mais puis qu'Amours si pesant fais me baille,
>Ce sera fort se je vif longuement![17]

[16] Ibid., p. 170, No. XLII.
[17] Ibid., p. 88, No. LXXXVIII, ll. 9–16.

It is evident that Christine believed that even for faithful lovers, punishment and sorrow are the only possible outcome of a clandestine love affair. Even a faithful lover was doomed.

A final presentation of the problems inherent in this sort of love is to be found in the *Cent Balades d'Amant et de Dame*, which was apparently composed somewhat later than the other cycles, for it appears only in the collection of Christine's writings which is now British Library, Harley Ms. 4431, assumed to have been compiled around 1410. This series is opened by a sort of introduction in which Christine confesses that these poems were written on command, apparently as a sort of penalty for having undertaken to turn the thoughts of noble ladies away from love.[18] It is evident, however, that Christine had not changed her views on so-called courtly love.

This time the lady begins by resisting the lover's advances, but in Ballade VIII, the God of Love himself appears to warn her that her youth is slipping away. She wavers, but finally succumbs to the lover's advances, in spite of a few lingering doubts as to his intentions. After a certain amount of happiness together, the lovers experience the usual difficulties: gossip, separation. When separated, they exchange a series of poem-letters in which both complain of their loneliness. In spite of a joyful reunion they eventually quarrel and separate. The lady, who has come full circle in her emotional experience, recalls her initial misgivings and laments too late her indiscretions:

> O Amours dure et sauvage,
> Certes, qui te fait hommage
> Se met en divers servage,
> Et si se puet bien attendre
> Que par ce dueil et dommage
> Lui vendra, c'est l'avantage
> Que tu fais au las courage
> Qui se laisse a toy surprendre.[19]

This same sort of moral vacuum, the price of such a love affair, is summed up in the *Livre du Duc de Vrais Amants* in a letter written to the lady by an old friend and confidant, a letter which apparently expressed Christine's own views so well that she repeated it in the *Livre des Trois Vertus*:

> Disons du cousté des amans, encore que tous fussent loyaulx, secrez, voir disans, ce qu'ilz ne sont mie, ains scet on assez que communement sont fains et pour les

---

[18] Ibid., Vol. III, pp. 209–10, ll. 17–24:

> Or pry je a Dieu que n'en soye lassée,
> Car mieulx me pleust entendre a autre afaire
> De trop greigneur estude, mais taussée
> M'i a personne doulce et debonnaire
> Pour amende de ce que ay dit que traire
> En sus se doit d'amoureux pensement
> Toute dame d'onneur; si m'en fault traire
> Cent balades d'amoureux sentement.

[19] Ibid., pp. 308–17, *Lay de Dame*, ll. 1–8.

dames decepvoir dient ce qu'ilz ne pensent ne vouldroient faire, toute fois est chose vraye que l'ardeur de telle amour ne dure mie longuement, meismes aux plus loyaulx et c'est chose certaine. Ha! chiere dame, comment cuidiez vous, quant il avient qu'icelle amour est deffaillie et que la dame qui ara esté aveuglée par l'envelopement de fole plaisance se repente durement quant elle s'avertist et pourpense les folies et divers perilz ou maintes fois s'est trouvée, et combien elle vouldroit, qu'il lui eust cousté, que oncques ne lui fust avenu et que tel reproche d'elle ne peust estre dit, certes vous ne porriez penser la grant repentence et desplaisant pensée qui ou cuer lui en demeure.[20]

This is not to say, of course, that Christine was against love as such. Young love was capable of bringing joy, but in the long run it was marriage and a well-ordered domestic life which provided lasting rewards. She was not unaware of the drawbacks of contemporary marriage laws, as can be seen from the advice she had to offer to the unhappily married in the *Livre des Trois Vertus*, but her own experience of marriage had been rewarding, if all too brief. Christine's poem in praise of marriage, 'Doulce chose est que mariage',[21] is unique for its day but, together with the *Livre des Trois Vertus*, is especially interesting as a forerunner of Italian humanistic views on the virtues of marriage and family life, of which Francesco Barbaro's *De Re Uxoria* and Leon Battista Alberti's *Della Famiglia* are perhaps the most celebrated expressions. Nor can one overlook the recollection of Christine's own emotion in certain other poems, especially several which associate the joys of young love with springtime. It is noteworthy that the emphasis is always on the rewards of *loyal* love, as for example:

> Or sus, or sus, pensez de bien amer,
> Vrais amoureux, et joye maintenir
> Ce moys de may, et vuidiez tout amer
> De voz doulz cuers, ne lui vueilliez tenir,
> Soiez joyeux et liez sans retenir
> Nul fel penser, car resjouïr se doit
> Tout vray amant par plaisant souvenir;
> Amours le veult et la saison le doit.[22]

A completely different group of poems is devoted to the rewards of true chivalry, especially Renown. Thus Christine offers advice to a young nobleman who wishes to achieve these rewards:

> Gentil homme, qui veult prouesce acquerre,
> Escoute cy; entens qu'il te faut faire:
> Armes suivir t'estuet en mainte terre;
> Estre loyal contre ton adversaire;
> De bataille ne fouïr, non sus traire;
> Et doubter Dieu; parolle avoir tardive;

---

[20] Ibid., p. 169, *Le Livre du Duc des Vrais Amans*.
[21] Ibid., Vol. I, p. 237, *Autres Balades*, No. XXVI.
[22] Ibid., p. 217, *Autres Balades*, No. IX, ll. 1–8.

> En fait d'assault trouver voye soultive;
> Ne soit ton cuer de lascheté repris;
> Des tours d'armes duis dois estre et apris;
> Amer ton prince; et a ton chevetaine
> Estre loyal; avoir ferme couraige;
> Croire conseil; promesse avoir certaine;
> S'ainsi le faiz, tu seras preux et saige.[23]

Such poems as this provide a key to Christine's humanistic concept of man's possibility of overcoming the uncertainty of Fortune through virtue. This is even more explicit in the lines:

> Assez acquiert tresor et seigneurie,
> Trés noble avoir et grant richece amasse,
> Qui par bonté, qui nul temps n'est perie,
> Acquiert honneur, bon renom, loz et grace.
> Car au monde n'est chose qui ne passe
> Fors que bienfait, tout ne vault une miche
> Autre tresor ne chose que l'en brace;
> Car qui est bon doit estre appellé riche.[24]

Christine considered some of her contemporaries worthy of such a reward along with heroes of the past. Thus she cited the virtues of Charles d'Albret, Constable of France, whom she compares to Brutus, the Roman founder of England,[25] of Jean de Werchin, the Seneschal of Hainaut, to whom she also dedicated her longer poem *Le Livre des Trois Jugements*,[26] and of Louis, Duke of Bourbon.[27] By a quirk of Fortune, which nobody could then foresee, two of these model knights were killed at Agincourt in 1415, and the Duke of Bourbon, taken captive there, died in England, still in captivity, in 1434. Fortune, indeed, abandoned them.

Although Christine believed, in common with other early humanists, that the search for non-material values was more successful in defeating Fortune's designs than dependence on worldly success, she was convinced that human hope must ultimately rest in God, as she says in one of the last of the *Cent Balades*:

> Si comme il est raison que chascun croie
> En un seul Dieu, sanz faire aucune doubte,
> Qui aux esleus son paradis ottroie
> Et les pervers laidement en deboute,. .
>
> Et non obstant qu'en peschié se desvoye
> Tout cuer humain, et que le monde boute
> En maint meffais, si doit on toutevoie
> Soy retourner vers Dieu;. .[28]

---

[23] Ibid., pp. 264–5, *Autres Balades*, No. L, ll. 1–13.
[24] Ibid., p. 207, *Autres Balades*, No. I, ll. 1–8.
[25] Ibid., pp. 208–11, 225–6, *Autres Balades*, Nos. II, III, XVI.
[26] Ibid., p. 245, *Autres Balades*, No. XXXIII; ibid., Vol. II, pp. 111–57.
[27] Ibid., Vol. I, pp. 277–9, *Encore Aultres Balades*, Nos. VII and IX.
[28] Ibid., p. 99, No. XCIX, ll. 1–4, 9–12.

Thus in the end divine salvation would appear to triumph over the whims of Fortune, which all too frequently victimise the human race.

As for Christine herself, however, one sees developing across these early poems her own way of dealing with the world. Reflections of her reading of Boethius, Ovid, Trojan history, and to some extent of Roman history indicate that she was already starting on the 'chemin de long estude' which was her personal salvation. Already towards the end of the *Cent Balades* she was writing of the rewards of learning:

> Si doit on bien mettre force et devoir
> A acquerir si trés noble richece;
> Car qui bien l'a, trop est grant son pouoir.
> Trés eureux sont ceulz dont elle est princece
> De gouverner tous leurs fais com maistrece.[29]

It was only later, however, in the *Mutacion de Fortune*, that she gave a more personal expression to this idea. At the end of her long allegorical poem about the machinations of Fortune she explained her own way of coping with the volatile goddess:

> Et, pour ce que partout Meseur
> Frequante, pour avoir moins noyse,
> Nonobstant que partout il voise,
> J'ay choisie pour toute joye
> (Quelqu'aultre l'ait), telle est la moye,
> Paix, solitude volumtaire,
> Et vie astracte [et] solitaire.[30]

One sees that in the course of about fifteen years, Christine had succeeded in working her way from her black despair at her husband's death, the punishment of Fortune which inspired her first poems, to a means of overcoming Fortune's adversities. On the way she had developed an independent view of society's punishments and rewards, beginning to see them across a study of the past which would remake her life and prepare the way for her most important writing, leading eventually to her final triumphant poem inspired by the appearance of Joan of Arc, seemingly the reward of her efforts.[31] The germ of much of this later writing is already to be found in the early poetry, far more than can be mentioned here.

In reading Christine's writings, one is always surprised by the complexity of her thought. Far from always following outworn models, she views the world from a remarkably independent point of view, frequently giving expression to

---

[29] Ibid., p. 98, No. XCVIII, ll. 15–19.
[30] *Le Livre de la Mutacion de Fortune*, ed. Suzanne Solente, SATF, Paris: Picard, 1959–66, 4 vols., Vol. IV, pp. 79–80, vv. 23630–6.
[31] *Ditié de Jehanne d'Arc*, ed. by Angus J. Kennedy and Kenneth Varty, Oxford: Society for the Study of Mediaeval Languages and Literature, 1977.

ideas which can only be associated with the humanism which was already making its way north from her native Italy: the value of patience and virtue against Fortune, the superiority of marriage over the much vaunted *fin'amour*, the fragile rewards of earthly renown, and, especially, the value of the lessons of history. Her writing, above all, reflects the instability of the times in which she lived, with their extremes of punishments and rewards.

# Tabula Gratulatoria

Professor H. T. Barnwell, Barnt Green, Birmingham
Dr Michael Bath, Department of English Studies, University of Strathclyde
Emmanuèle Baumgartner, Paris
J. H. B. Bennett, French Department, University of Glasgow
Elisabeth J. Bik, Amsterdam
Dr Fanni Bogdanow, Cheadle, Cheshire
Dr G. N. Bromiley, Department of French, University of Durham
Keith Busby, Instituut voor Algemene Literatuurwetenschap, Utrecht
Mr P. W. Byrne, French Department, University of Glasgow
Dr John Campbell, French Department, University of Glasgow
Dr N. T. Clanchy, History Department, Westfield College, University of London
David Clandfield, Department of French, University of Toronto
A. E. Cobby, Edinburgh University Library
Professeur André Crépin, Amiens
Edinburgh University Library
Professor R. G. Finch, Department of German, University of Glasgow
Naoyuki Fukumoto, Tokyo
Glasgow University Library
Professor Dr Jan Goossens, Niederlandisches Seminar, Munster
Dr P. B. Grout, Department of Romance Studies, University College, Swansea
A. J. Holden, Department of French, University of Edinburgh
Dr Stanley Jones, Modern Language Building, University of Glasgow
Dr E. M. Kennedy, Reading
Professor J. C. Laidlaw, Gonville and Caius College, Cambridge
Professor Rex Last, University of Dundee
Miss H. C. R. Laurie, Glasgow
Professor A. H. T. Levi, St Andrews
Dr Brian J. Levy, Department of French, University of Hull
Heather Lloyd, Department of French, University of Glasgow
R. A. Lodge, Department of French, University of Newcastle-upon-Tyne
Dr Jill Mann, Cambridge
Jean-Claude Mühlethaler, Baden
Professor Gianni Mombello, Turin

Xenia Muratova, Paris
Dr Venetia Newall, London
Dr Joy Newton, Department of French, University of Glasgow
Masami Okubo, Paris
Noel A. Peacock, Department of French, University of Glasgow
Thérèse Saint-Paul, Bearsden, Glasgow
Dr Jeremy J. Smith, Department of English Language, University of Glasgow
P. South, Colchester
R. H. Spencer, Cardiff
Michel Stanesco, Université de Paris-Sorbonne, Paris
Jean Subrenat, Aix en Provence
Elina Suomela-Harma, Helsinki
Toshiyuki Takamiya, Department of English, Keio University, Tokyo
University of Birmingham Library, Birmingham 15, England
The University Library, Dundee
Colette-Anne van Coolput, Brussels
Dr Erwin Verzandvoort, Rosmalen, The Netherlands
Professor David H. Walker, Department of Modern Languages, University of Keele
Jeanne Wathelet-Willem and Paul Wathelet, Liège
Gareth O. Watts, National Library of Wales
B. Woledge, Wendover, Aylesbury
Professor Dr F. Wolfzettel, Institut für Romanische Philologie, Giessen